Surviving Graduate Sch

Surviving Graduate School in Psychology

A POCKET MENTOR

Tara L. Kuther

American Psychological Association

Washington, DC

Published by
American Psychological Association
750 First Street, NE
Washington, DC 20002
www.apa.org

To order
APA Order Department
P.O. Box 92984
Washington, DC 20090-2984
Tel: (800) 374-2721; Direct: (202) 336-5510
Fax: (202) 336-5502; TDD/TTY: (202) 336-6123
Online: www.apa.org/books/
E-mail: order@apa.org

In the U.K., Europe, Africa, and the Middle East, copies may be ordered from
American Psychological Association
3 Henrietta Street
Covent Garden, London
WC2E 8LU England

Typeset in Meridien by Circle Graphics, Columbia, MD

Printer: Sheridan Books, Ann Arbor, MI
Cover Designer: Minker Design, Bethesda, MD
Technical/Production Editor: Emily Welsh

Cover art: Richard L. Dana, *Wise Guy,* 2005, 37 in. × 19 in., mixed media on canvas.

Kuther, Tara L.
Surviving graduate school in psychology : a pocket mentor / Tara L. Kuther.
p. cm.
Includes bibliographical references and index.
ISBN-13: 978-1-4338-0346-8
ISBN-10: 1-4338-0346-1
1. Psychology—Study and teaching (Graduate) I. Title.

BF77.K86 2008
150.71'1—dc22

British Library Cataloguing-in-Publication Data
A CIP record is available from the British Library.
Printed in the United States of America
First Edition

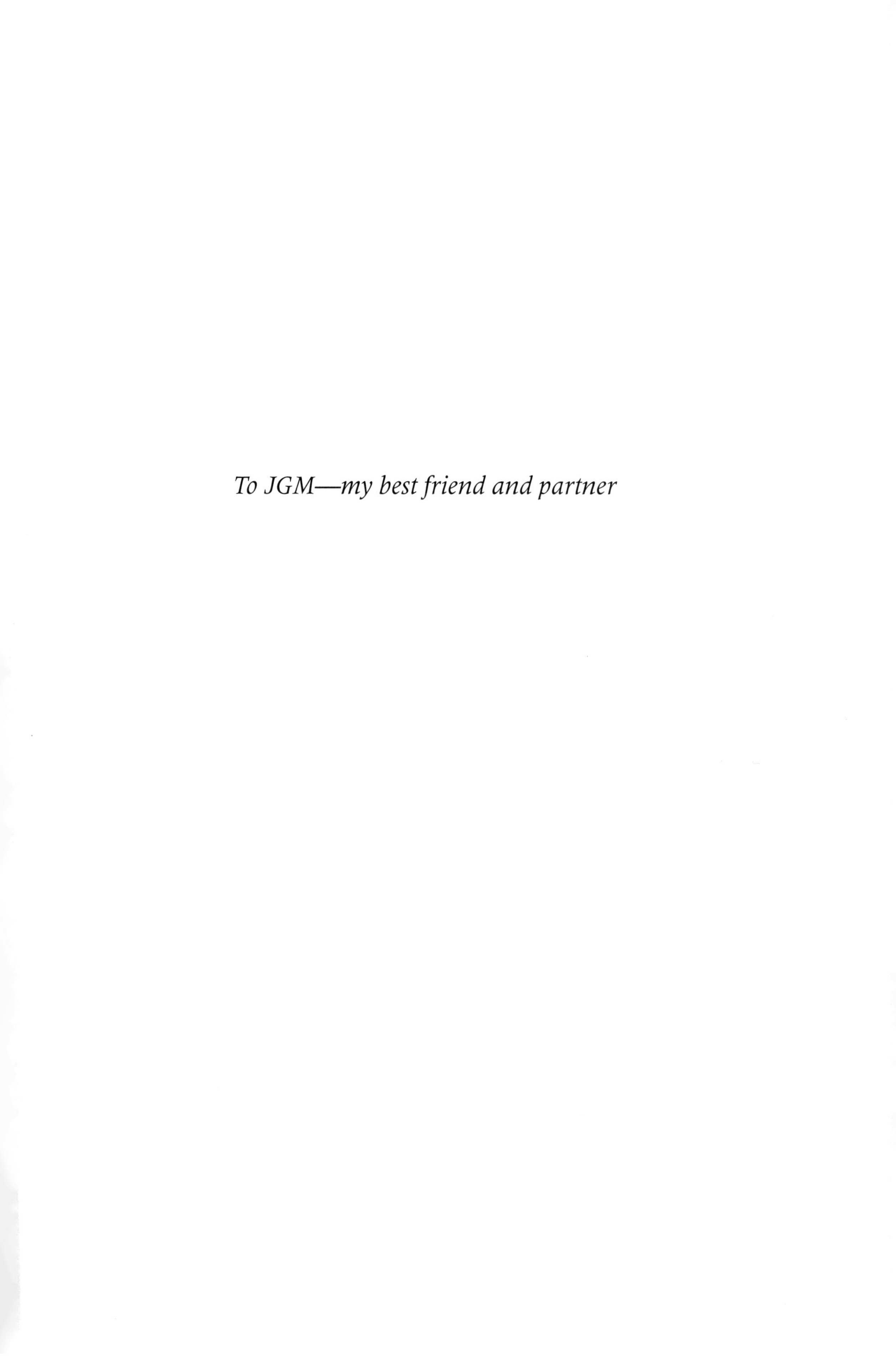

To JGM—my best friend and partner

Contents

Acknowledgments

Although writing may feel like a solitary endeavor, this book owes much to the encouragement and assistance of others. I thank Linda McCarter at the American Psychological Association for her guidance in shepherding this project through the publication process. Emily Leonard and Emily Welsh were especially helpful in managing the myriad tasks and details that arose during development and production. I am grateful to Lansing Hays, who first saw the merit in this project and signed it. Thanks to my colleagues Bob Morgan and Corey Habben for the many conversations we have had about graduate study and the needs of graduate students and early career psychologists.

I am especially indebted to my family, whose understanding is boundless. Over the last few decades, Phil and Irene Kuther have provided the multiple forms of support that characterize exceptional parenting. I greatly appreciate the assistance and warmth from my dear friend Calvin. And finally, I thank John Mongelluzzo—my rock—whose love and support is my foundation, for the solid encouragement that both motivates and calms me, making this period, and much of my life, serene.

Introduction

Graduate study in psychology is a wondrous opportunity to be surrounded by smart people—psychologists and students—who are working toward a common goal: improving human life, whether through basic and applied research, scholarly activities, or clinical work. Graduate school entails working alongside skillful researchers who are making strides in understanding the bases of human nature and uncovering the knowledge that will fill tomorrow's textbooks. Graduate students learn the practice of psychology from master practitioners.

Graduate school is a restricted world, not open to everyone. Success in graduate study requires initiative. In college, students are often taken by the hand and led through the ropes; they are told of the expectations and hurdles that earning a bachelor's degree entails. Graduate school is much less clear-cut. Most psychology students do not receive explicit guidance on what to expect and what to do—or not do. Generally, there is no set timetable, agenda, or map on how to navigate graduate study in psychology. It is vague and open-ended; some students finish before others. Although all psychology graduate students may take courses on research methods or techniques in therapy, there is no one path to becoming a skilled researcher or practitioner. The graduate school years can be lonely as professors usually do not stand alongside students and spoon-feed them all there is to know about being a psychologist. Even graduate students who are blessed with ideal mentors who are accessible, warm guides will often feel adrift during graduate school. It is the nature of the beast.

Surviving Graduate School in Psychology: A Pocket Mentor is intended to guide students through the process of graduate study by emphasizing the pragmatics of completing a graduate degree in psychology, including how to balance life with academics and how to build an identity as a psychologist. Graduate students are free to use their time as they see fit; therefore, discipline and self-management are critical to success. Choices regarding mentors, research projects, and applied experiences can mean the difference between completing a doctoral degree in 4 years and taking much longer. Mentors are essential to student success, but the sheer number of students entering graduate programs means that not all receive the mentoring they need. Although no book can substitute for interactions with an experienced professional who can mentor and guide one through the hurdles and decisions of graduate study, this one is a start.

Surviving Graduate School in Psychology begins with a discussion about the practical side of entering graduate school, offering advice on moving to a new town or city, funding graduate study, and managing money. How well students transition to their new graduate school environment influences their overall success. Chapter 2 discusses the transition to graduate school, describing how graduate school differs from undergraduate study and how to ensure a quick and effective adaptation. Chapter 3 examines the ways in which graduate students spend their days: attending seminars and colloquia and engaging in reading, research, and writing.

After an introduction to the basis of graduate study, chapters 4 through 7 discuss personal skills that are needed to succeed in graduate school, such as self-management skills that include organization, time management, and goal setting. Many students are surprised to learn that people skills are perhaps the most important tools for success in graduate school. Chapter 5 examines the people part of graduate study: getting along with mentors, other faculty, and peers, as well as departmental politics. Relationships outside of school also influence students' ability to juggle the multiple demands of graduate study. Chapter 6 also discusses people skills, specifically the challenges and rewards of maintaining outside relationships during graduate school. How do students balance the needs of friends and family with their academic demands? How do dating and romantic relationships fit in? Is it ever okay to date within the department? Perhaps it goes without saying that graduate school is a stressful time in most students' lives. Chapter 7 discusses coping with stress and managing conflict, a way of reducing and avoiding stress.

As students progress through graduate school, they take on more sophisticated and demanding tasks and roles. Chapter 8 discusses the applied part of practitioner training: practicum and internship. How should students prepare for these experiences? What do applications entail? What can students expect during the internship? Another challenging role that many graduate students adopt is that of professor. Chapter 9 explores teaching: how to prepare a course, develop teaching skills, interact with students, and balance teaching with the myriad other roles juggled by graduate students. Perhaps the most demanding task that graduate students face is completing the dissertation. Chapter 10 provides a detailed overview of the dissertation process, including writing the proposal and dissertation, managing the committee, and completing the dissertation defense.

As students complete their training, their task is to transform from student to professional. Chapter 11 examines the ways in which students hone their professional voices as psychologists. It is by interacting with the field at large—by participating in professional societies, contributing to the scholarly literature, and networking—that students become part of the larger community of psychologists. Chapter 12 discusses the multiple developmental transitions that occur over the graduate school years, including student transitions, changes in relationships with mentors and supervisors, and developing a professional identity as a psychologist. The final step in transitioning to the professional world is to obtain a position. Chapter 13 discusses career moves for emerging psychologists: jobs as postdoctoral fellows, practitioners, and academics.

Many of the issues discussed in this book are particularly salient for doctoral students; however, master's students in psychology encounter many of the same issues and can also benefit from the advice in this volume. Students often find graduate study especially challenging because it entails so much more than coursework, yet there are few stated rules. No one explains exactly what students must do to become a psychologist, apart from earn a graduate degree. Make *Surviving Graduate School in Psychology* your pocket mentor, offering the knowledge, support, and encouragement you need to become a confident professional.

Surviving Graduate School in Psychology

Pragmatics of Graduate Student Life

1

The transition to graduate school begins at home, perhaps with a move to a new town or city. Many students relocate to new cities and states, requiring them to find a place to live, transport their possessions, and get settled in a new home right before beginning graduate school. Graduate school holds new financial challenges for students, even those who remain in their hometown. In this chapter I discuss the pragmatic and domestic aspects of beginning graduate study: how to manage your home and your money.

Find an Apartment and a Roommate

The first step in transitioning to graduate school, for many students, is a geographical transition—moving to a new town or city, often several states, or even a country away. Moving is one of the more stressful experiences that someone can undergo. Think about other changes that a new graduate student experiences: starting graduate school, meeting new friends, getting used to a new place, graduating from college, or leaving the world of work to return to school. Change is stressful. Even good change is stressful. Accept that—and then do what you can to manage the stress. One of the best ways to ward off anxiety is to plan and take control of the situation. Any move, even one to the other side of town, can be overwhelming. Factor in distance, and simply imagining the steps entailed in moving can be incapacitating. Where do you start? With a plan: The first step is to secure an apartment.

> "Victor, have you begun looking for an apartment? It's June already and you need to be settled sometime in August." "Mom, I know. Don't worry. It won't take much time." "Finding an apartment in New York City isn't as easy as you think," Victor's mother says. "OK. I'll start," sighs Victor. A month later, he searches the online listings at the *New York Times* Web site. "Wow, there isn't much I can afford," he thinks to himself. After searching Craigslist.org, Victor realizes that he underestimated the challenge of finding an affordable apartment. He travels to New York and hires a realtor. Most of the apartments he sees are not habitable, at least to his standards. He finally sees one that he likes. He tells the landlord that he does not have his checkbook or the information needed for the credit check. He returns the next morning, but the apartment is taken.

Preparation and an early start are critical to success with real estate. Begin looking for an apartment long before the semester begins. Some places, like New York City and San Francisco, have particularly challenging housing markets. Get to know the peculiarities of the housing market in your new town. Contacts at your new school, especially other graduate students, can provide housing information. Current graduate students are an important source of advice about your new town, especially advice on which neighborhoods to avoid. Your new colleagues may even have leads on apartments. Tell everyone you know that you are moving and looking for an apartment because it is a small world; networking sometimes can turn up valuable housing leads, even in other cities. Online listings, such as those at Craigslist.org and Realtor.com, can turn up useful housing leads. Many local newspapers have searchable Internet listings of rental properties; check these and do not forget to use an Internet search engine such as Google.com to locate online rental listings specific to your new town. If you are short on time and nervous, or if the rental market is especially bleak, seek help from a real estate agency, but note that agencies charge fees that can range anywhere from $50 to 2 months' rent.

Attend to details inside as well as outside the apartment. Exhibit 1.1 lists considerations when visiting apartments.

As you visit apartments, keep your checkbook with you and be prepared to put a deposit down on an apartment if you decide it is the one. In some competitive markets a decent apartment does not last an afternoon; by the time you run to get your checkbook or transfer cash, it may be rented. Understand the rental market in your new town. Will you have to jump on the first good apartment you find? Be prepared to write

EXHIBIT 1.1

What to Look for When Considering Apartments

- ☐ Is the building clean?
- ☐ Are common areas of the building well kept or are they run down?
- ☐ Is there evidence of pests in the cupboards and closets?
- ☐ Are there outlets for your appliances, such as for a coffee pot and microwave in the kitchen and hairdryer in the bathroom?
- ☐ Do the refrigerator and stove work?
- ☐ Is there enough counter space to work?
- ☐ Look for outlets in each room and consider whether the outlets will accommodate your needs.
- ☐ What lighting source is there in each room? Will you have to purchase floor lamps?
- ☐ How large are the rooms? Will they hold your furniture?
- ☐ Check all faucets and sinks for leaks.
- ☐ Check all windows. Do they open?
- ☐ Is there adequate closet space?
- ☐ How is the apartment heated? Is heating included in the rent?
- ☐ Are utilities included? If not, can you fit them into your budget?
- ☐ How secure is the building?
- ☐ How long is the lease?
- ☐ When is the rent due?
- ☐ Is there a fee for late rent payments (and how is it calculated)?
- ☐ Are pets allowed?
- ☐ If you have a car, where can you park it? Is there off-street parking?
- ☐ How close is the apartment to school? (You will spend a lot of time on campus, thus a long commute is not desirable.)
- ☐ Are laundry facilities available?
- ☐ Where is the nearest grocery store? Bank? Drug store?
- ☐ Is public transportation available and nearby?
- ☐ Is it conducive to your work? Some people need silence and may find it difficult to work on a busy street; others prefer street noise while they work.
- ☐ Don't be afraid to ask questions about anything that seems broken, unusual, or off.

a check for the first and last month's rent as well as a deposit (usually equal to a month's rent). Note that most landlords will want to check your credit, a list of references, and financial information (e.g., how you will pay the rent). Come prepared with whatever information and documentation needed to submit an application for the apartment you want. Although some busy housing markets require you to move quickly to secure an apartment, be sure that you really want the apartment before you put down a deposit because the deposit likely will not be returned if you change your mind.

Most landlords require that you sign a lease; if a lease is not offered, request one. Sometimes landlords rely on verbal agreements, but always get a written lease to protect yourself against sudden rent increases or eviction. You will not want to worry about getting thrown out of your apartment when you are eyeball deep in your research. Carefully read a lease before signing. Be certain that this apartment is the one that you want because once you sign a lease you have committed yourself to its terms. If you decide to move and break your lease, you could be held liable for the balance.

Perhaps the most important consideration in choosing an apartment is the rent: What can you afford? Draw up a budget before shopping for apartments; later in this chapter I discuss budgeting and provide relevant resources. According to experts, your monthly housing expense should amount to no more than 25% to 30% of your monthly income. How do you manage it? A roommate is often the answer.

A roommate can make housing costs more affordable because you share the cost of rent and utilities. Select your new roommate carefully, or you could be disappointed to learn that your lifestyles do not match well or that your roommate does not honor his or her financial obligations (leaving you in the lurch for rent and utilities). Remember that friends are not always good choices as roommates. Seek someone with a similar lifestyle. Check the bulletin boards at school and speak with other graduate students, and you may find a roommate with similar needs for quiet study time. Roommate matching services are also available and are particularly helpful if you are moving to a new town. One of the biggest advantages of a roommate matching service is the screening process (financial as well as lifestyle). Find a roommate matching service in the Yellow Pages or online (search "roommate matching service") and check with the Better Business Bureau for complaints before choosing a service.

The most important consideration in choosing a roommate is whether your lifestyles match. Ask yourself the following beforehand to know what you will and will not tolerate:

- Will you consider someone of the opposite sex?
- Will you consider someone with a live-in girlfriend or boyfriend?
- Will you consider someone whose girlfriend or boyfriend spends lots of time over?
- Will you consider a smoker?
- Will you consider someone who regularly engages in substance use?
- Will you consider someone of a different sexual orientation?
- Will you consider someone with a pet?
- Will you consider a morning person versus a night owl?
- Do working hours matter?
- What is the person's ideas about tidiness? Do they match your own?
- What are your preferences for inviting people over? How often do you have friends over and how many at a time? Overnight guests?
- Are any hobbies off limits (any loud or space-hogging hobbies like drumming or carpentry)?
- How will your new roommate pay his or her half of the expenses?

Trust your gut. If you do not feel comfortable, even if you cannot articulate why, go with your instinct. Although the search for a roommate can be daunting and the idea of sharing your space with someone else can be scary, the financial realities of graduate school make roommates a non-negotiable option for most students. Graduate school is enough of a challenge without adding extra financial pressures. Roommates share the burden of rent and utilities, and they can provide much needed companionship during what will be some of the most stressful—and exciting—years of your life.

Homeownership and Graduate School

Entering graduate students who own homes will find that moving to a new town or city is not as simple as renting an apartment and hauling possessions. Instead, they must determine whether to purchase or rent a home in their new city—and whether to sell their existing home. Is graduate school the right time to buy a home? Students who move to areas of the country with very affordable real estate prices may wonder if it makes more sense to buy a home. This is especially common in areas where mortgage payments are similar in cost to rentals. Is buying a home in graduate school a good idea?

Consider the pragmatics. Can you afford a down payment, closing costs, and renovation costs? Although it may appear that buying a home is cheaper than renting, affording a home means more than making mortgage payments. Property taxes, home insurance, maintenance, and emergency repairs are part of a homeowner's budget. Will a $5,000 emergency repair to the roof or furnace deplete your savings? Aside from the financial realities, are you prepared for the day-to-day work that homeownership entails? Mowing the lawn, yard work, cleaning gutters, and other routine maintenance will eat into your study and relaxation time.

What happens after you graduate? Most new graduate students are unable to predict their whereabouts after graduation. Will you relocate after graduate school? Where? How easy will it be to sell the property? Will you sell for a loss? Will you be able to rent the home for at least the cost of the mortgage? Are you able to maintain the property from a distance?

Why purchase a home during graduate school? Homeownership, with all its stresses, provides a sense of stability that many students find attractive. Students who plan to remain in the same town or city after graduate school might consider homeownership. However, plans change, so homebuyers need an exit strategy right from the beginning. If you choose to purchase a home, consider what is entailed in renting it and selling it.

Being a landlord entails more than getting tenants to sign a lease and send monthly rent. Are you prepared to repair and maintain your property from afar? Can you afford to let the property sit vacant between rentals? How long can you afford to wait for a tenant? Are you prepared for tenants who do not pay the rent on time, let the property get run down, or break things? Although the idea of renting a home often is intuitively pleasing ("We don't have to sell it, it's still ours, and it pays for itself"), the reality of an empty home or difficult tenants surprises many new landlords. Research your options before you purchase a home.

How about selling a home? Financially established graduate students as well as new graduates are often faced with selling a home before entering graduate school or a new career. Proper pricing of a home is the most critical factor affecting the time it takes to sell. Many homeowners find it difficult to estimate the value of their homes. One way is to compare your home with those on the market and recent sales. A real estate agent can help with making pricing and other decisions. Although sellers must pay an agent a percentage of the sale price, entering students who are busy and need to sell their homes quickly might consider hiring a real estate agent a necessity. The recommended readings at the end of this chapter offer advice on managing real estate decisions.

Move to Your New Home

The lease is signed and it is time to move. How do you get all of your stuff to your new home? Do you find the prospect of loading all of your possessions into a truck and trekking to your new place stressful? You are not alone. Nearly everyone finds relocation challenging. Should you move yourself or do you hire a mover? Most graduate students self-move, but the method you choose depends on the following:

- Where are you moving from and to? If you are moving from or to a dorm, a self-move probably is the way to go. A move between apartments or houses usually entails more furniture and boxes and can be more complicated.
- Do you have the time to pack and move?
- Do you have helpers (friends and family) to move large and heavy objects?
- Can you drive a rental truck, or do you know someone who can?
- How heavy, awkward, and expensive are the items? If you are moving an antique armoire or a 250-pound television (you will not need that in grad school!), consider hiring movers.
- Would breaking or damaging an item be devastating and put strain on a friendship? If so, then a self-move may not be right for you.

- How far away is your new home? Long-distance moves are better suited to professional movers; otherwise you will ask your friends to go away for the weekend—a major favor.

If you opt for a self-move, your next concern is soliciting person-power. Line up volunteers ahead of time, and make sure that you can count on them. Pizza and promises to reciprocate usually work well. Hauling capacity is the second essential. Rent a larger truck than you think you need so you can move all your stuff in one trip. Do not waste time on moving day trying to fit everything into a truck that is too small. Compare deals with several moving truck rental companies. Ask the following questions:

- How early do I need to book?
- What is the cancellation policy?
- Is a deposit required?
- What size trucks do you have, and how do you determine what size is needed?
- Where do I pick up and drop off the truck?
- Are there any time restrictions?
- What are the daily charges?
- Are there charges for mileage, drop off, or anything else?
- Are there driver age restrictions?
- Can more than one person drive?
- Must I refill the gas tank?
- When do I pay?
- Am I covered by my auto insurance?
- What are the insurance options?
- What happens if I am not insured?

Sometimes a self-move is not the way to go. If you are moving a long distance, have few friends to rely on, or cannot spare the time, hiring a mover might be a better option. If you decide to hire a mover, be sure to do your homework. Locate movers by asking friends and family for recommendations. If you do not have firsthand knowledge about a small local mover, you are better off going with a national mover. Approach several companies at least a month in advance and request a free home visit to receive accurate estimates. Some will give estimates over the phone or over the Internet. Ask for a binding estimate, which means that the company is committed to moving you for that fee. Ask for a written contract and be sure that you understand it. Most important, seek enough insurance to cover any losses. Insurance adds to the price but is essential for peace of mind.

Regardless of which way you choose to move—by yourself or with a mover—be sure to notify your current landlord and your new landlord of your moving date. If you are moving into an apartment building, you likely will have to notify the superintendent, too. Be aware that some apartment buildings have rules limiting when moves can take place (e.g., only on weekdays between 8 a.m. and 4 p.m.). Learn those rules before moving day to avoid unpleasant surprises.

Tip

Place everything that you will need for the first evening and morning after your move into one box and label it so that you can find it. This will keep you from having to unpack that first night when you are exhausted. Include sheets, toiletries, a change of clothes, coffee pot, utensils, and anything else that you think you will need to make that first 24 hours in your new home more comfortable.

Aside from unpacking, there are several other things you need to do to complete your move, many of which can be completed before your moving date:

- Use mail forwarding to route mail from your old address to your new address.
- Change addresses on bank statements, magazines (most permit you to make address changes over the Web site), credit card bills (you do not want these to get to you late or get lost as it could damage your credit rating), car payments, and car insurance (moving may change your insurance plan).
- If you move to a new state, consider whether you need to change your driver's license, car registration, license plates, and car insurance.
- Check on phone installation (if you maintain only a cell phone, check to see you have adequate coverage in your new home and enough minutes in your plan).
- Find out who is responsible for the following:
  - Electric and gas
  - Cable
  - Trash collection
  - Water

Although moving is stressful, it serves a useful purpose (aside from getting you closer to school): It marks the transition to a new lifestyle, that of graduate student. The act of moving signifies that this is a new period in life and makes it easier to change old habits and establish new ones. Graduate school is a whole new animal and requires a different perspective on life and different work habits than when you were an undergraduate. Use your move as an opportunity to establish new habits that will foster success during graduate school.

Beyond Loans for Funding: Graduate Assistantships

Funding is critical to success in graduate school. The more funding you can get for the least amount of work, the better because you will have more time for study and research and be able to finish sooner. Many psychology PhD programs try to support all PhD students during the 5 or so years the university deems necessary to complete the program; some PhD programs support students only after the first year of graduate school.

Most students take out loans to pay at least some of their expenses during graduate school. Sixty-eight percent of 2003 psychology doctoral graduates reported debt, with 35% reporting a debt of $75,000 or higher (Wicherski & Kohout, 2005). PsyD students and master's students often receive little to no financial aid from the school and often rely on earned income and loans. Many books cover the process of seeking financial aid and the forms of aid available, such as government loans (Stafford and Perkins loans) and outside grants and scholarships (see the list at the end of this chapter).

Assistantships are the most common form of financial aid awarded to graduate students. They require service from the student in exchange for a tuition waiver and living stipend; the stipend can range from $5,000 to $14,000 per year. The philosophy behind assistantships is that doctoral students are seen as apprentice members of the department; therefore they are used to inexpensively fill departmental research and teaching needs. Doctoral students are more commonly awarded assistantships, although master's students can also receive them.

Assistantships are awarded by faculty, so relationships with faculty members have everything to do with whether you are awarded one. Faculty seek to work with students who are competent and dependable. Assistantships offer opportunities to develop and strengthen relationships with faculty who can also influence your tenure in school—as committee members as well as leads for jobs when you graduate. It is not uncommon for graduate students who do not receive funding during their first year of graduate school to develop good working relationships with faculty and later be invited to work as assistants and get their tuition paid the following years. Be good to faculty; they can help you in more ways than you can imagine.

TEACHING ASSISTANTSHIP

Graduate students who are assigned teaching assistantships are assigned to assist an instructor (or instructors) for typically 20 hours per week. Usually a teaching assistant (TA) will help the instructor by attending lectures, grading papers, supervising labs, and leading classroom discussions for introductory undergraduate courses. More advanced graduate students may be asked to teach a course and may have the freedom to choose a textbook and create a syllabus for the course; these more advanced teaching assignments may be called teaching fellowships or may simply be called teaching assistantships (though it is not really assisting if you are teaching the course, right?). Most departments offer orientation seminars for TAs, especially those who will have full responsibility for teaching a course; these seminars help students become acquainted with the basics of teaching, including university requirements for textbooks and syllabi.

A teaching assistantship can be a welcome change from coursework and research. As a TA you will have the opportunity to work alongside several professors. For example, one student was a TA for the discussion sections of one professor's introductory psychology class and the next semester graded papers for another professor's social psychology class. Working as a TA can be a good way to get to know different professors, to get recognition from faculty, and to decide if an academic career as a professor is for you. That said, a teaching assistantship can be a time suck. Although it is supposed to be a 20-hour per week assignment, it can entail many more hours, especially if you are preparing lectures or grading lengthy papers. Teaching assistants spend time in the classroom, and outside of the classroom their time is spent preparing and grading as well as holding office hours to answer student questions. Teaching experience is valuable, particularly if you seek a career in academia, but it can also slow down your progress because it eats into study time and research time.

RESEARCH ASSISTANTSHIP

A research assistantship requires engaging in laboratory or other work under the direction of a faculty member. Research assistants (RAs) are paid by grants that professors obtain from funding agencies, such as government agencies and foundations, to support their research. Professors use grant funds to support all aspects of their research, including equipment, technology, travel, and staff (i.e., graduate students) to carry it out. As an RA, you will be asked to work about 20 hours per week, although the exact hours can vary week to week and by faculty member. Often the hours are flexible, varying over the semester and over the course of a research project. You might be required to work many more hours during critical phases of research. If you take on a larger role that merits coauthorship on a research project, then your work likely will continue well after the assistantship ends, but the reward is experience and coauthorship on a paper or article. Sometimes students are asked to work during the summer; often supervisors may ask you to work less during the summer or will offer summer salary for the work.

As an RA, you are an essential component to the business of academia. Professors handpick RAs to help them get the research proposed in their grants done. If the work is not completed, the funding agencies may withhold grants and the professor will lose funding as well as the ability to conduct research. Research funding is competitive, often a source of financial support for faculty positions, and the basis for faculty promotion and career opportunities. Professors have a personal stake in getting their projects done right and efficiently, so they seek students who can follow instructions, take initiative, and work independently to complete research projects.

Research assistants' activities vary. Many RAs perform tasks that are closely connected with the research project, such as literature searching, data entry, statistical analyses, and writing, but they may also perform more mundane tasks, such as compiling surveys, stuffing envelopes, searching for references, and typing reference lists. Although boring, these tasks are an essential part of conducting research. Sometimes supervisors may ask RAs to do nonresearch-related clerical work and filing that are mundane tasks but a necessary part of academic life. Occasionally RAs are faced with helping their supervisors with more personal matters that are not part of the job description. One first-year graduate student was asked by a supervisor to search the university library for books on art history to help the supervisor's young daughter complete an art project for school. Another graduate student was asked to transport office supplies and campus mail to her supervisor's home each week during her sabbatical (a semester or year break that professors earn after several years of service). Although it is not appropriate for faculty to request assistance with personal matters, such as their children's homework assignments, students are in a bind as to whether to speak up or complete the tasks so as to maintain the relationship. This is a challenging decision with possible implications for students' graduate careers. There is no right or wrong response on your part. Carefully consider what you can bear and the potential consequences of each route of action.

The relationship with your supervisor and the project may be particularly challenging if the supervisor is also your mentor and advisor. The lines between the assistantship and your own research as well as collaborative research may blur. Graduate students whose supervisors are also their advisors may find it particularly hard to say no. Later in this book I will discuss the role of politics in graduate school. For now, recognize that assistantships are not a free ride. Research assistants work hard for their funding, and some RAs may have more relevant and rewarding experiences than others. Some may work harder than others. It is not fair, but it is a fact of life as a graduate student.

However challenging, there are many benefits to working as an RA. First and foremost is that you learn how to do research: You get to see a scientist at work distilling problems, generating hypotheses, designing methodologies, analyzing data, and drawing conclusions. Your assistantship may spark research ideas for your own projects and may offer a springboard in creating your own research agenda. Some graduate students find that their dissertations grow out of their work as RAs. Others become coauthors with faculty on papers resulting from the research conducted as an RA.

Generally speaking, a research assistantship is more desirable to students than a teaching assistantship because of the opportunities to develop methodological, statistical, and practical experience. Even if it is not your own research area, an RA position will provide excellent training, experience, and perhaps papers and publications. A research assistantship is even more valuable if it is in an area related to your research because you will be paid to conduct research that will aid your own projects. Regardless of whether you are awarded a teaching or research assistantship, treat it as a job. Show that you are dedicated and responsible and that you can get the work done, be a team player, and communicate effectively with others.

Tip

Keep a record of your assistantship. What hours did you work? What activities did you complete? Update these each week and carefully maintain your records. These records will be useful if a disagreement ever arises between you and your supervisor. They are also useful documentation of your research skills and experiences.

Do Work and Graduate School Mix?

Once you obtain a master's degree, a new work option will open up to you: being an adjunct instructor. Adjunct instructors are part-time college teachers hired at both 2- and 4-year colleges. As an adjunct instructor, you will be given full responsibility for teaching a course. Departments vary in their policies regarding curricula and books, but usually you will design your own syllabus and assignments and choose your own textbook. The autonomy that adjunct instructors receive to teach courses as they see fit is a double-edged sword. It is exciting to create your own course and design your own methods for imparting knowledge to your students, but it is also very time consuming. As graduate students teach their first courses, they quickly realize that teaching takes much more time than they anticipate. Hours will be spent designing assignments, preparing lectures, doing outside reading, preparing overheads and handouts, writing tests, conferring with students, and grading assignments. Teaching as an adjunct instructor is excellent experience for graduate students who expect to become professors, but the drawback is that it eats up valuable research time. Research is an academic's currency; teaching experience is helpful in getting a job as a professor, but a solid research program is essential.

What about other work, aside from teaching as an adjunct instructor? Generally speaking, full-time graduate study should be treated as a full-time job. This is especially true if you have an assistantship or were awarded a fellowship or scholarship; if you have these forms of financial aid, faculty will expect you to devote all of your time to graduate school. In fact, many faculty and departments frown on students working outside of the program. Some schools and departments have regulations forbidding students to work outside of the university, especially if the students receive funding. Sometimes students take on outside work secretly, hiding it from faculty.

> Terry had a hard time making ends meet. His assistantship covered his tuition, but the stipend was too small to meet his expenses. He detested the idea of taking out loans and did not want to worry about health insurance or a drop-in income, so he decided to continue working full time. He worked at an inpatient clinic, a job that was related to his interest in psychology. He worked overnight shifts, which were generally quiet. Most nights he stayed up reading and studying and was not interrupted. However, he was required to stay awake. After working a night shift he often felt like a zombie, making it hard to participate in class. Some nights were very busy, with troubled patients in need of assistance. Although this was a seemingly easy job that provided lots of study time, Terry found it hard to maintain his energy. Plus he had to keep his job a secret because graduate students in his department were encouraged to not work. He is unsure if it is an official rule, but the unwritten suggestion is that graduate students who receive funding should treat their studies and assistantship as a full-time job. Some mornings Terry arrived exhausted. His advisor asked if everything was all right. Terry hated lying but knew that telling Dr. Smith about his job could jeopardize his funding and perhaps even his slot in graduate school.

The downside of working during graduate school is that it may be overwhelming and may contribute to a sense of stress over trying to be all things to all people (student, researcher, employee). Hiding employment is troubling to many students. Is working during graduate school, secretly or otherwise, worth it? The time you take to work will slow down your research, and you will take more time to finish your degree. If you must work, choose something that is not too mentally taxing. One student worked as a bartender 2 nights a week at a busy establishment and earned enough to support himself while not eating into his research and study time. A job where you can also do homework may also be appropriate.

The final word on working during graduate school? Try to avoid it if you hope to finish your degree on time and with your sanity intact.

Manage Your Money

Funding graduate study is not just about getting money; it is also about keeping it by spending what you have wisely. No matter how large your stipend or how many classes you teach as an adjunct instructor, you will run short on funds to cover living expenses. That is simply reality. The vast majority of graduate students take out loans, if not for tuition then to cover at least some of the costs of living. Make what you have work for you, and avoid taking out additional unnecessary (and costly!) loans by drawing up a budget and sticking to it.

Draw up a budget. Record all sources of income: loans, stipends, work, and family. List all monthly expenditures, including rent, utilities (phone, cable, Internet); food (groceries, lunch, dinners out); transportation (car payment, subway fare, parking, maintenance, gas); insurance (medical, disability, etc.); entertainment (movies, travel, clubs); clothing (also laundry and dry cleaning); personal care (toiletries, gym membership, hair cuts, manicures); health (out-of-pocket expenses for doctor visits, prescriptions); credit card payments; school expenses (tuition, books, photocopying); and miscellaneous (gifts, unanticipated expenses). Once you have your income and expenditures on paper, compare them. Do you have money left over? If so, it means that you are spending less than you are earning—congratulations! Use extra cash to pay down credit card balances and to save. Most graduate students will find that their expenses exceed their income and will have to look for places to save. For example, transportation often is a major budget item for students. Is a car really necessary? Is public transportation available? Reconsider your needs and your wants. Sometimes wants masquerade as needs: Know the difference.

Track your spending for 2 to 4 weeks to see where your money goes and to discover places to save. Some things you believe are necessities are really luxuries in disguise. Consider that mocha latte from the coffee shop. You might pick one up each morning without thinking twice. A $3 latte daily is $90 per month. If you skip it, make your own, or have a cup of coffee from the deli even a few times per week, you will have more cash for things that are truly important to you. Many graduate students scoff on spending $3 on a cup of coffee and instead drink coffee at the university's student lounge. Even cheap university coffee can add up. Two large coffees each weekday at $1 each amount to $40 each month. Consider putting a coffee pot in your office. Many students are surprised by what they learn by tracking their spending. Try it. You will learn where your money goes and will identify ways to curb expenses. The fewer expenses you have, the less you will need to take out in loans or put on credit cards, and the less worry you will have later on.

Tip

Many students, especially those who are on internship or externship and in professional settings, find themselves spending more than they can afford on clothes and luxuries. Avoid prematurely living like a professional. There will be plenty of time to upgrade your lifestyle later—if you avoid racking up unnecessary debt now.

Managing your money is not just about managing what is in your pocket. It is about planning. Medical insurance is an important need that students must plan for. When you are young and healthy it is hard to justify paying for medical insurance, but trying to get through graduate school without medical insurance is a serious risk. If medical care is needed it could result in devastating financial problems that put schooling in hold. Medical insurance is a form of financial protection. If you do not have insurance, you will have to pay the full cost of any medical services without being able to file an insurance claim and be reimbursed. Without medical insurance, you might forgo care, get substandard care, and pay the full cost of any medical care you receive. If that care entails even a short hospital stay or a few tests, the expense can be quite damaging.

If you are no longer covered on your family's insurance plan, look for other options. There are two ways of obtaining medical insurance: through a group or as an individual. Group insurance is eligible to a group of people because of their relationship with a particular company or organization. Some universities give graduate students the opportunity to purchase insurance at group rates. Group insurance is mainly sold to employers who pay at least a portion of the premium for their employees. Individual health insurance is sold to individuals and families. If you obtain individual insurance, shop around because coverage and premiums can vary substantially. Forgoing medical insurance is not an option. Even a routine illness requiring several doctor's visits or a short hospital stay grows expensive very quickly. A serious illness can be financially devastating. Where can you find affordable insurance?

- Contact your state department of insurance by phone or through their Web site to get information about types of plans and reputable sources. The National Association of Insurance Commissioners (http://www.naic.org/state_web_map.htm) maintains links to all state departments of insurance.

- Community-based organizations including churches, synagogues, chambers of commerce, and women's centers sometimes endorse particular programs or can make suggestions.
- Your alumni association may be able to suggest a medical insurance carrier.
- Student Resources (http://www.studentresources.com) is an insurance company that caters to students and is owned by United Health, one of the largest insurance carriers in the United States.

The challenges of graduate school are well under way by the time classes begin. Carefully plan your move and get your finances in order and you will ease the transition and give yourself the opportunity to focus your attention on the intellectual and emotional transition, which we discuss in the next chapter.

Recommended Reading

Allen, J., & Regelman, K. (2005). *How to survive a move: By hundreds of happy people who did and some things to avoid, from a few who haven't unpacked yet.* Atlanta, GA: Hundreds of Heads Books.

Bowers, L. J. (2001). *On your own for the first time: A guide to starting off in the real world.* Cincinnati, OH: Pyramid.

Davis, S. (2004). *A survival guide for buying a home.* New York: AMACOM/ American Management Association.

Davis, S. (2005). *A survival guide for selling a home.* New York: AMACOM/ American Management Association.

Hamel, A. V., Heiberger, M. M., & Vick, J. M. (2002). *Graduate school funding handbook.* Philadelphia: University of Pennsylvania Press.

Lawrence, J. (2004). *The budget kit: The common cents money management workbook.* Chicago: Dearborn Trade.

Rich, J. R. (2004). *Make your paycheck list: How to create a budget you can live with.* Franklin, NJ: Career Press.

Wilner, A., & Stocker, C. (2005). *The quarterlifer's companion: How to get on the right career path, control your finances, and find the support network you need to thrive.* New York: McGraw Hill.

Transition to Graduate School 2

As a first-year graduate student, you are about to enter a whole new world, one vastly different from your undergraduate experience. This is especially true if you are a doctoral student. In graduate school you will be immersed in a learning environment and surrounded by like-minded folk who are interested in improving human life by making and applying psychological findings. You will work under the tutelage of master researchers and practitioners who are making discoveries that will fill tomorrow's textbooks. You are one of the fortunate few people who inhabit this world of discovery. Recall the graduate admissions procedure: Remember how grueling it was? The admissions process is intended to weed out those who are not ready for or capable of engaging in the extended study and critical analysis needed to become a psychologist. This chapter explores the process of graduate study, how it differs from your undergraduate experience, and how to ease your transition to this new phase in your education.

Orientation to Graduate School

Your first few days as a graduate student serve as a foundation for your academic career. Remember this, begin on the right foot, and do not follow Robert's lead.

> The first week of graduate school has barely begun and Robert feels out of breath. He explains, "There's so much to know. It seems that there is much more to know than there was in undergrad. It doesn't look like anyone is going to offer much help." And it seems that whenever he asks a question someone says, "That was covered in orientation." Robert didn't attend orientation, reasoning, "They're just going to hand out the course catalog and tell you where the library is." Now he feels that he's begun graduate school at a disadvantage relative to the other students.

Orientation events are important opportunities to get to know your new school. Most graduate departments offer an orientation session during which students learn the lay of the land, including how courses are selected (you may even register during orientation), program requirements, and how departmental resources like office space, lab time, and technology are allocated. What are the purposes of orientation? What should you get out of it?

LEARN PROGRAM OVERVIEW AND REQUIREMENTS

Orientation sessions cover detailed information about the program. You will learn about coursework: What courses are required? What courses are free electives, courses that are not required but can enhance your marketable skills and serve as the basis for a specialty area of competence? You will learn which courses have prerequisites and the degree of flexibility in satisfying prerequisites. Are there opportunities to take interdisciplinary courses, and how many classes in other disciplines will satisfy degree requirements? Orientation should explain the minimum standards for performance, grade point average requirements, how advisors are assigned, and internship and externship requirements. Expect to learn about qualifying or comprehensive exams and the requirements for advancement to doctoral candidacy.

Orientation can be overwhelming because you will be given a large amount of information in a short period. Remember that the most important information is repeated in writing, usually in student handbooks and the graduate catalog. Most departments publish their own student handbooks, detailing specific information that entering graduate students need to know about the department and program. After orientation, read all of the materials distributed, especially the student handbook and graduate catalog. Knowing departmental and program policies, procedures, and requirements will help to prepare you for the demands of graduate school and avoid embarrassing mistakes. After studying departmental and program handouts and publications, if you have additional questions, approach faculty for assistance. However, attempt to find the answer on your own first, because asking questions about material that is explained thoroughly in the student handbook will send the message that you are not an independent and motivated student but instead require hand feeding of information, which is not a message that you want to send.

Tip

Keep the course catalog that you receive at orientation because it spells out all of the requirements for your degree at the time of entry. If the program is changed, students who enrolled before the change are grandfathered in.

GET TO KNOW OTHER STUDENTS

An important reason to attend orientation is to get to know other students. You will get a profile of your classmates. How motivated do they appear? What kinds of questions do they ask? Are they competitive? Who might you befriend? Most people feel shy during orientation. It is normal to feel a little bit awkward. Remember that the other students are in the same boat: They likely also feel awkward. You will likely make small talk about basic background information such as where you earned your degree, where you are from, where you live now, and perhaps the most common issue over which to bond, parking. The important thing is that you start meeting and getting to know students who will become colleagues. Graduate school is stressful, and a social support system is important to success. Sure, you have friends from college, but graduate school is unlike the "real world." It is important to have friends who understand what you are going through—fellow graduate students.

IDENTIFY DEPARTMENTAL ROLES

One of the confusing parts about graduate school entails determining who is who in the department (Bloom, Karp, & Cohen, 1998). It is not just a matter of learning names. The world is no longer broken down into the simple categories of faculty and student anymore. What are the various roles in a department?

- *Research assistant:* Typically a graduate student, but can be an undergraduate, who is paid to carry out research for a faculty member.
- *Teaching assistant:* A graduate student who is paid to assist in teaching a course, usually including grading, proctoring exams, and leading discussion sections.
- *Postdoc:* A postdoc or postdoctoral fellow has a doctoral degree, works as a researcher for a faculty member, and is paid from a

faculty member's grant. Postdocs may range from new doctorates to experienced researchers.

- *Lecturer:* In the United States, a lecturer often is a college teacher who does not have a doctoral degree. Outside of the United States, "lecturer" is often a title used for professor.
- *Adjunct instructor:* A professor who teaches part time.
- *Assistant professor:* An entry-level professor position, without tenure. The assistant professor works toward gaining tenure, which typically is applied for after 6 years of service.
- *Associate professor:* The second level of professor hierarchy. Associate professors have gained tenure.
- *Professor:* A full professor is the highest level of distinction, the most senior rank.
- *Department chair:* A professor who is the administrative head of the department, sometimes selected by departmental vote and other times appointed by an administrator.
- *Support staff:* Administrative assistants and secretarial staff offer more than office skills. They are the eyes and ears of the department and important sources of information. Establish relationships with support staff as they can offer a great deal of assistance in answering questions about departmental policies, securing resources, and learning about faculty.

MEET FACULTY

Orientation often includes a mixer or social hour in which faculty, staff, and graduate students mingle. The purpose of these events is to meet other people, but remember that this is the graduate school equivalent of an office party: Although it is social in nature, faculty are observing and learning about students. Make sure that your first impression is a good one. That said, do not feel pressured to be brilliant in front of faculty. Simply be friendly and ask appropriate questions about the program, if you have any, and show genuine interest in others' work.

Tip Be genuine in all interactions with faculty, staff, and graduate students.

Meeting faculty is an important purpose of attending orientation. Faculty attend to get a peek at the incoming students from which their advisees and assistants will come. You will have an opportunity to get to know faculty and get ideas on who might be good mentors. Good relationships with faculty will aid you throughout graduate school, not simply through mentorship, advisement, and training but also with the support and political savvyness that are necessary for success. Relationships with faculty can be the ticket to participation in research as well as assistantship opportunities, not to mention letters of recommendation when you apply for internship and jobs after graduation.

Tip

Remember that faculty are not necessarily middle-aged or older and male. Many faculty are young, female, and dress similar to students. It is sometimes hard to tell who is a faculty member and who is a student because some faculty may look like students. Beware. You are better off assuming that a graduate student is a faculty member than the reverse.

ASK QUESTIONS

Before you begin asking questions, remember that contrary to what children and students are told, there are stupid, or bad, questions. In a formal orientation session, bad questions are those that cover material that was presented before you arrived (if late), cover material presented without seeking additional clarification about an issue, or pertain to only your personal concerns (and are not relevant to other students). All questions related to concerns about your particular situation should be held until you meet one-on-one with an advisor or other faculty member; these questions are not appropriate to ask in a group orientation setting.

What should you ask during a group orientation? There are many good questions to ask. Be sure not to ask them all at once: Pace yourself and ask questions about relevant material as it is covered. Compare the information you receive with your questions and then seek clarification about anything you do not understand or that is not covered. Basic information about your program that you should know after orientation includes the following:

- What are the regulations for adding and dropping courses?
- How are advisors assigned?
- Are thesis and dissertation advisors assigned?
- How are internship and externships selected? Do students have input in selections?
- When are students eligible for comprehensive exams?

- What happens if a student does not pass the comprehensive exam?
- What are the steps in the thesis and dissertation process (i.e., is it simply proposal defense and thesis or dissertation defense or is there another step, such as a progress report)?

Remember that you have lots of opportunities to ask questions; you do not have to ask them all during the orientation session. Some of your questions will be answered during your self-orientation, as described next.

GUIDE YOURSELF

Supplement the orientation session by independently seeking answers to your questions (Mitchell, 1996; Peters, 1997). Seek information about the more subtle aspects of graduate life. Approach multiple sources because you may find that a graduate student may have a different perspective on a question about the pace of proposal writing, for example, than a more senior student or faculty member. Seek overall consensus and compare the answers you receive because they may not always match up. The truth is often a mix depending on perspective and circumstance. Discussions with students and faculty should give you a sense of the departmental culture.

In addition to seeking answers to specific questions, your self-orientation should provide you with all the information and resources that you need to start the school year, including the following:

- Obtain your school ID.
- Get to know the different campus buildings and the layout of campus.
- Locate the gym.
- Locate computer labs, printers, copies, and wireless areas.
- Learn whether you need a network ID to log into the campus computer or wireless system.
- Locate the library.
- Understand the organization of the library. Are all library resources housed in one building? Some university libraries are fragmented over several buildings; others separate and house library holdings by field.
- Locate where the most recent periodicals are kept. Which journals are available online? Where are the copiers and printers? How do you access library resources online?
- Locate the cafeteria and nearby cafes. Where can you get a cup of coffee?
- Locate parking lots near buildings as well as alternative places to park in the likely event of crowding.
- Locate the departmental offices. Are they located on the same floor in the same building?
- Determine whether medical insurance is available through the university.

- Set up your university e-mail account and use that for professional correspondence and professional e-mail lists.
- Many universities block free e-mail addresses (e.g., Hotmail, Yahoo, AOL) and treat them as spam, so use your university e-mail instead of your personal account for school-related communication, such as e-mails with professors.

Understand How Graduate School Is Different

Many things about graduate school are different from undergraduate school. Master's programs are more advanced than undergraduate programs, with more seminar-style classes, heavier reading loads, and more papers. Doctoral programs are radically different, as described below (note that, depending on the program, many of these characteristics describe some master's programs).

STUDENTS ARE THEIR OWN GUIDES

Most undergraduate students receive frequent feedback and are told all the important information about their program that they need to know. Do not assume that is the case in graduate school; do not wait to be told (Frank & Stein, 2004). Actively seek out information about course, experiential, and dissertation policies. Many students only ask questions when something is wrong, like when they are locked out of the university computing system. By waiting until something is wrong, students often miss the opportunity to fix the problem. Ask questions early and often, but judiciously. Seek information from multiple sources, including faculty, staff, and other graduate students.

Graduate students must learn to guide themselves. Except for coursework, which is a small portion of the overall requirements of the doctoral degree, the only person who will monitor your progress in graduate school is you (Bloom et al., 1998; Frank & Stein, 2004). No one cares as much about your success as you do. No one will monitor your progress or advocate for your interests as well as you do. You cannot expect anyone to keep track of what courses you have taken, whether you meet the prerequisites for required courses, or whether you have filed necessary paperwork. You are your own guide, and autonomy—the ability to self-govern—is rewarded. This applies to the mundane details of graduate school, such as meeting fellowship application deadlines, completing coursework on time, and selecting and registering for courses, but it also applies to the big picture issues, such as preparing for comprehensive exams, choosing thesis and dissertation topics, and carrying out the thesis or dissertation. Many students find the heightened autonomy a culture shock. Not everything is clearly laid out, and you must take the initiative in seeking information, assistance, and feedback.

EXPECTATIONS DIFFER AND GRADES DO NOT MATTER (MUCH)

One difference between graduate school and college that most students immediately notice is the class size. Depending on the level and course, most graduate school classes are capped at 10 to 25 students. Graduate courses are often taught as seminars, entailing a great deal of reading and advance preparation for in-depth class discussions and extensive involvement with faculty (Colón Semenza, 2005). Graduate students also encounter different expectations for learning in graduate classes. Absorbing facts and content is no longer enough to earn good grades. Professors are interested in seeing how students think. Expect to be asked to read complex texts and demonstrate that you can manipulate the information (i.e., apply, evaluate, analyze, and synthesize it) to draw conclusions. Rote memorization is no longer enough. In graduate school, success requires the ability to think and to articulate a line of thought.

Coursework and grades are not important in graduate school—to an extent (Bloom et al., 1998; Frank & Stein, 2004; Mitchell, 1996). Grade inflation is rampant in graduate school, so very poor grades are rare. Grade inflation is common because graduate students are excellent students. Exceptional grades and GRE scores are required to gain admittance to graduate school. Good students tend to earn good grades. Second, most graduate programs require that students maintain a B average; faculty award very few Cs. A grade of C is nearly equivalent to an F in graduate school.

Although students will enroll in courses in the beginning of graduate school, the later years of graduate school are not course-based. Instead, graduate students' work is focused on research problems. Faculty are less concerned that students learn facts than how to be psychologists. What students really learn in graduate school—how to do research and practice—happens outside of class, by doing. Successfully completing graduate study, specifically a doctoral degree, does not come from completing a set of required courses but rather from carrying out a program of research. That said, graduate study entails some classes.

GRADUATE SCHOOL IS AN APPRENTICESHIP

In graduate school, courses matter less than experience. Most of what you learn will come from professional activities: from conducting research and engaging in applied work. You will work as an apprentice to a faculty member on his or her research, getting hands-on experience selecting research problems, designing and carrying out experiments, and disseminating the results. Slowly you will learn the skills it takes to be a scientist and design your own research program. Applied training also takes the form of an apprenticeship whereby you will first observe expert clinicians, then accept your own clients under a faculty member's guidance, initially through direct observation and, later, through more informal supervision. There is no instruction book on how to become a psychologist. Learning occurs through immersion, by spending time observing, working alongside, and interacting with master psychologists.

GRADUATE SCHOOL ENTAILS SPECIALIZED STUDY

Undergraduate education provides a broad-based foundation in a given field. Psychology majors receive a general introduction to the field of psychology through a broad range of courses in the various subdisciplines. In graduate school, work is much more focused. Training is centered on one psychological subdiscipline, such as developmental or social psychology, but students specialize in a particular content area such as adolescent risk behaviors, alcoholism, social cognition, or persuasion. As a graduate student, you will not study textbooks, as you did in college. Instead, expertise in a psychological specialty comes from extensive study of classic and new scientific literature as well as interaction with peer and more senior colleagues.

GRADUATE STUDY TAKES TIME

You will find that it takes much more time to succeed in graduate school than it did in college. Moreover, how you use your time will change. You will spend less time in class and more time doing research, completing assistantships, attending lectures and symposiums, and fulfilling practicum requirements. Much of your time will be spent reading. You will read for class, for your advisor's project, and for your own research, and the reading will be more challenging than what you have encountered as an undergraduate student. You will also find that you spend more time on campus, in the department, your advisor's lab, your own office, and the library than you did as an undergraduate student. You will likely work at least some evenings and weekends. New students are often unaware of how their work will spill over into other areas of their lives. If you have a significant other or family, these new drains on your time will be challenging. Tell your loved ones about the new demands on your time and what help you need to succeed. Try to get more help around the house: Ask older children to take on chores to ease your burden, ask a relative to babysit while you work or take time to yourself, and ask your spouse to help in figuring out how to juggle the demands of graduate study with that of a family.

Graduate study challenges your intellect, time management capacities, coping resources, and energy. You will find that work is nearly constantly on your mind. You will get an idea for a paper, a solution to a problem, or insight into a finding while you complete everyday mundane tasks like driving to work or grocery shopping. Moreover, there is a mental toll to graduate school. It is not uncommon to be preoccupied with work while you are trying to relax and spend time with family and friends. Because your mind is always at work, you will make strides in your research, but family and friends will have to understand that you may sometimes be preoccupied with work.

Adapt to the Game

We have seen that graduate school is a different beast as compared with college. It also entails different, often unstated, rules. For example, as an undergraduate student, it was grades that mattered; a 4.0 grade point average was the measure of success. Not so in graduate school. Instead, it is experience that matters, namely in the form of research and applied experiences. Publications are the currency of academia and the major indicator of research productivity. Becoming involved in your advisor's research and establishing a research program of your own are critical to your success in academia, as a graduate student and prospective faculty member (Bloom et al., 1998; Peters, 1997). Students interested in applied careers should focus on developing practitioner skills through supervised experiences in a range of settings. Succeeding in this new game called *Graduate School* entails following a new set of rules.

EXPECT AMBIGUITY AND BE FLEXIBLE

Always remember that requirements and rules are much less explicit and structured in graduate than undergraduate school (Frank & Stein, 2004). Much of what will be expected of you and what you will encounter is not laid out in course catalogs and student handbooks. There is no standard timetable for navigating the graduate years; some students finish before others, and students set their own timetables. Although there are some required courses, most students tailor their curriculum to meet their anticipated needs. There is no one path toward becoming a skilled psychologist. Anticipate the ambiguity and provide your own structure by seeking the information that you need to make choices about your education.

Students who are flexible take advantage of opportunities that come their way. As a graduate student, you have very little power and control over your situation. Instead, you react to the demands of the department, faculty, and your advisor. If you are flexible, you are better able to manage change and seize opportunities that arise. Flexibility also means being intellectually open. For example, your advisor's research may not be exactly what you want to do, but approach your work with an open mind and you will learn from your experience. Being open to new ideas will help you to pick up a lot of information over your graduate school years that might help you to refocus your own research or direct you to a new line of research. Most students write dissertations on topics that they would not have predicted on entering graduate school.

PUT IN THE TIME

Graduate school is a full-time commitment. To be successful, you must put in hours of reading, study, and research. Conducting research is not just a matter of getting ideas but entails long hours of library research, reading, and planning. What many students are unprepared for is that there are also mundane tasks that are not interesting but must be completed, such as entering data, sorting surveys, stuffing envelopes, scanning data for errors, and soliciting participants. All of this takes time, in addition to producing research results while managing coursework, assistantship, and other duties.

Successful students do not just put in a lot of time, they put in face time. They spend time in the department and make themselves visible; they let their faces be seen. Sure, putting in time will ensure that you complete your work, but putting in face time makes it more likely that faculty will get to know you and identify you as a hard worker and team player. Spend time working in the department and other highly visible places like your office, the lab, the department lounge, and student lounge. Do not hang around aimlessly wasting time, because that will earn you a negative reputation; instead, make yourself visible around the department.

TAKE INITIATIVE AND BE TENACIOUS

The thesis or dissertation is your ticket out of graduate school. Master's students typically complete a thesis, a research project or lengthy review of the literature conducted under the guidance of a faculty member. Doctoral students complete a dissertation, an empirical research study designed to make new discoveries within a given field. Completing a thesis or dissertation is no easy feat. It is requires focus, dedication, and the ability to take the lead in designing, carrying out, and disseminating a research project. You may turn to your advisor for guidance, but, especially when writing your dissertation, no one will hold your hand and tell you what to do. Initiative—the ability to take charge and carry out decisions—is essential to completing the thesis or dissertation. Initiative comes in handy throughout graduate school because students who take initiative by seeking opportunities to assist faculty on research projects are more likely to earn publications and establish solid research programs.

Students need more than initiative to succeed in graduate school. Initiative might get you started on a project or task, but you will never finish unless you are tenacious. The ability to stick to a task and complete it slowly and surely despite conflicts and boredom is essential to completing a yearlong thesis or a multiyear dissertation project. The dissertation is likely the biggest project that students ever encounter, and it is uncertain how long it will take to complete. Students often underestimate the time to complete it because it is not uncommon to encounter obstacles that add months or years to the project. Many students lose their motivation and do not complete the dissertation at all. Tenacious students stick with it and work on the dissertation consistently despite feeling unmotivated or depressed.

DEVELOP INTERPERSONAL COMMUNICATION SKILLS

You may have enrolled in graduate school to become a researcher, assuming that you will not have to "deal with people," but it will be difficult to succeed without developing interpersonal skills. Success in graduate school (and everywhere) depends on your ability to get along with others and to build and maintain relationships with others—fellow students, faculty, staff, and your advisor. Interpersonal skills permit you to communicate your needs and interact with others in ways that help you to achieve your goals. Interpersonal skills are essential for acquiring the resources, such as equipment and assistance, you need to do research. If you are unable to work with others (e.g., your advisor or other members of the lab) you will not get access to the resources you need to do your research.

Communication skills are also vital to your career. You will write articles, grant applications, reviews, and patient assessments. You will make presentations, defend your dissertation, and give lectures. If you can write and speak well, you will stand out from the crowd. Moreover, self-expression is a major part of the job of psychologist; professors and researchers must communicate research results, interact with students, and teach, and clinicians must communicate with patients, staff, and other professionals.

BE ORGANIZED

As an undergraduate student, your main academic responsibility was to complete your coursework and earn decent grades. Students' responsibilities multiply in graduate school. In addition to class times, you will have many other obligations: lab meetings, advising meetings, assistantships, lectures, and so on. To keep track of and meet these obligations, you need to be organized. Misplacing papers, showing up late, and forgetting tasks and meetings will not make people perceive you as an absent-minded genius. Instead, you will simply appear careless and disorganized, nether of which are helpful to your standing. Learn how to organize your time and your work.

FIGURE OUT WHO YOU ARE

In addition to learning how to become a psychologist, during your graduate school years you should also learn about yourself. It is important to become aware of your issues and define your values because they influence how you perceive and solve interpersonal, scientific, and everyday problems. Self-awareness is especially important for clinicians, whose own perspectives and biases influence their interactions with others. You need to understand yourself to work effectively with others.

FIND A MENTOR(S)

A mentor is a guide. Find one mentor, preferably more. Only by observing expert models, asking questions and picking their brains, and soliciting feedback and constructive criticism of your work can you become an expert in your field. Graduate school takes the form of an apprenticeship whereby you learn alongside a master psychologist. Seek multiple mentors, and you will be exposed to multiple perspectives. Mentorship is discussed in more detail in chapter 5, but for now remember to seek out mentors who can serve as models and guides to your training.

How Learning Takes Place

There are no explicit courses on how to be a psychologist; no one will pull you aside and give you the secret to becoming a psychologist. You will find that you learn about science and practice by being immersed in it, in the same ways that you learned about the world as a child, through observation, imitation, reading, direct guidance, talking with others, making mistakes, and receiving feedback about performance. In short, people learn through experience. There are many experiences that scaffold one's learning.

OBSERVATION

When you first begin graduate school, you will probably spend a lot of time learning through observation, by watching how others use lab equipment, interact with others, and get work done. You will learn from listening in on conversations among students, postdocs, and faculty. You will also learn from casual conversations with others. For example, it is not uncommon to talk casually about research project and results, considering alternative explanations. These kinds of conversations occur routinely in graduate school, and they are how you learn. In some cases you may be asked to watch particular lab members while they work with sensitive equipment, for example. Remember that although you are observing in these situations, you must be a fast learner. You must learn from what you observe and be able to perform.

LAB AND ADVISOR MEETINGS

Meetings with your advisor or lab meetings in which all those who work with a professor meet are important learning opportunities. It is during these meetings that research that is in process is discussed: How is data collection going? What are obstacles? Are there any quirks in the data? What are plans for analyses? Can you explain findings? Are there unexpected results? It is during these meetings that the limitations of research are discussed. A good researcher will try to poke holes in findings and explanations. These discussions are learning opportunities. This is how you learn to think like a scientist and critique and evaluate a study. In one-on-one meetings with your advisor, you get to see the workings of a psychologist's mind up close. You may have similar discussions at the lab meetings, or they may be more focused on theory or on your own work.

Tip

Listen and learn during lab meetings. Get a feel for all the members of the lab and the general dynamics before diving into any debates so as to not inadvertently join in on a faction within the lab or unintentionally alienate anyone.

READING

Much learning in graduate school is a solitary endeavor. You will spend countless hours reading. The hours you spend immersed in journal articles and books will shape your thinking. You will learn about the history of the field, current findings, and where it is going. You will also learn about how science is done; each journal article is a scientific study, an illustration of science in process.

ATTENDING CONFERENCES

As a graduate student you will begin to attend scientific conferences such as the annual meeting of the American Psychological Association as well as conferences that are specific to your field. At these conferences you will hear talks by renowned psychologists, attend poster sessions that permit you to interact with scientists and discuss their research, and get a close look at research in progress because most of the work discussed is unpublished and its next destination is a scholarly journal.

DOING

Much of your learning will take place through immersion. The only real way to learn psychology is to do it. As you carry out a research project, your own or your advisor's, you will discover that even the best laid plans often require tweaking. It is by collecting and working with data and making the adjustments needed to keep the research process going that you learn how to be a scientist. It is by working with people, conducting assessments, and engaging in therapy that you learn how to be a practitioner. Reading and advance preparation is essential, but much learning occurs by doing.

WRITING

Many hours will be spent writing. Learning to organize a coherent argument, using literature to support your rationale and major points, entails learning not just how to write but also how to think, locate, understand, assimilate, integrate, and manipulate information to construct a persuasive argument. Preparing papers for classes and manuscripts for submission to conferences and journals gives you lots of experience in making arguments and supporting them with data, thought work that serves as the backbone of scientific thinking.

MAKING MISTAKES

You will make mistakes in graduate school. Everyone does. From using the wrong analysis to deleting data to mixing up patient files, mistakes are part and parcel of graduate school. The critical question is whether you can identify your mistakes, rectify them, learn from them, and not repeat them.

FEEDBACK

Not all feedback that you receive in graduate school will be positive. Even the best of evaluations will include constructive criticism and comments on aspects of your work that can be improved. Considering and responding to criticism is an important avenue for learning; use these opportunities. Sources of criticism are many: course instructors, advisors, applied supervisors, other mentors, dissertation committee, advanced students, and peers. It is hard to hear that your work is not perfect, but remember that no research study or paper will be perfect. There are always ways to improve research; even research conducted by top scientists can be improved. Likewise the work of master practitioners can also be improved. Take advantage of the feedback you receive to improve your skills.

Stages of Graduate School

The stages of college are easy to understand: 4 years, each with a different name (freshman, sophomore, junior, senior). The ambiguous nature of graduate school means that its stages are not as clear-cut as undergraduate school.

COURSEWORK

In your first few years of graduate school, you will take a variety of courses, required and elective. Most will be in your specialty area. Others will provide you with the basic tools of a psychologist. Methodology and statistics courses will provide you with a base of knowledge from which to conduct research. Courses in your specialty area will give you the foundational knowledge to start your research program. Courses in therapy techniques and assessment protocols will educate you in the clinical tools of your trade. During these years you will spend a lot of time reading, preparing for classes, writing papers, and preparing for exams. Often coursework is taken concurrently with research and applied experiences, requiring students to manage their time carefully. Master's students will often find that coursework is the foundation of their degree; only some master's programs require that students complete comprehensive examinations.

COMPREHENSIVE EXAMINATIONS

When coursework is completed, you will face your biggest challenge until now: You must pass a comprehensive exam, also known as a qualifying or preliminary exam (students often refer to these exams as "comps," "quals," or "prelims"). All doctoral programs require that students complete comprehensive examinations; however, only some master's programs require comps. The comprehensive exam is a test of an entire field, covering material in coursework, reading lists, and other sources such as recently published journal articles. Each department administers its own exam, so content and expectations vary widely. The exam is written but sometimes also oral. Some exams take the form of complicated essay questions that require library research and analysis and must be completed within a certain number of days. More often comps entail a series of challenging essay questions that must be completed in 1 day within a proctored testing room. To pass the exam, students must demonstrate the ability to assimilate, integrate, and synthesize a vast literature to provide a comprehensive response to a question. Preparation entails extensive study of the field by reading new and classic publications and considering potential questions for weeks or even months. Students who fail the exam usually are given another opportunity to take it; students who fail twice leave the program.

MASTER'S THESIS

The master's thesis is the final requirement for completing the master's degree. Some master's programs give students the option of completing either master's comprehensive exams or the master's thesis. Other programs require both. Doctoral programs that award the master's degree as a stepping stone to the doctoral degree often require that students complete a master's thesis.

The master's thesis is a paper in which the student demonstrates that he or she understands the content of the field and is able to apply it. Master's programs vary on the required content of the thesis. Some programs require that students complete empirical research studies, whereas others require that students write literature reviews that discuss the theoretical basis, empirical findings, and applied value of a field. The master's thesis conveys mastery of a field but does not require that students make new discoveries or extend the field. Doctoral dissertations, in contrast, generally require that students make significant contributions to the literature, advancing the field.

DOCTORAL CANDIDATE AND INTERN

Once the student has passed comps, he or she is referred to as a doctoral candidate, often referred to as ABD ("all but dissertation") to reflect that all he or she must do is complete the dissertation to receive the doctoral degree. Although it may seem as if doctoral candidacy is the home stretch in a long run, it is a marathon unto itself. Students in applied programs and especially clinical psychology programs are required to complete a 1-year internship, typically in the 4th through 6th year. During that year you work full time in a clinical setting such as a hospital, clinic, or mental health center. Students must apply for internships in a process similar to applying to graduate school. Internships typically are not connected with your graduate program and may be in a different part of the country. Many students also work on their dissertation during their internship year. All students complete the dissertation, which entails three major steps: writing the proposal, researching and writing, and defending the dissertation.

Proposal

In many respects this is the most challenging stage of dissertation writing (see chap. 10, this volume). Your goal is to come up with a plan for the dissertation. You will read widely in your area of interest to get an idea of a topic. You will discuss potential ideas with your advisor and perhaps a few faculty who you will ask to compose your dissertation committee (a group of faculty, usually four to six, who evaluate your dissertation and decide whether you have conducted the work that is entailed to earn a doctorate). Once you have an idea, have conferred with your advisor, and have agreed on the content of the dissertation project, you begin writing the proposal. The dissertation proposal is a lengthy document in which the student discusses the proposed research within the context of the existing literature. In a lengthy literature review the student discusses the background of literature on his or her topic and places the proposed research within this literature, explaining why it is important and what it will add to the existing literature (Cone & Foster, 2006). During graduate school you learn not only to apply knowledge but also to contribute to it, to create it. Your dissertation is where you demonstrate that you are a creator of knowledge. After you have reviewed the literature, described the problem, and explained how the study will add to the literature, you must describe the design and methods to be used.

The proposal is submitted to your advisor and your dissertation committee, who will make the judgment if you have passed. Usually this committee evaluates the oral defense but not always. During the proposal meeting, a proposal defense that is sometimes referred to as a preliminary oral exam, the student presents the research to the committee and the committee asks questions to determine the value of the work and the student's knowledge of it. The committee may accept the proposal; ask for changes to the research, sometimes entailing that the student submit a revised proposal; or reject it with suggestions on how to revise the idea or ask the student to begin again. That is why it is important to seek advice throughout this stage, so that everyone is on the same page and you are not surprised by a rejection. Students who fail are given another opportunity to construct and present a proposal. This stage can be quite lengthy (it took me a year) and stressful.

Dissertation Research and Writing

Once you pass the proposal defense, you are ready to begin your dissertation and carry out the plan you articulated in the proposal. During this phase you carry out the research, enter data, conduct analyses, and figure out what happened. The dissertation research phase can take years. These years are the core of graduate school because it is when you learn how to be an independent researcher. As will be discussed in chapter 10, this time can be lonely and requires initiative, motivation, and tenacity. The challenging part is that you are working independently; it is how you show whether you will sink or swim as an independent scholar. Some departments request progress reports, either annually or once the data are collected and analyzed, before writing of the dissertation. Other departments do not require progress reports and instead let the student work on his or her own timetable without intervention or instruction. The final dissertation contains the updated literature review, statement of the problem and rationale for the research, along with statement of methodology carried out, a section presenting statistics, a discussion section describing what was learned, and a conclusion section (Cone & Foster, 2006). The dissertation is submitted to the advisor and committee.

Dissertation Defense

Once the student submits the dissertation and the committee has reviewed it, the dissertation defense, also known as the final oral exam, occurs. The defense is the culmination of the years of writing and research, when the student presents his or her research. The committee (a) questions the student on the dissertation, (b) evaluates the student's knowledge of the literature, and (c) assesses the student's ability to explain why his or her method was the appropriate choice for the problem, explain limitations and how they have been addressed, and explain future research (Cone & Foster, 2006). The committee evaluates the dissertation and decides whether the student will be awarded the doctoral degree. After passing this defense, the student has obtained the doctorate.

These are the steps entailed in graduate study. There is no definitive timetable that applies to all students in all programs. Even within a program each student proceeds at his or her own pace depending on his or her characteristics, characteristics of the advisor, relationship with the advisor, and the nature of the work. Every student has a different time schedule; it is not uncommon to be a year or two ahead or behind a student who started with you.

Recommended Reading

Frank, F., & Stein, K. (2004). *Playing the game: The street-smart guide to graduate school.* Lincoln, NE: iUniverse.

Peters, R. (1997). *Getting what you came for: The smart student's guide to earning an M.A. or a Ph.D.* New York: Farrar, Straus, and Giroux.

3 The Daily Grind
How Graduate Students Spend Their Time

I have discussed the ways in which graduate study is different from undergraduate study, but what is it like to be a graduate student? How do graduate students spend their days? Graduate students spend their days juggling coursework, with reading, writing, and research, for their own and their advisor's projects. It is easy to focus on the here and now—on getting through the days, weeks, and semesters—but graduate students should also plan ahead and keep the big picture, progressing through the milestones in graduate study, in mind.

Coursework

There are many ways in which graduate study is different from undergraduate study. Coursework itself is not one of them. Graduate students, like undergraduate students, are required to complete coursework; however, the nature of courses is likely to be quite different. Most graduate courses meet for a 2- to 3-hour period once a week. There are common requirements that all students take and then more specialized courses (i.e., seminars) that only a handful of students take. Graduate study is characterized by small classes; your largest class will hold about 30 students at most, whereas seminars will enroll fewer than 15 students.

THE GRADUATE SEMINAR

The seminar is at the heart of graduate study, especially doctoral study (Bloom, Karp, & Cohen, 1998). Typically these courses are composed of between 2 and 15 students who often sit casually around a table rather than in a traditional classroom-desk setup. The seminar has less structure than traditional courses; the professor generally does not lecture but instead exchanges ideas with students about the assigned readings. Seminar classes tend to be more specialized and focused classes that cover topics of expertise to the professor. Students observe the thinking of an expert and get an insider's view on his or her work and the field at large, including who the major players are, what is known and unknown, and where the field is going (Bloom et al., 1998). Professors guide students through a casual, collegial discussion of important articles and chapters.

Student participation is critical to the success of the seminar class. The student's role in a seminar class is to contribute; professors tend to interpret silence as a lack of engagement or unpreparedness. Participate to show professors and classmates that you are prepared, interested, and thoughtful about the material. If you find it extremely difficult to speak up in class, try writing out some of your observations and discussion questions ahead of time so that you can feel more comfortable joining in the discussion by knowing that you are prepared (Colón Semenza, 2005).

Most students are shy, but graduate students are expected to overcome their shyness and speak out passionately about their field (Colón Semenza, 2005). Students may be asked to present a particular article or chapter to the class. Although leading a discussion may seem intimidating, remember that it is a small group of fellow students, and everyone will be asked to complete the same task. Make your presentation in a conversational style and create meaty questions to entice others into a hearty discussion.

During class discussions, make an effort to listen to other students, acknowledge their statements, and give them credit when credit is due. Be considerate and always respond to classmates with respect. However, do not shy away from challenging them to explain their ideas and do not be upset when you are challenged. Graduate study, and academics in general, is all about intellectual dueling. Good seminars consist of passionate conversations about a topic in which basic rules of etiquette, such as respect for others, apply (Colón Semenza, 2005).

Although graduate classes often have a more casual atmosphere than your undergraduate classes, attendance is expected. Attendance is even more important in graduate school because classes meet only weekly, there is much to learn, and, most important, instructors often take absence from classes, especially small seminar classes, personally (Colón Semenza, 2005). Chronic absenteeism may alienate the instructor, and you do not want to alienate any professor because all faculty are in positions to help or hurt you. If you must miss a class, notify the professor beforehand if possible. Explain that you understand that absences are unacceptable, and then be sure to attend every class afterward.

Tip

Use professors' office hours judiciously. All professors post office hours, hours that they are in their office and available to meet with students. Take advantage of these times and get to know your professors. Consult with them about your class paper, but be informed before you do so. For example, prepare one or two paper topics by identifying the main idea, potential sources, and basis for your argument. Do not simply show up seeking help on your topic without having considered it and created a plan beforehand. Office hours are a chance for professors to get to know you outside of class. Present yourself as a serious and motivated student. Such meetings send professors positive messages about your organizational abilities and professionalism. Visiting professors during office hours is a useful political strategy, but you should also be careful not to hog their time. Be sensitive to cues that you have overstayed your welcome. Professors are busy people, and although they enjoy getting to know students, they have a great deal of work to complete.

Preparation is essential when you attend class. Participation is the foundation for nearly all graduate courses; attending class without having completed the assigned readings is nearly the same as being absent. Do not try to fake having completed the assignment because most professors can tell and will resent it. As described in the next section of this chapter, preparing for class entails more than simply reading the assignment (Frank & Stein, 2004). The goal is to understand the concepts, not memorize the assignment. Consider the overall value of the theories or findings: How do they fit with the existing research, what you have discussed in class, or the real world? Are there other ways of studying the topic or other conclusions that could have been drawn? What are the limitations of the work? Finally, why did your professor assign the reading? That is not a facetious question. What does the professor want you to get out of the article?

Tip

Sometimes students encounter a problem with class, say an instructor who is unfair or who does not cover the material in the syllabus. Evaluate the nature and extent of the problem. If the problem persists over several classes, there are several options: (a) speak with the instructor, (b) speak with your advisor, (c) speak with the program or department head, or (d) do nothing. Speak with classmates and determine if they experience the same problem. If you are the only student who feels that the class is not going well, then it may be a matter of adjusting your expectations and perspective. Should others agree, consider acting. If the professor seems unfair, it is unlikely that speaking with him or her will resolve the issue and may instead direct negative attention your way. Soliciting help from your advisor should be your first step. Do not go over the instructor and your advisor's heads without approaching your advisor first. Speaking with your advisor about the course is a good strategy if you have decided that the problem is affecting your learning and is unlikely to stop. It is more effective if classmates also speak to their advisors. If you decide to approach the program or department head, do so as part of a group of students because there is power in numbers. Finally, sometimes it is best to simply do nothing. How far along is the semester? How likely is it that you will encounter the professor again and need his or her assistance? Sometimes the politically correct but personally frustrating solution of doing nothing is in your best interest. Consider this carefully and discuss this with your classmates, advanced students, and perhaps your advisor.

Much time will be spent preparing for and attending classes. Classes, though important, are not the heart of graduate education. There is a core body of knowledge that students must learn, and class work should be taken seriously because it introduces them to that body, but graduate school is about becoming a psychologist and emphasis should be on research and therapeutic skills.

JOURNAL CLUBS, BROWN BAG LUNCHES, AND COLLOQUIA

By now you realize that there is much to learn in graduate school and that there are many ways to learn. In addition to formal coursework, you will also participate in less formal learning communities such as journal clubs, brown bag lunch groups, and colloquia. The scientific literature is continually advancing. The journal club (in some departments referred to as a brown bag lunch) provides a mechanism for keeping abreast of current research and gaining experience critically evaluating the literature (Bloom et al., 1998). Students and faculty meet at a set time to discuss an agreed-on article. All are expected to read the article beforehand and engage in the review of the article, discussing its merits, strengths, and weaknesses. Students can learn simply by listening to the reviews because skill in critiquing research comes with experience. The club may or may not be required, but savvy students know to always attend because this activity permits faculty and student to participate as colleagues, all input is welcome, and everyone can learn something from the discussion (Bloom et al., 1998).

Many departments also hold informal discussions during "brown bag lunches," where a student or professor gives an informal conversational presentation of his or her research including its basis, methods, current findings, and future directions. The presentation is intended to begin a constructive discussion of the project in which participants discuss potential problems, loopholes, and significance to the field and provide helpful feedback.

Colloquia are another informal learning opportunity. Most departments hold colloquia, presentations by faculty, students, and outside guests, on a regular basis, sometimes weekly. By attending these presentations, students learn more than research and theory. Students will have the opportunity to study various ways of presenting information and identify what makes a good presentation. Frequently a department will invite researchers from other universities to present their work. It is a courtesy to see invited speakers and a good opportunity to learn about new research from an expert, get a glimpse into the mind of an expert researcher, and network.

Overall, new graduate students generally feel most prepared for the coursework component of graduate study. Remember that classes are not simply hoops to jump through but important preparation for learning how to think and work like a psychologist. Take coursework and informal learning opportunities seriously. Try to make conceptual connections among ideas, consider the applied value of ideas, and see where they fit in your own conceptual framework of human behavior and how the world works.

Ongoing Activities of Graduate Students

Coursework is important, but do not take it too seriously because there are myriad other learning and thinking activities that compose a graduate student's days. As mentioned earlier, graduate study does not mean simply learning and regurgitating facts. Instead, graduate study is about thinking—weighing ideas and constructing a framework of knowledge. Graduate students engage in a variety of activities that aid their construction of knowledge.

READING

The first thing that many students notice about the workload in graduate school is that reading takes up much more of their time than ever before. Professors assign reading for every meeting. Sometimes it will be a reasonable amount, a few articles or chapters, and other times it may seem ridiculously large, such as several books. Determine how to keep up with the reading, and understand what is important without wasting too much time on nonessential material. This is one of the biggest challenges of graduate school. How do you cut your reading down to the bare minimum while still permitting comprehension and retention? There is not one strategy.

Although students learn to read in elementary school or beforehand, graduate study entails a different set of reading skills, partly because of the difficulty of the material, but more so because of the vast quantity of required reading. Most people do not read scholarly books from first page to last. Instead, successful students skim and read with a purpose (Colón Semenza, 2005). For books, begin with the table of contents. Are there any chapters that cover information that falls within your research or interest area (this is particularly helpful for edited books in which each chapter is written by a different author)? In some cases, reading the table of contents is enough to tell you if you want to read all, parts, or none of the book. Your next step is to read the introduction; this is where the author or editor frames his or her argument and the book's content.

For articles, read the abstract for a general overview. If the article still seems worthwhile, then read the last two paragraphs of the introduction for information on the research question and purpose of the study, then the final summary, conclusion, or last three paragraphs of the discussion (if there is not a summary or conclusion), and you will get the overview of what was found and why it was important. If you deem the study worthy of more attention, then read the entire article. Do not feel obligated to read every word. The first and last sentences of each paragraph will tell you the most important information. Do not waste time reading if you do not have to; this technique will work in most cases. However, this strategy will not work if it is an important article in your area of study that you need to know thoroughly. Professors will often identify such articles. Do not try to take the easy way out on these articles. Read them carefully and know them well. The other case in which articles must be thoroughly read is when the author is a professor within the department and especially when the author is your course instructor. Be sure to know these readings well.

Tip

One common way in which graduate students manage the sheer quantity of readings is to break them down into sections and divide them up. Everyone skims all of the reading or as much as they can manage. Each student reads his or her assigned section and distributes detailed notes to the other students. Should you choose this route, team up with students who are competent and dependable.

Reading is a skill necessary to conduct professional work because keeping up with the latest developments in the field is critical to your success as a scholar. By doing so, you can determine what line of research to develop and what questions remain unresolved. Your reading list will encompass much more than class assignments. Once you broaden your research to include your topic area, you will realize that the research literature in your area is voluminous. Only selective reading will do (Dee, 2001). Keep abreast of the new publications and then select the needed articles. Organize regular scans of the literature. Compile a list of key words and important authors' names. Then simply remember to run your search periodically to pull out new articles. Many journals offer free e-mail alerting services to permit you to view tables of contents when new issues are published. These are useful for critical journals, but if you subscribe to too many it can become overwhelming. Next is to determine what to read because you will not be able to read everything. Survey the literature carefully and remember that no one can know everything and that knowledge is built slowly over time.

> Jeanne worked hard to keep up with the literature. She subscribed to services that e-mailed her links to the current contents of journals she identified as critical to her discipline; some weeks she'd receive links to eight new journal issues. Jeanne routinely ran literature searches to hunt for new articles. She scoured the reference lists of articles she deemed important. Her list of relevant literature was both broad and deep. Coursework, research with her advisor, and her assistantship left Jeanne with little time to read. She dutifully made copies of all the articles she found, piling them on a chair in her office. As the semester ends, Jeanne looks forward to thinking about her own research and doing background reading to prepare her research study. "I do not know where to start," she says, looking at the 3-foot mound of articles on her chair. Jeanne decides that she should sift through it, organizing it by topic area and importance to her research. Several hours later she has only scratched the surface of the pile, about 3 inches worth of paper. Frustrated, she decides to scrap the pile and start from scratch.

How do you select what to include on your reading list and what to store or delete? Some students, like Jeanne, copy or print everything. This can lead to an overwhelming stack of research to sort through. You will end up with no clue of what is in there, what is of value and what is not. Sifting through the pile to figure out what to read is time consuming. If you are dealing with such a pile, quickly sort articles into three stacks: essential reading, background reading if you have time, and delete. In the future, copy articles selectively. Read the abstract first to determine if it may be useful to your work. If you are unsure, save the reference and return to it later. As you download or copy articles, organize them into piles or folders so that you know what is there. Most important, only download or copy articles that are essential; keep a running reference list of background research to review should you need to or have time. Do not waste space storing articles that you only might read and use.

Tip

Use your time wisely and read anywhere you can: while taking the subway to school, waiting in the doctor's office, between classes, and so on. Always carry an article or something else to read.

RESEARCH

Given the apprenticeship model of graduate study, most students become engaged in research early by assisting more advanced researchers and working on simple projects. Assisting others helps students learn research techniques and observe and participate in scientific thinking (Bloom et al., 1998). Students who make significant contributions by working long and hard may even earn credit on a presentation or publication. New students often begin working on faculty projects before they understand the meaning of their work. Take time to review the relevant literature and learn about the background and history of the project.

Always keep your research in mind because you will encounter background material and ideas when you least expect them. Students in the hard sciences have long maintained lab notebooks in which they record the details of each experiment, equipment, techniques, and findings so that they have an enduring record of their research. Graduate students in psychology can also benefit from such notebooks. Create a research notebook to collect all of your research-related ideas, thoughts, and activities. As you read, note relevant information and ideas in a research notebook. Record reflections regarding potential research topics, critical articles, insight into how to analyze data, and interpretations of the data. With a research notebook, you will no longer forget that great idea. Moreover, the act of writing out your ideas for topics, arguments, data analyses, and interpretations will force you to articulate the relevant information and get a better understanding of what you mean. The research notebook will capture many thoughts and will make it easier to design your research and later write up your findings.

The aspect of research that seems to evoke the most anxiety in students is statistics. Many graduate students in psychology dread taking courses in statistics. Yet training in statistics is one of the most important parts of doctoral work in psychology because statistics are the tools by which discoveries are made, and doctoral work in psychology is all about making discoveries. Whereas master's students are expected to become informed consumers of research, doctoral students are to become producers of research. Statistics competence is essential. Knowledge of statistics aids finishing the dissertation; students frequently submit the proposal, collect data, then stumble on what is next. Do not find yourself faltering when it comes time to analyze the data. Fluency in statistics will make your research go more smoothly, including your dissertation, and will aid your career because research proficiency is an important component to a successful academic career and is a highly marketable skill outside of academia. Take basic and advanced courses in statistics and get hands-on experience by analyzing datasets. Many students remark that they did not truly understand statistics until they worked with real data and were able to apply the numbers to something tangible. Hands-on work is invaluable.

Juggling research with coursework, assistantships, applied activities, and reading will keep students busy during the early years of graduate study. Although students are busy with coursework, they are expected to spend a great deal of time on research and applied activities. Coursework is important, but it often will come second to these other responsibilities. At some times of the semester coursework will take more time. It is a constantly shifting ratio.

Graduate school is a special time. Students identify their interests, pursue their own research questions, and have freedom to explore human behavior using sophisticated techniques. They can conduct their research without much worry about securing or maintaining grants as their work is funded through their advisor's research. Discovery is exciting and energizing. At the same time, there is much about research that is mundane, like entering and checking data, conducting literature searches, and setting up equipment. There are also times when students feel like they are not making progress and not making discoveries, as well as times when things go wrong, like losing data, incorrect analyses, and unsuccessful experiments. Most researchers agree that these mundane aspects of research are outweighed by the joy of discovery.

WRITING

Graduate students write. A lot. Period. Students cannot avoid writing; that is the nature of graduate school. Many people find writing painfully difficult; however, usually the real challenge is in starting. Writing is simply communicating ideas. If you can talk about your work, you can write. There are several strategies that can help you break through the inertia and begin writing.

One way to start is to pretend that you are talking to a friend and telling the story of your research (Rugg & Petre, 2004). How do you explain your research? What questions might the friend ask and how would you answer them? Run a digital recorder, and you will have a record of you describing your research in a conversational style that you can transcribe into a first draft of your paper.

Another way of starting is to deliberately write it "wrong" (Rugg & Petre, 2004). Get out the ideas as quickly as possible, even if they are not entirely right, so that you can move from initial generation of your paper to rewriting it. Most people find rewriting easier than writing because there is something to work with. Writing something that you definitely will want to change will give you something to react against, and it will give you a lot to work with. Many students find it helpful to not start at the beginning and instead write whatever sections flow most easily. Write whatever sections you are ready to write, and you will find that the pages fill themselves.

Strive for concise, simple, yet eloquent communication that is understood by your audience (Frank & Stein, 2004). The purpose of scholarly writing is to communicate information, so be sure that your message is understood as intended. Sometimes students become so concerned with sounding like an expert in their field that they hide behind big words, long sentences, and jargon and write in ways not easily understood by their readers. It is often easier to write badly using jargon than to write clearly, because to write using simple language you must understand exactly what it is you want to say (Peters, 1997). The purpose of writing is to communicate ideas. Do not hide yours in confusing language. Keep your writing brief and tight. Use big words sparingly but when you do so, use them carefully and well. When you must use jargon, explain it clearly. Try to write as if you are engaging in a professional conversation with a colleague (Frank & Stein, 2004).

Tip

Back up all of your writing (as well as data and anything deemed important). Invest in an external hard drive to back up electronic computer files. Also use a flash drive to back up each day's work. Computer viruses, hard drive failure, and accidental deletions happen to everyone—and usually at particularly inopportune times. Protect your work (and your sanity) by devising a system to regularly back up electronic files.

Writing becomes less overwhelming when you remember that it is a process. The initial draft will not be polished. View writing as a series of steps. The first step is getting something down on paper; dump all of your ideas without slowing to evaluate them. In the second draft, place the ideas in order. Construct full sentences in the third pass. Later drafts permit you to reconsider the organization of ideas throughout the paper and within each paragraph. Finally, consider grammar, word choice, and spelling (do not trust spell checkers—reread the corrections). Most of writing is editing. All good writers know this and schedule plenty of time in their writing schedule to edit their work multiple times before it is due. What do you look for while editing?

- Begin paragraphs with topic sentences to guide the reader and explain what is to come.
- Do not put too many ideas into one paragraph. Clear writing includes one main idea per paragraph. Otherwise ideas compete and your reader must choose which to focus attention on.
- Use key words to guide your reader. Key words are the important terms in your paper. Despite what your English composition might have taught, do not vary your language by using synonyms for your key words because it confuses the reader. For example, if you are writing a paper on free will, use that phrase throughout; do not vary your word choice to include terms (e.g., volition, choice) other than your key phrase free will (Peters, 1997).
- Break up your writing. Avoid overly long paragraphs (i.e., a paragraph that spans a double-spaced page is too long) because they are harder for readers to understand. Writing is a form of communication; your intent is to write for understanding.
- Summarize repeatedly. Whenever you have made a conclusion and presented a series of ideas, summarize it for the reader. At the very least, summarize at the end of each section of your paper. A transitional phrase or sentence between paragraphs will ensure that your reader gets the point.
- Many writers identify errors, inconsistencies, and stylistic problems when they read their work aloud. Print out your work and read the hard copy; sometimes a paper reads differently on the computer screen than on paper. Another way of giving yourself enough distance to objectively consider your work is to put it aside for a few days before editing.

All students, regardless of how well they write, will encounter criticism. It is a part of graduate school and academic life. A professor's job is to help students to become better writers. There will always be ways to improve writing; expect professors to provide comments on all of your papers. Some professors offer constructive comments; learn from these. Other professors may simply tear the work apart. Take combative comments with a grain of salt, but try to find the truth within because there always is an element of truth from which you may learn. Learn how to respond to criticism without becoming defensive and emotional. One of the best ways to manage criticism is to read comments, then put the paper aside for a bit. When you return to it, read it with a critical eye and try to understand the comment. Perhaps one of the best pieces of advice about writing is: Do not get emotionally attached to your words.

The Big Picture

The day-to-day deadlines and stresses of graduate school life keep most students more busy than they imagined. It is easy to focus on keeping your head above water and forget the big picture: where you are going and how you are getting there. Most students do not think about the various hoops in their programs until they must jump through them (Mitchell, 1996).

> Miguel excelled in his classes, kept up with reading, and balanced his teaching assistantship with assisting his advisor with research. As he begins his final semester of coursework, he feels a sense of relief that this stage of graduate school is over. The semester progresses and his classmates talk more and more about the upcoming comprehensive exam. Many began preparing the previous summer, completing readings and writing summaries. Over the fall semester, they carved out a few hours each week to review old examinations and construct outlines of the literature in several areas. Miguel feels confident in his ability as a student, but as he listens to his peers, he wonders whether he should have already begun preparing. Although he always knew he'd have to take comps, it somehow always seemed very far away. "I have a lot to catch up on, I guess," Miguel thinks to himself, "And I can't believe that I'll start the dissertation right after. Maybe I should think about that too."

The next stages in the graduate program, comprehensive exams and the dissertation, can pop up, seemingly out of nowhere, leaving most students feeling unprepared. It does not have to be this way. One theme throughout this book is the importance of planning ahead to prepare for each stage of graduate school, keep progressing toward your ultimate goal, and avoid unpleasant surprises.

COMPREHENSIVE EXAMS

Comprehensive examinations (comps) are considered the culmination of study for the graduate degree and are designed for students to demonstrate mastery of their program of study. Comps are typically taken during the last semester of coursework or immediately after coursework is completed. Passing the comprehensive exam is a milestone in graduate school; once students pass they are admitted to candidacy and become doctoral candidates, free to embark on the dissertation. Doctoral candidates have completed all requirements for the doctoral degree except for the dissertation; for this reason, as mentioned earlier, doctoral candidates are often referred to as ABD, "all but dissertation."

Comprehensive exams most often are written and can take anywhere from 2 hours to 2 days. No two universities or programs within universities have identical comprehensive exams. Some schools also include an oral exam designed to show mastery of the content of the discipline and how well students reason on their feet. Comps may be individualized or standardized. In some programs students take comprehensive exams that are tailored for them; the advisor prepares questions and obtains additional questions from faculty (Rossman, 2002). Programs that administer a standardized comprehensive exam give all students the same exam on the same day. Questions are usually drawn from a pool of questions developed over the years, and new questions are added to reflect trends in the field.

It is common to feel nervous about the exam. The best way to combat anxiety is to prepare. Discuss questions and concerns with your mentor. You are not the first student to worry about comps. Your mentor can give advice on how to prepare as well as share his or her experience in taking comps and in supervising students who have passed the comps.

Preparation should be your primary concern. Carefully plan your time because you will have a lot of information to absorb and retain; it is impossible to cover everything, so you will want to make good use of your time. Review course notes and course readings but remember that you cannot memorize them all—do not waste time trying. Instead, pull ideas from the readings. Review your marginal notes and summaries from courses. Do not assume the exam will be restricted to material covering your courses; graduate students are expected to go beyond the courses and be familiar with the current literature in the field. Create brief summaries of readings as you prepare. Organize these summaries logically to present a body of research findings.

Try to anticipate what topics will appear on the exam. Professors' specialties and research areas can guide your study. Questions might concern background research for a problem a professor studies or may request analysis of current research in that area. Review syllabi for your courses; many professors provide lists of suggested readings. Review these. Your professor identified them as important enough to get prime real estate space on the syllabus; they are likely to inform your responses to comp questions. Also read the current literature because professors often create questions that tap the latest research and controversies. What are the current hot topics? Be familiar with them. Some departments create reading lists to guide students' preparation for the comprehensive exam. Other departments, especially those that administer individualized comprehensive exams, require students to create their own reading lists. Students who create their own reading lists should organize empirical and review articles by topic area and ask their mentor as well as other professors to review it.

If possible, review past comprehensive examinations. Some programs provide lists of prior comp questions to help students prepare. Many students find the lists overwhelming; do not spend time drafting responses. Instead look at patterns: the types of questions asked (e.g., research methodology, history, application), the specific fields covered, overall complexity, and topics or types of questions that arise often. If your program does not provide students with past exams, talk to students who have passed the comps to get information about the kinds of topics that appeared and the type of reasoning tapped by questions (e.g., analysis, comparison, application). Ask for suggestions on how to prepare, but also take their advice with a grain of salt remembering that memory can be faulty, students vary in ability ("hard" and "easy" are relative terms), and you will not see the same questions on your exam.

Make sure to allow adequate study time. Most students set aside time to do nothing but study for weeks and even months. Being holed up with your books can be isolating. Seek social support; take breaks to spend time with family and friends. Form a study group with other students who are studying for comps. Explaining ideas to a peer increases your own understanding. Different perspectives on problems and issues will expand your own perspective. Learning that other students also are struggling with the task will help you to feel less alone and realize that this is a hurdle that all students must clear.

Schedule breaks. Go for a walk. Do some housework. Run an errand. Zone out. Stay healthy throughout your study period. Exercise regularly. Get enough sleep. Both sleep and exercise will help you stave off depression, maintain your functioning, and improve your retention. Make time for you to do the things that help you relax and make you feel good. After you take the exam, celebrate by doing something special for yourself, whether it is getting a massage, going to a play, or taking a small trip. Celebrate that you have finished the exam for which you have spent a great deal of time preparing.

What if you do not pass? Some students do not pass the comprehensive exam on their first try. It is a cliché, but it is not the end of the world. Programs usually give students two opportunities to pass. Now that you have taken the exam you know the kinds of questions that are asked and the ways in which they are asked. You might have insight on the content areas that you did not focus enough attention on. Determine the material to cover and create a plan. Return to studying. Remember that the real measures of success are tenacity and how hard you work. Successful people keep trying until they succeed; it is not a one-shot deal. The period in which you prepare for comprehensive exams is a gift; you do not have to attend class and your job is to read, study, and think. No other point in your career will you immerse yourself so deeply in the literature or days simply thinking.

DISSERTATION

Once students pass the comprehensive exam and become doctoral candidates, their next step is to complete the dissertation. Period. No more coursework. As a doctoral candidate, your research time is your own. The dissertation is the culmination of your graduate school experience; it is the gateway to your career as a psychologist. If simply reading about this makes you feel pressured, you are not alone. Although the dissertation is the final graduate school hurdle, successful students do not wait until they are doctoral candidates to begin it.

Over the graduate school years you are expected to become an expert in your topic area. The dissertation is where you demonstrate your expertise. However, you should attempt to build that expertise throughout your graduate school years. Start thinking about your dissertation the moment you enter school. Although you will not have a specific project planned, and should not at that stage, you should have ideas about potential areas on which to specialize (e.g., risky behavior in adolescence, older adults' functioning, or mood disorders). Use your class papers as opportunities to research aspects of your topics. For example, in a cognition class you might study cognitive influences on risky behavior, cognitive functioning in older adults, or the cognitive basis of mood disorders. The research you do for these papers will serve as background research and will help you evaluate potential topics. The feedback you get on course papers will help you narrow your topic and flesh out your ideas. This strategy will also help you determine whether your topic will hold your interest over the next few years; if the course papers are painful to write, your dissertation will be worse, so change your topic. I discuss the dissertation in great depth in chapter 10.

It is easy to look at each course and required activity as an obstacle to clear and not think about how it fits into the big picture. Use your class work as opportunities to prepare for your dissertation. Likewise, all of the ways in which graduate students spend time (coursework, reading, research, and writing) interact and influence each other, and they can help students keep the big picture in mind and prepare for the two largest hurdles of graduate school: the comprehensive exams and dissertation. Successful students plan ahead and complete their coursework, reading, writing, and research with their ultimate goal in mind—completing graduate study.

Recommended Reading

American Psychological Association. (2001). *Publication manual of the American Psychological Association* (5th ed.). Washington, DC: Author.

Klump, P. (1998). *Breakthrough rapid reading.* New York: Prentice Hall.

Leong, F. T., & Austin, J. T. (2005). *The psychology research handbook: A guide for graduate students and research assistants* (2nd ed.). Thousand Oaks, CA: Sage.

Ostrov, R. (2003). *Power reading* (3rd ed.). North San Juan, CA: Education Press.

Strunk, W., & White, E. B. (1999). *The elements of style* (4th ed.). New York: Longman.

Zinsser, W. (2006). *On writing well* (30th ed.). New York: Collins.

Self-Management for Graduate School and Beyond

4

What accounts for success in graduate school? Entering students have what it takes. Graduate admissions are based on academic performance and potential as indicated by grades, GRE scores, personal statements, and recommendation letters. No student wins admission without the expectation that she or he has the capacity to complete the degree. So then why do some students swim while others sink in the often treacherous waters of graduate school? Perhaps the one message you should get from this book is that intelligence is not enough to ensure your success in graduate school. Instead, it is the ability to manage yourself—to organize your space and your thoughts, to use effective time management strategies, and to set goals, devise plans to achieve them, and make consistent progress on them—that ensures success.

Get Organized

Organization is one of the most critical components of success. Organization does not just refer to managing clutter (though that is an important part); it means managing your physical and mental resources. Successful graduate students are able to organize information and ideas.

WORK SPACE

Where you work influences the quality and quantity of your work. Your surroundings influence your productivity.

> "Feels like I've read this a hundred times but I still do not get it." Jane once again attempts to plod through and take notes on the paragraph she's rereading but her eyes feel heavy from the strain of trying to concentrate. Her pen jerks across the page as her chair is bumped. Jane looks up to see a boy brushing by, likely a first-year undergraduate student. As he walks off, Jane looks around. Conversations hum throughout the student lounge, computer keys clatter. Jane turns up the volume on her MP3 player to mask the sounds and returns to her work.

Graduate students have a qualitatively different workload than do undergraduate students. Not only is it more work, but it is more challenging work. You will no longer be able to complete all of your work while in the library or on campus because you will be spending more time working and will often work at off-hours, such as in the evening (sometimes late at night) and in the early morning. More important, you will need to be able to concentrate, and computer labs can often become quite noisy, especially during evenings and busy times of the semester. Carve out a space to work at home.

Avoid the classic habit of spreading out your work on the kitchen table. In graduate school you are studying to become an expert, and that takes space. You will need space to organize articles and notes in meaningful ways that are easily accessible as you prepare papers. You will work on more than one paper and project at once (e.g., papers for two courses as well as writing for your advisor's project and perhaps your own). Books for classes, papers, and your own research will multiply throughout the semester. The articles and books that you read for your courses, let alone for your advisor and your own research, will quickly fill the kitchen table. Clearing the table each time a member of the household wants to eat will waste precious time. This is especially true if you have a family because your time is likely a very scarce commodity. You will lose startup time if you must pull out and organize your materials each time you work, and you will work way too frequently to do that. Moreover, you will be more likely to procrastinate and put off working because of the setup time required. Sometimes you will need to be able to sit down and work for a short period of, say, 30 minutes. If you must arrange all of your materials before you sit down to work, you will likely not use those small but important windows of time.

Your desk does not need to be expensive. An inexpensive card table can be tucked into a corner as a place to organize your work. The goal is to organize it efficiently once and stick to the organizational scheme; avoid continually reorganizing it. If you have the space, a folding conference table is especially effective because it is large enough to hold your computer and printer and provides space to organize papers for multiple projects. Better yet, if you have the space, purchase an inexpensive door (defective doors are the cheapest and the defect usually is not visible) and rest it on two or more filing cabinets. You will have a large work space as well as file space.

Also ensure that you have space that is yours and yours alone, because you need to be able to arrange your materials in ways that make sense to you and that will not be disturbed by others. If you share a computer with others, then that computer table cannot be your work space. A lot of time can be lost looking for something that is misplaced by someone else who is working in your space. Relatedly, if you do not have your own computer, invest in one now. In this day and age, it is impossible to complete graduate school without having your own computer. Whether you use a desktop or laptop is your choice, but owning one is essential. The benefit of a laptop is portability: You can use it to take notes in class or at the library; to work at school, at home, or wherever you go; and to access e-mail and online databases from coffee shops or wherever there is a wireless connection.

You will need a comfortable and supportive chair. Do not underestimate the need for this. You will spend a great deal of time reading (and the bed is no place to read as you will quickly find out that some scholarly reading can put you to sleep!). You will also spend many hours writing and your back will be stiff even with a good chair. If you try to get by with a kitchen chair or folding chair, you will find yourself looking for reasons to get up while working. Spend more on a good chair; you can save money on other office furniture that can be used or even makeshift. Likewise, seek excellent lighting. A halogen lamp with a dimmer will permit you to adjust the light to your needs. Flooding your work area with light reduces your chance of falling asleep and also reduces eyestrain.

Invest in supplies and arrange them in useful ways so that you are more likely to use them. Anything that makes your work easier or more enjoyable is worth it. It is easier to get organized when you have the right tools, such as Post-it notes in various sizes. Large ones can be used to write to-do lists or lists of needed references that you stick on your notebook or in your appointment book. Small ones can be used to mark pages to copy or important passages of books.

Tip

Buy supplies in bulk. Paper is cheaper by the case. Purchase boxes of paper pads, file folders, pens, and Post-its rather than individually packaged items because you will often save money on bulk items, and office supplies will always come in handy.

A quiet study place is conducive to work. You will need your full attention as the reading and work you do in graduate school will be difficult and complex. Many students find that household sounds are distracting. It is easy to be distracted by others who want or need attention (e.g., those pesky children). Ambient noise from the home also filters into the study area and is distracting. Close the door, if possible; arrange for a family member, spouse, older child, or babysitter to watch over young children (more on this in later chapters); and use white noise (ocean sounds or even radio static) to mask household sounds. I discuss ways to minimize and manage distractions later in this chapter.

ORGANIZE IDEAS

You cannot communicate ideas effectively, or make sense of others' ideas, without organizing them. There are a variety of techniques for organizing information. Use what works for you and what is appropriate to the task.

The most common way of organizing ideas—your own and others—is to create an outline. The outline highlights the major points in the message, whether that message is delivered in a paper, book chapter, or dissertation. Outline what you read and the structure of the author's argument, and the points the author used for support will be apparent. Similarly, outline your own writing to clarify your argument and supporting material.

Another way of outlining material for a paper or project is to think of it as a book and make a provisional table of contents as soon as you begin. The table of contents provides the framework for the project: It gives structure to the work, and it forces you to consider how each piece fits together to make a whole. For example, in organizing a research article, the table of contents will list lines for the following: Purpose and Background, Methods, Results, Discussion, and Conclusion. The table of contents for a paper on treating depression might include the following headers: Scope of Depression, Medication, Therapy, Combined Approaches, Group and Family Therapy, Conclusions, and Research Needs. As soon as you begin a project, construct a provisional table of contents. It will likely be sparse and contain gaps, but it focuses you to consider the project as a whole and the end goal. Elaborate the table of contents as you read and learn more.

A concept map is another way of organizing material: class lectures, articles, chapters, and your own work. The premise of a concept map is that it permits a nonlinear and visual organization of information. A concept map is created on a large piece of paper. Begin by writing a word or concept at the center of the page. Then list related concepts and use lines, arrows, and words to illustrate relationships among items. This makes it easier to see connections among ideas, assess the issue under study, and brainstorm new ideas. Figure 4.1 illustrates a student's initial concept map for a paper on depression.

FIGURE 4.1

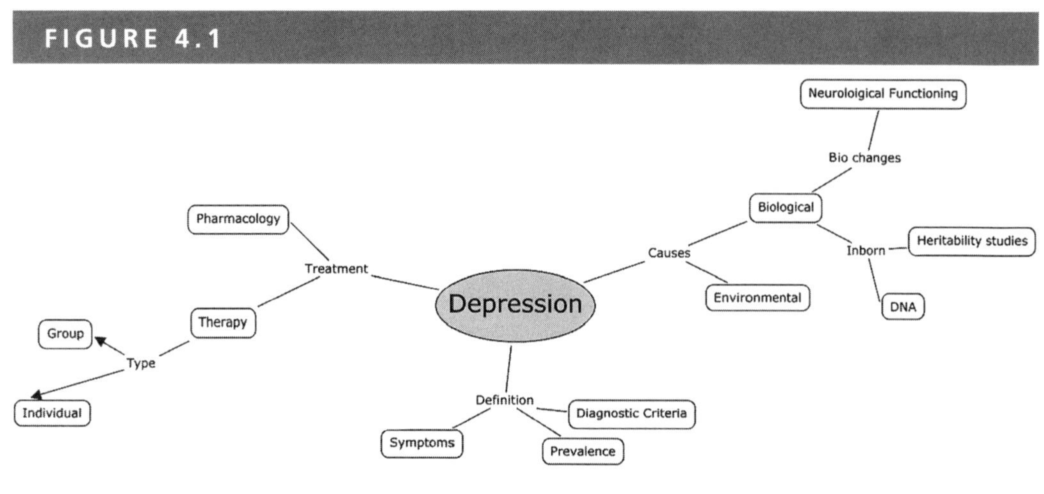

An Example of a Concept Map for a Paper on Depression

ORGANIZE FILES

Your desk will accumulate a great deal of material: references for papers, course reading, and material for your advisor's and your own research. The key to managing these multiple projects is to stay organized. Arrange your books and papers in meaningful ways, keeping resources for a given project together, for example. A critical task in managing your desk is to periodically clean the area and examine every stray scrap of paper. If the paper is part of your research, file it with the other material for that project. If it is a random scrap or article, reassess its usefulness. If you have not used it for months and do not see the need to do so, throw it away. Articles can always be downloaded again. If a paper is essential to keep but not related to current work, file it away.

Given the degree of organization demanded by graduate school, the ability to find what you need, when you need it, is essential. A filing cabinet is a necessity. Used filing cabinets often are very affordable. If a filing cabinet is too expensive, an alternative is to use file crates, cardboard boxes that are sized to hold files. Office supply stores sell file crates that are cheap but do the job. The disadvantage about using file crates is that the crate must be lifted to access the file below it, which might prevent you from filing all that you should. You may be more likely to put off filing because accessing the file space is challenging. You might also consider using the cartons in which copier paper is packed. They are sturdy and the perfect size. Universities go through a lot of paper; simply ask support staff and they are usually happy to help. Again, the challenge is that if you are dealing with more than one file box, then you will need to shuffle boxes around. Although paper cartons are great for storing archival material that you will not go into frequently, a filing cabinet is your best choice for current material. Get a good quality one with a smoothly working drawer mechanism: You will be opening and closing it often and will be more likely to stick to it and file regularly if it is easy to use. Keep your filing cabinet within reach and you will be more likely to use it. Likewise, buy lots of file folders and do not scrimp because once you do you will likely file stuff in places where it does not belong and lose it.

How you organize your files is entirely up to you. Choose an organizational scheme that makes sense and then stick to it. Create categories to hold the various scraps of paper that you retain. Label one drawer or section *Personal* and fill it with folders containing the assorted paperwork of life, such as car insurance, lease, and so on. Another drawer will be labeled *Coursework,* and one or several drawers will be labeled as *Research* and contain materials organized by research project. You might begin with just one file folder in the *Research* drawer: *Ideas,* where you will store research ideas that arise in your class activities, assistantship work, reading, and so on. As you develop each idea, give it a new file. Eventually the research sections of your filing cabinet will consist of several subsections referring to the research notes and materials for several projects. Other files that you are likely to keep concern your comprehensive exams: copies of past exams, practice tests, and reading lists.

Early in graduate school, expect to keep at least the following types of files:

- Research and thesis ideas
- Comprehensive exams
- Professional credentials (curriculum vitae, sample cover letter, statement of research and teaching interests)
- Life (bills, taxes, forms)
- Teaching materials (organized by course/topic)

Coursework can be organized in a variety of ways. One of the easiest is to use large binders to hold course material with dividers for notes, assignments, readings, and so on. Often the amount of material that you will use for a given course is too large for a binder. In this case use a section of your filing cabinet, creating files for the syllabus and assignments, readings, notes, and so on.

Tip

Buy file folders in bulk. Ensure that you have extra folders so that you are not tempted to skimp and file too many different kinds of materials in one file. Skimping on folders is tempting, but it will cost you time and effort when you cannot locate what you need.

Label the sections of your file cabinet in ways that make sense to you. Frequently, students prefer to use categories to organize the sections of their file cabinets. For example, within the *Personal* section, categories might include Bank Account, Car, and Medical. Folders might include Bank Account: Chase; Bank Account: Citibank; Car: Insurance; Car: Registration; and Medical: Prescriptions. Whatever labeling method you choose, make your system obvious, and use it consistently to make filing and retrieval intuitive and easy.

Use a label maker. Many organization pros, like David Allen, the author of *Getting Things Done,* recommend that you use a label maker for creating labels. Many students and faculty simply use a pen to label a tab, and when they want to reuse a folder they cover the old label with tape or Wite-Out; however, handwritten and corrected labels are messy and difficult to read (as students go through graduate school, many find that their handwriting deteriorates). Label makers are inexpensive and make a difference. Open a file cabinet with neatly labeled folders and you are more likely to want to retain the organization. Over time it is easy to let your filing cabinet grow out of control with extra files. Every now and then, reassess what is in there and determine what can be purged or archived.

Tip

Retain a copy of all syllabi for classes you take in a separate file because you will need to document your training, experiences, and skills when you apply for internship, licensure, and other opportunities.

ORGANIZE ELECTRONIC INFORMATION

An organized file cabinet is not enough to keep casework and research organized. Given the amount of work that graduate students do on the computer, it is absolutely essential to keep electronic files organized so that you can find what you need when you need it. Organizing your electronic files will also permit you to clear away the clutter that can slow the operation of your computer.

Neaten Your Hard Drive

Set up a simple organizational system on your hard drive, creating electronic folders to categorize and organize electronic files, much like you do for your paper files. Create electronic folder categories using clear, concise, and descriptive names like *Coursework, Research, Teaching,* and *Personal,* and use subfolders within to organize related material, such as folders for each class under *Coursework* and for each research project under *Research.* Consider how to look for the material and organize it in ways that will enable you to quickly locate what you need. Subfolders aid in organizing large bodies of electronic files; however, too many levels can become cumbersome. Create an archive electronic folder separate from your main files to hold files for completed projects, previous classes, and prior drafts of papers. Periodically burn these to CDs to ensure that they are saved.

Streamline Your E-mail

An orderly computer entails carefully organizing electronic files, but it also entails utilizing computing resources such as e-mail effectively.

- *Keep your e-mail inbox clean.* As you read a message, decide what to do with it: delete it, file it, or act on it. If you can act on the e-mail and the task takes 2 minutes or less, do it immediately. If responding will take longer than 2 minutes, flag the message for a follow-up and place that message in an e-mail folder marked "Follow-up." With this system, the only material in your inbox will be new mail. The key is to not let flagged mail sit, so each day devote a small chunk of time to working through the flagged e-mail file.
- *Create an e-mail filing system.* Similar to your electronic files, create a filing system for e-mail that organizes mail in intuitive ways: Follow-up (for e-mails that need to be returned), Personal, Coursework, Listservs, and Research, for example.
- *Clean your e-mail folders.* Periodically sort through and delete e-mails from your send file as that clutters the system. Do not wait until you run out of space on the server or your hard drive.
- *Save e-mail addresses.* Add e-mail addresses to your address book often. It takes just a moment and will save time when you look for e-mail addresses later.
- *Filter your e-mail.* Put spam filters on your e-mail to limit junk mail sent to your inbox.

Tip

Purchase (and use!) antivirus and firewall software, especially if you have a broadband connection to the Internet. Update your software regularly to ensure that your computer is protected from viruses and malicious software. A computer virus can strike with little warning and can destroy your work and even your computer itself. Fixing your computer, restoring software, and locating or retyping files (if you have saved them as electronic or hard copies) will take time away from your work and delay your progress toward your degree.

Use Bibliographic Software

Your computer itself is an organizational tool. One thing that can offer immeasurable help in managing reference lists and articles is bibliography software such as EndNote or ProCite. These programs allow you to make a separate entry for each reprint that contains bibliographic information, whatever notes you create, and key words that you choose, and these can be linked to a copy of the article that you have saved as a PDF file on your computer. In addition, the software can create a reference list as you write, eliminating the need to hunt down and type references later. Bibliographic software programs come with referencing styles for thousands of journals, which will save you hours of work spent adjusting references to a journal's specific format by hand. That may not seem like a big deal now, but you will probably have references for hundreds of articles in your dissertation. Start using it now, and bibliographic software will save you a great deal of time later.

Back Up Your Computer Early and Often

Computer backups are your friend. Computers are indispensable to graduate students' work. A computer is used for everything: communicating with others, searching for references, writing, analyzing data, organizing material, and more. All of this electronic information is vulnerable. Protect electronic information by backing it up regularly and by keeping up-to-date antivirus software. All computers crash; everyone experiences it. For example, one student suffered through more than one computer crash that destroyed important files that could not be replaced. A computer crash can destroy months or even years of work in an instant.

Make multiple copies of important work. Each week back up your computer onto an external hard drive. Save your work as you go, and each day back up the files you have changed onto a flash drive or e-mail them to yourself. Keep electronic folders that you use regularly synched to a flash drive so that you can use them anywhere. Even when deadlines are tight and you are only working on one project, back up your work each night, even if is just the one or two files. E-mail the latest version to yourself.

Save work as you go, and you should avoid much of the misery associated with lost work. What if you do lose something? Despite all of this, you will lose some work at some point in graduate school—everyone eventually loses data. For example, at the end of a long day you might accidentally delete your work by clicking "no" when the program asks if the changes should be saved. This happens at one time or another to everyone. What do you do? Immediately try to restore the document by writing as much as you can remember. You will likely find that the structure and even a large part of the material will come back to you. Do not wait because as time goes by it will be harder and more frustrating.

Goal Setting and Time Management

A critical part of self-management is allocating your time and effort effectively by determining what is to be done, prioritizing your tasks, and allocating your resources accordingly. This sounds like a lot of work because all you really need to do is buckle down and produce something, a paper, dissertation chapter, lecture, right? Do not fool yourself. Graduate students never have only one task to work on. In addition to that paper, you have got to put in time for your assistantship, read those chapters for class, begin thinking about that other paper for that other class, and try to come up with ideas for your own research. The only way to juggle these competing demands on your time and intellectual energy is to prioritize them and make a plan for attacking them.

SET GOALS

Setting goals is simple. Determine your objectives. What do you hope to do? Think big. Yes, your ultimate objective is to write your dissertation and get out of graduate school, but that is probably years away. Commit some concrete goals to paper, and you will avoid feeling overwhelmed with the big picture—how you will get from an entering graduate student to a PhD—and frustrated by slow progress. Moreover, you will have a plan to guide your efforts so that you use your time and energy in ways that propel you forward toward completing your goals. You can only achieve your goals by identifying them and then coming up with an action plan.

Clarify your goals. Look at the big picture: What is your ultimate goal? Graduate. Then list all the things that you need to do to reach that goal, working backward: write the dissertation, complete comprehensive exams, complete predoctoral research, complete coursework, and so on. Now consider what is realistic to accomplish within this next year: Select tasks to address, and determine what progress you can make on each. For example, continue with coursework and carry out predoctoral research. List all that you will need to do to accomplish the selected goals. For example, to complete predoctoral research: identify the problem and agree on scope of project with advisor, gain institutional review board approval, complete the literature review, choose measures, determine methodology, collect data, enter and analyze data, discuss results, draw conclusions, edit the manuscript. Then devise a timetable for completing the tasks, working back from your endpoint of 1 year. Recognize that these objectives may change over time. Students often complain that it is difficult to plan for coursework when they do not know course expectations until after it begins. For this reason, construct a set of goals and timetable each semester that lays out all that you must accomplish to complete your coursework along with your other goals, in this case predoctoral research goals, along with time frames. Work backward to determine what needs to be done when. Finally, look at the next month and outline your goals for that month. Look at your list. Are your goals concrete and measurable? How will you know if you have achieved them?

Write down strategies for achieving your goals. For example, if your goal for this month is to gain institutional review board approval, determine how you will do this and write down a list of action steps that will help you do so, such as gather appropriate forms, draft the introduction/ problem statement, draft descriptions of measures, draft consent forms, and compile and edit the proposal. Write down all the steps you need to get from Point A to Point B. You will do this for each of your goals.

Once you have considered strategies and action steps, prioritize your action steps. As you consider how to prioritize tasks, remember that tasks vary in their urgency (deadline) and in importance. Prioritize them, indicating their relative importance to your career or personal development so that you can work on the one that is most important first (see Table 4.1). Prioritize your actions so that you will first do what is most important or time efficient.

As you use this system, you will find that many tasks are not easily classifiable into dichotomous yes/no categories by urgency and importance. Rank items based on how urgent and how important each is. Essentially all of this is a to-do list, a list of tasks that you need to complete, broken down into small action units.

After you have compiled your prioritized list, consider a time frame and construct a plan for completing your list of actions. Make sure that your plan is doable. Can you realistically carry out the set of steps that you have allocated for a given time frame? Do the steps fall into a logical sequence? Note your tasks and time frame in your calendar; later in this chapter I discuss calendar methods.

As you implement your plan, monitor your progress. Give yourself positive feedback for what you do accomplish rather than punishing

TABLE 4.1

Prioritizing Tasks

Priority	Urgency	Importance
1	Urgent	Important
2	Not urgent	Important
3	Urgent	Not important
4	Not urgent	Not important

yourself for what you do not. Assess the feasibility of your plan, and make adjustments if needed. Most people find that their action plans require at least some adjustment. People often make unrealistic plans. Modify yours into more realistic ones (be sure to look over your big plan too). Finally, remember that these techniques can also be applied to short-term goals—monthly, weekly, and even daily sets of tasks.

Finally, remember that you are not alone. Other students struggle with these issues too. Take advantage of that and work together: Use the buddy system. Work with a friend to increase your sense of accountability and help you to stay in track. Find people with whom to share your goals and time frames. It is better if you have someone to bounce ideas off of and to work with in tracking your progress. Make contracts with your friend; promise that you will have a task done by a specific day. The deadline you have set creates a social responsibility, and you will feel embarrassed if you do not comply with the contact. Be realistic. If you are certain that you can complete the task on a given day, set a contract with your advisor. Set deadlines that will not embarrass you. This is a great way of keeping yourself moving, showing your advisor what you can do and that you are responsible and motivated.

MANAGE YOUR TIME

Once you have identified your goals, time management becomes critical to achieving them. Ever have that feeling like there are not enough hours in the day to accomplish everything? Everyone has the same 24 hours each day. How do some people manage to do so much more with those hours than others? It is a matter of how people use those hours. Good time management will help you achieve your goals and give you a sense of control by permitting you to get done what you need to and still have time for yourself.

Recognize Demands on Your Time

Before discussing how to manage your time, consider the demands on your time. During work days, people direct their time toward several different sources: advisor/supervisors, the system, self, and peers. Consider how you spend time in each of these four categories, and consider how to make improvements in each.

- *Advisor/supervisor-directed time:* time you spend meeting with, waiting for, and completing tasks for your advisor or supervisor. You cannot do much about these demands, although you can work around them. For example, if like many students you find yourself waiting around for an advisor who is running late, make that time your own by bringing pocket work with you, whether it is an article to read, paper to grade, or manuscript to proof.

- *System-directed time:* time you spend meeting departmental, lab, and program demands such as departmental paperwork, coursework, and teaching. Again, you cannot avoid these tasks, but you can find ways of streamlining them, like creating e-mail templates and grading protocols to make everyday tasks move more smoothly.
- *Self-directed time:* time you spend directing your own activities. Time spent working toward your goals is well spent, but many people direct their own activities in ways that are not useful to making progress on their goals, like surfing the Internet, e-mailing and chatting with friends, and playing video games. One solution is to set a timer to limit your nongoal-directed activity. For example, suppose that you want to take a 10-minute break. That 10-minute break can easily turn into an hour and derail your work, so set a timer to ensure that you stick to it.
- *Peer-directed time:* time you spend on activities that are subordinate or peer driven. For example, another graduate student asks for your help with a research problem, an undergraduate asks you to tell him where to apply to graduate school, or a friend asks you to proof a paper for a class. Consider where to cut back. For example, the undergraduate student can be encouraged to research specific programs and then return.

You can never escape these demands on your time, but you can become aware of them and consider how to become more efficient so that you have more time for the tasks that are truly important to you.

Log Your Time

How do you spend your time each day? Classes, reading, writing, studying, right? How much time do you really spend working? As a student of psychology you have learned that people do not always perceive reality accurately. One way to learn more about how you use time as well as find ways to use your time more efficiently is to keep track of your time by maintaining a time log.

Record your daily activities: What do you do and how long does it take? The trick to making this work is to diligently record every task and every minute. Consider setting a timer to ring every 15 minutes and then record your activities. If you are like most people, you will be surprised by what you learn: You are wasting much more time than you think. When you track your time, you will learn about your patterns of work and distraction. Where does the day go?

> Ted sits down to work, ready to open his word processing software and begin writing. "First, I'll quickly check my e-mail," he thinks to himself. After reading and responding to the 38 e-mails in his inbox, Ted breezes by the American Psychological Association Web site and notices that the new issue of the *Monitor* is posted.

> "Some of these articles look critical," he says to himself and begins reading. An hour later he checks his e-mail and remembers that he forgot to complete his statistics homework that was due yesterday. Two hours later he completes the assignment and submits it, late. Ted takes a break for lunch and goes to the diner with some other graduate students on his floor. The remainder of his day was taken up by a lunch that took too long, responding to e-mails, checking *The New York Times* on the Web, talking to people who duck their head into his open office door, and a quick meeting with his advisor. Ted realizes that he's put in a 10-hour day but does not know where the time has gone.

We have all had days like these, but it is only after recording how time is spent that we take action and devise ways of saving our most precious commodity. A benefit of charting your time is that you will get to see your own energy patterns. You probably know if you are a morning or night person, but when are you most productive? Your productivity varies based on your sleep, eating, temperature of the room, stress, and so on. By tracking your time use, you will get a better picture of how your energy and productivity shift over time and will identify your peak energy periods and be able to schedule your time to take advantage of those peak times. For example, use those times for writing and the off-times for e-mail.

Schedule Your Time

Goal setting and action plans are important, but you will only complete your action plan if you have worked it into your schedule. This is where a calendar comes in. Do not just use one calendar; instead, use several to indicate long-term, short-term, and current plans and activities. Right from the beginning of graduate school, you should set up a calendar system that works for you.

Five-year calendar. To facilitate long-term planning, use a calendar that covers the entire period of your graduate school program (e.g., a 5-year calendar). Mark important deadlines such as financial aid requirements and testing periods, as well as self-set requirements such as goals for taking comprehensive exams and submitting the dissertation proposal. Refer to this calendar frequently, making new entries as they arise (e.g., goals for submitting articles for publication, grant deadlines, and so on).

Year calendar. Although it might feel like keeping track of your day is challenging, it is more difficult to keep track of what you need to do 6 or 8 months from now. For example, conference deadlines are often posted a year in advance, yet it is not uncommon for graduate students (and faculty) to realize that they have forgotten a pending deadline (and therefore drop all of their current work to frantically complete a proposal, leaving them exhausted and behind on their work). It is easy to focus on the here and now, getting through this next exam, for example, and forget to think about the big picture and your long-term goals. If you want to make progress on these goals, you have to keep them in mind. Record your long-term goals and action plans into your annual calendar to ensure that you make consistent progress on the big picture items that matter to you, such as completing your dissertation.

Month calendar. This calendar shows your month in detail and illustrates when you will work on specific tasks. Note all important deadlines and dates, pulling deadlines from your year-scale calendar. Pay particular attention to items at the beginning of the upcoming month that may be overlooked when you are focused on the end of the current month. Post this in a visible place so that you have a visual of your month. Try to post at least 2 months at a time so that you can see the overlap between the present and upcoming month.

Day and week calendar. This is the calendar that you will carry. It might be electronic, a weekly planner, or some other format. The important thing, regardless of format, is that you record all of your daily and weekly activities. Record times for class meetings, advisor meetings, assistantship hours, office hours, and so on. This is where you schedule specific times to complete your action items. Schedule time to study, write, and complete other tasks. If you take online classes, schedule time to log in. If you teach online sections of your classes, list log-on times as well.

Do not schedule all of your time. Keep your schedule flexible because most tasks will take longer than you intend, and you do not want to schedule your time too tightly and set yourself up for failure. Perhaps most important is that you should factor into your schedule time to recover and recharge. Do not plan more than a half day's worth of work over the weekend because you will need time to rest as well as time to catch up should you run behind. If you spend your weekends working, you will burn out and find that 1 or 2 days during the week are not very productive. Take vacations, too—time completely away from work.

Every week stop and assess your progress. What was your action plan? What did you intend to accomplish? What did you accomplish? What were obstacles? Were there any unexpected events? Was your plan realistic? How would you change it? Then look over your short-term goals and action plan and modify them, if necessary, in light of what you have learned. Adjust your weekly and monthly calendar accordingly.

Reduce Distractions and Eliminate Procrastination

The graduate school years are filled with days that fly by. Sometimes the hours pass too quickly with not much to show for it. If you have lots of bad days when you feel that you are not getting as much done as you would like, step back and assess the situation. Do you recognize any of these distractions?

DISTRACTION DISGUISED AS PRODUCTIVITY

Have you ever noticed that the minute you sit down to work, a list of undone tasks come to mind? You finally sit down to read or write and you remember that you have not paid the bills, fed the dog, replied to that e-mail, or done the dishes? Each of these tasks seems very important and pressing; it drives you crazy that they are undone. These thoughts are distracting, and they are a popular form of procrastination. How do you know? Force yourself to work instead; after putting in an hour's worth of writing you will find that the task seems much less urgent.

Procrastination takes many forms and this one—telling yourself that there are other pressing tasks to complete—can be particularly effective at derailing your work because the task really does need to be completed. The dishes really do need to be done, the dry cleaning needs to be dropped off, and your MP3 player really does need to be organized. What is the solution to balancing your work with all of the pesky tasks that come to mind? Write them down.

Keep a pad of paper and a pen next to your work area. Each time your mind wanders to a new task that needs to be completed, grab the pad and write it down. It takes 5 seconds but will record the task and let you get back to work. You can make yourself feel better by telling yourself that you have written it down and will not forget it, but now you have time to work. The challenge is that often these distracting thoughts will disguise themselves as research needs and solutions. For example, you might think of a new way to analyze the data or something that you may have missed in your last set of analyses; new books and references that you must get; places where you might find the perfect quote or reference; or new ways of accounting for your finds. The danger here is that the task is work related. Is it okay to shift tasks? Should you run that PsycINFO search, e-mail that noted researcher, or open SPSS? No. Instead, jot down the task or idea and keep on working. Finish the work that you have promised yourself to complete. When you are done with the day's work, reevaluate the idea. If it truly is an epiphany, it still will be of value when you return to it.

COMMON DISTRACTIONS AND SOLUTIONS

Successful graduate students know that planning ensures that the work is completed. However, allocating time and resources is not enough; you also must reduce the distractions that keep you from fulfilling your plan.

E-mail

It is easy to succumb to the urge to open every e-mail that works its way into your inbox. Limit your use of e-mail. Turn off the announcement. Check e-mail at the beginning or end of the day. If you must check e-mail more often, then restrict it to every 2 to 3 hours. Limit the time you devote to e-mail by setting a timer and sticking to it. Otherwise e-mail can take up much more time than you intend.

Internet

The Internet is the biggest of distractions. It is a tremendous resource for research, but it is easy to find yourself with multiple browser windows open, surfing for news and celebrity gossip while searching for references on PsycINFO. News, blogs, and shopping can be addictive. Pace yourself. Use your Internet surfing as a reward and closely monitor the time you spend. Set a timer to remind you of how long you want to surf and to help you stop when you wish.

Phone

Turn off your phone while you are working to avoid distracting calls. You might promise yourself to not answer but it is very hard not to. Even the phone ringing will set you off task; you might check to see who it is and engage in a mental struggle as to whether you should answer it. Avoid the time waster. Like e-mail, check it after you work.

Self-Defeating Thoughts and Emotions

Sometimes we are our biggest sources of distraction. Unwanted thoughts and emotions can pervade our minds while we are trying to concentrate on work. Negative beliefs such as "I'll never finish" or "I do not have the skills to do this" detract from our self-confidence and motivation, sapping our energy and creating self-fulfilling prophecies. The stress of graduate school often leads to anxiety. Feelings of overwhelm and fears of failure are big distracters. In chapter 7, I discuss emotional regulation and self-management, important influences on a person's success.

Social

Social breaks are important; everyone needs to gab with peers who are also struggling with coursework, research, assistantships, and more. Plan your social breaks, however, to avoid the following: A colleague stops by to ask a quick question. An hour later you are talking with your office mate about departmental politics and then the latest *Grey's Anatomy* story line. Does this sound familiar?

When possible, close your office door, and you will get more accomplished. A closed door tells others that you are working and makes them rethink their reason for interrupting you. Closing your door also helps you concentrate because it eliminates outside distractions, like people walking by. The drawback to closing your door is that it can make you seem unfriendly. Assess the habits of people in your department. If most have their doors open most of the time, then close yours only when you really need to catch up on your work. Another way to manage social distractions is to work on off-times. You can get a lot accomplished if no one is around. Typically before 10 a.m. and after 5 p.m. are quiet times in most departments. Consider shifting your hours or working early or late a couple of times a week. You will find that you can accomplish more during these times.

Some distractions are necessary and ones that you ought to be doing, like maintaining collegial relationships with others. Casual conversation serves a variety of purposes: relationship building, education (graduate student talk is often interspersed with passing on of research gems), and blowing off steam. The challenge is not to lose your day to it.

Success in graduate school entails self-management skills. Organizational skills (i.e., managing space, files, and time) create structure that makes it easier to complete tasks. Learn techniques of managing yourself, setting goals, devising plans to achieve goals, and reducing distractions, and the challenges entailed by graduate study will be made easier.

Recommended Reading

Allen, D. (2002). *Getting things done: The art of stress-free productivity.* New York: Penguin Books.

Blair, G. R. (2000). *Goal setting 101: How to set and achieve a goal!* Palm Harbor, FL: Blair Publishing House.

Burka, J. B., & Yuen, L. M. (1983). *Procrastination: Why you do it, what to do about it.* Reading, MA: Addison-Wesley.

Covey, S. R. (1989). *The 7 habits of highly effective people.* New York: Simon & Schuster.

Crouch, C. (2005). *Getting organized: Learning how to focus, organize and prioritize.* Memphis, TN: Dawson.

Dodd, P., & Sundheim, D. (2005). *The 25 best time management tools and techniques: How to get more done without driving yourself crazy.* New York: Peak Performance Press.

Fry, R. (2005). *Get organized.* Clifton Park, NJ: Thomson.

MacKenzie, A. (1997). *The time trap: The classic book on time management.* New York: American Management Association.

Merson, L. (2005). *The instant productivity tool kit.* Naperville, IL: Sourcebooks.

Morgenstern, J. (2004). *Time management from the inside out: The foolproof system for taking control of your schedule and your life* (2nd ed.). New York: Henry Holt.

Department Relationships

Mentors, Peers, and Politics

5

Graduate school is about becoming a psychologist by learning how to do the work of psychologists, which includes making new research discoveries; sharing them with the world; encouraging and assisting others (e.g., media, policymakers, and educators) in interpreting and applying relevant research results to real-world problems; and, when relevant, applying them in clinical practice. Relationships are critical to your success in this endeavor. Smart graduate students learn how to establish and sustain good working relationships with faculty and peers. In this chapter we discuss the people part of graduate study.

Relationships With Mentors

Mentoring relationships are an important predictor of success in graduate school and afterward (Clark, Harden, & Johnson, 2000; Johnson & Huwe, 2003; O'Neill & Wrightsman, 2001). The terms *advisor* and *mentor* are often used interchangeably; however, they are not the same. An advisor is someone who oversees your study; he or she may be assigned or chosen through mutual agreement, depending on graduate program. Your advisor will help you select courses and usually supervises your research, including your dissertation. The function of the advisor is to act as a mentor and to guide your professional growth and development throughout the graduate and postdoctoral years. Although advisors generally provide supervision in research and practice, not all provide mentorship, a nurturing relationship, to students. Mentoring generally takes the form of an apprenticeship. The mentor provides instruction, but perhaps more important, socializes the student to the norms of the scientific and professional community of psychologists.

Ideally your advisor will also act as your mentor, but unfortunately that does not always happen (Colón Semenza, 2005). Sometimes students work under the supervision of advisors who do not provide professional guidance.

> Christina completed her dissertation under the supervision of Dr. V. She complained to graduate students of a lack of guidance; each week she brought topic ideas into her meetings but Dr. V. offered little feedback, criticism, or guidance on whether the topic was feasible. Nevertheless Christina plugged away at her topic, chose measures, passed her proposal meeting, and collected and analyzed data. Throughout the process she felt alone. Christina would approach Dr. V. for feedback, for example, explaining her problem with missing data and how she would like to approach it, and receive nothing but a nod in return. The final straw was when Christina received an invitation to interview for an assistant professor position at her dream institution: an active research department with a graduate program located in a liberal arts institution in a highly desirable geographic area. She excitedly told Dr V. and asked for advice on how to prepare and what to expect. Dr V. only offered congratulations. Christina went to the interview, asked questions, and gave her job talk. Afterward Christina realized that she bombed the talk by presenting too much background literature, dumbing down the work, and not being prepared to answer rudimentary questions. Years later Christina laments, "I had no clue what I was getting myself into. I really think Dr. V. should have helped me prepare."

In Christina's case, her advisor Dr. V. supervised her progress in graduate school and her dissertation but did not guide her socialization into the discipline of research psychology and the culture of academia. What are the activities of mentors? The following sections discuss the activities of mentors, the benefits of mentorship, what to look for in a mentor, and how to manage the relationship.

Your mentor will share knowledge as well as provide emotional and moral support, giving honest feedback and constructive criticism on your performance. The mentor is a master to which the student is apprentice. The mentor is a sponsor who is a source of information about and aid in obtaining opportunities, a model of what it is to be a psychologist. Mentoring goes beyond advising because it includes support and nurturing, not simply information passing. The mentoring relationship changes as students move through the program. When entering graduate school, students need information about courses and the program as well as guidance in learning the ropes of research and practice; later the emphasis shifts to professional issues such as publishing, grant writing, and managing complexities that arise in practice. In chapter 12 I discuss the phases of the mentoring relationship within the context of professional identity development.

WHAT DO MENTORS DO?

Mentors provide career guidance, helping protégés learn how to be psychologists and advance in the field, as well as psychosocial support, enhancing self-esteem, professional identity, and sense of competence. Mentors guide students in several ways (Johnson & Huwe, 2003; Kram, 1985; O'Neill & Wrightsman, 2001).

- Mentors provide sponsorship, smoothing the path for students by recommending them for awards and positions, promoting their work, and advancing their careers.
- Mentors challenge protégés, providing direct training and encouraging them to work on projects and complete tasks that push them to advance their competence and develop and hone skills.
- Mentors provide protégés with opportunities for exposure and visibility by inviting their participation in research projects and other professional activities and providing opportunities for them to demonstrate their competence and advance in their careers.
- Mentors provide protégés with professional coaching, encouraging and offering them information about departmental politics, the role of power in professional psychology, and how to manage interpersonal conflict.
- Mentors protect protégés, shielding them from undue criticism and supporting them when needed (e.g., during contentious meetings with their dissertation committee).

There are several ways in which mentors provide psychosocial support (Johnson & Huwe, 2003; O'Neill & Wrightsman, 2001):

- Mentors act as role models, demonstrating what being a psychologist entails; essential tasks such as conducting research, teaching, grant writing, or therapy; professional skills such as balancing personal and professional life; and conflict management and resolution.
- Mentors communicate acceptance and build confidence in protégés, facilitating their trust and encouraging them to succeed at challenging tasks.

- Mentors provide counseling to protégés, providing advice about career issues, decision making, and how to integrate and balance career and personal responsibilities.
- Mentors and protégés reciprocate a sense of being appreciated, valued, trusted, and respected.

There are many functions that mentors may serve. Remember that no one mentor relationship will fulfill all, just as no personal relationship fulfills all functions. Research suggests that graduate students most often report receiving direct training, sponsorship, role modeling, and acceptance from mentors (Clark et al., 2000). Seek the guidance of several individuals and you will benefit from multiple perspectives (Colón Semenza, 2005). Multiple mentors with different strengths will provide support on different aspects of professional life; for example, choose a faculty member who can guide your research endeavors and another who can model applied work.

Given the functions of mentors, there are a variety of benefits to being mentored (Clark et al., 2000; Johnson & Huwe, 2003; O'Neill & Wrightsman, 2001).

- Learn professional skills by observing and working alongside a master.
- Observe a model of what it is to be a psychologist, colleague, and ethical professional.
- Develop a sense of professional confidence and identity in response to your mentor's encouragement.
- Learn how to network and develop professional contacts in the department and field that will aid employment opportunities.
- Become a productive scholar.
- Develop and successfully carry out a dissertation.
- Secure internships and other training experiences.
- Be more satisfied with your graduate program.
- After graduation, be more likely to be employed and experience more career mobility and more career satisfaction.
- Learn to mentor others.

Although many entering graduate students do not question their need of a mentor, sometimes older, nontraditional graduate students may feel that a mentor is unnecessary (Johnson & Huwe, 2003). This is especially common among students who have left professional careers for graduate study. In some ways a mentor is even more important for older and nontraditional students because the transition to graduate school entails more change for nontraditional students, with many experiencing a change in status, from knowledgeable professional in a position of power to entering student and subordinate. In addition, older students may be significantly older than other students and may find it more challenging to establish relationships with their peers.

Everyone can benefit from the tutelage of a mentor. Even faculty members and professional psychologists seek mentors as they transition to the professorate and embark on careers in research and practice. Mentoring is not only for graduate students and new psychologists; mentors provide guidance to psychologists as they move up in professional ranks and progress to more senior levels. One of the challenges that older students face is seeking mentorship from a same-age or younger faculty member; sometimes if a student clicks with a faculty member it may be hard to remember the power differential in the relationship. Nontraditional students face challenging mentorship relationships indeed, which is why it is particularly important for them to consider the advice in this chapter and implement as much as feels comfortable.

WHAT TO LOOK FOR IN A MENTOR

By now you realize the importance a relationship with a faculty mentor holds in influencing your career. A good relationship with your advisor can ease your way through graduate school and enhance your opportunities after graduation. A poor mentoring relationship can halt your professional journey just as it is beginning. It is in your best interest to consider potential mentors carefully. There are several characteristics and qualities that are desirable in a mentor (Clark et al., 2000; Colón Semenza, 2005; Johnson & Huwe, 2003; O'Neill & Wrightsman, 2001).

Similar Research Interests

An initial consideration in choosing a mentor is his or her area of study. You will work alongside your mentor, conduct his or her research, and your own research will likely spin off of that work. While your potential mentor's current research project may not be on a specific question that you would have chosen, ensure that the topic area is of interest to you. For example, Amy is working with her mentor on a project examining the influence of parenting on delinquent activity in teenagers. Although Amy is not specifically interested in parenting, she is interested in adolescents' engagement in risky activities. Her mentor's work focuses on at least an aspect of Amy's topic area of interest. You will spend a great deal of time and creative effort working alongside your mentor. Interest in the research topic is unquestionably essential or you will find it very hard to summon the motivation needed to carry out the work.

Tip Do not rely only on conversations with professors to learn about their research. Read recent publications (before you speak with them!) and request copies of articles that are in press (not yet published but scheduled to appear in research journals) as well as recent conference papers to ensure that you are familiar with the full volume of the professor's work.

Personality and Compatibility

It is hard to work with someone whose personality clashes with your own. Choosing a mentor whose personality does not match your own (at least to a degree) and who you do not like will sabotage your graduate school career (Johnson & Huwe, 2003). Your mentor will supervise your own research, but his or her influence will extend well beyond the graduate school years; he or she will provide advice, career guidance, and letters of recommendation through at least the early years of your career, but often throughout its entirety. Characteristics to look for are warmth and empathy, humor, flexibility, patience, and dedication. Choose someone whose personality complements your own; you do not have to be best friends, but you will have to work together, often intensely, over a long period of time. Moreover, mutual respect makes the relationship work, and it is hard to respect someone you do not like.

Tip Speak to current graduate students to find out what it is really like to work with a potential mentor.

Productivity

Mentors who are productive and actively engaged in research and publishing provide many opportunities to learn the art of psychological research. To evaluate productivity, review the faculty member's publications. Are they all on the same topic, demonstrating a line of research, or are they on a variety of topics with little coherence? How recent are the publications? Some faculty may have been very productive early in their career, before they earned tenure, and then slowed their pace. Look for current publications, within the last few years. Also consider how often he or she publishes with students and the order of authors in those publications (the order of authors designates credit for the work with the first author receiving more credit). If the faculty member publishes with few students, it may mean that he or she does not invite students to work alongside him or her, or it may mean that students are not getting adequate credit for their work (it happens).

Scientific Reputation

Although it may seem that productivity and scientific reputation are linked (after all, famous professors generally are prolific), they are not. Many professors produce a great deal of research that is of good quality but do not receive a great deal of attention from the scientific community. All things being equal, it is advantageous to work with a mentor who is well known and active in the field. Mentors who are well respected by the scientific community will open many doors for you, from introducing you to leaders in the field to writing letters of recommendation that carry weight. The drawback is that the most famous professors are the busiest, working on multiple projects, reviewing grants and journal articles, and traveling often. You might find it difficult to get the attention you want. Talk with students to learn what it is like to work with famous professors and whether they get the guidance they had hoped for or if a postdoc working under the professor instead does most of the training.

Availability and Interpersonal Skills

Good mentors are available to students. They respond to student questions, e-mails, and phone calls within a reasonable amount of time (say 48 hours) and schedule regular meeting times (and keep them) for discussing research, student progress, feedback, and other issues. Availability does not simply refer to an advisor's physical presence but also to his or her capacity to relay information to students. Good mentors have interpersonal skills that permit them to communicate well. They are able to communicate expectations and provide feedback and constructive criticism in a way that does not demean others.

Student Success

The fate of former graduate students can tell you a lot about a faculty member. Ask other graduate students about who has worked with a given faculty member and their ultimate fate. If many students leave to work with other faculty or drop out of the program, it could tell you that the faculty member is challenging to work with. Instead, if the students continue to work in the lab or have graduated and moved on to postdoctoral fellowships, faculty positions, or excellent applied positions, then you can bet that the mentor is capable. It is particularly important to consider recent graduates; if they hold desirable positions, then it suggests that the faculty mentor is willing to give students credit for their work, promote them, and write letters or make calls for them. Finally, how long does it take the average student of a given faculty member to graduate? This information may be hard to come by, but ask current students how long they have been enrolled in graduate school, who are the most senior students, and whether it seems that students graduate in reasonable time frames. If most students who work under a given faculty member take a long time to graduate compared with their peers, it may mean that the professor is not available, gives poor advice, or does not guide student research well. Remember that there are always some students who are faster or slower than others, so consider the time to degree completion of most students, not simply individuals.

Tenure Status

Tenure provides faculty with a safety net; it was designed to protect academic freedom and permit professors to study and speak on topics as they see fit without fear of losing their jobs. Most faculty are not awarded tenure until their 6th year of work. Assistant professors are the most junior members of the department; they do not have tenure. To earn tenure, they must publish extensively, demonstrate their capacities as academics, and become well known. If they do not earn tenure, they must leave the university and search for a new job.

Working for junior professors can be very rewarding because they are conducting research, often state-of-the-art research on hot topics, at a rapid pace and publishing often. However, working for a junior professor can also be dangerous. If the junior faculty member does not live up to departmental expectations and does not earn tenure, you may lose your mentor. Even if the faculty member gains tenure, junior faculty may be so concerned with their own future that they may give students little attention. Of course, this is true of senior faculty too. On the other hand, new faculty may be closer to your own age and may be particularly generous because they are more likely to remember what it is like to be in your shoes.

Personal Factors

There are also personal factors to take into account when choosing a mentor (Colón Semenza, 2005; Johnson & Huwe, 2003). Some students, for example, feel that they must work with a same-sex mentor. They worry that they may feel uncomfortable asking for help and seeking mentorship by a faculty member of the opposite sex. Other students prefer to work with mentors of the same ethnicity or race. Students of color may feel that they will be better able to connect with a faculty member who has similar experiences and background and has overcome similar obstacles and struggles. Age may be a concern for older, nontraditional graduate students. Such students may fear age bias or may even encounter it. They may feel uncomfortable working with a faculty member who is younger than them, or a young faculty member may find it difficult to advise an older student.

Regardless of your situation, carefully consider your own mentorship needs. They may be for a faculty member of a particular gender, ethnicity, or age. Find a faculty member who is well suited to you because you will work as a partner with this person for the next few years of your life, and your career will be shaped by his or her influence.

HOW ARE MENTORS ASSIGNED AND WHAT DO THEY SEEK?

Now that you know the importance of mentors, how do you obtain one? Some mentors are not chosen. There are at least two different approaches to placing students with mentors. Many graduate programs assign students an advisor, matching incoming students to faculty on the basis of research interests, needs, and faculty funding; mentorships are expected to grow from these relationships (Clark et al., 2000; Colón Semenza, 2005; Johnson & Huwe, 2003). The faculty mentor assists the student's transition to the program and continues to work with the student through the dissertation years to graduation. An early student–faculty pairing is beneficial for students because it gives them a head start, immerses students in the faculty's areas of research, and provides research supervision from Day 1. Students are more likely to graduate with research-based conference presentations and publications, which aid in employment. The potential downside is that there may be few opportunities to work on research that is outside the mentor's area of interest (Johnson & Huwe, 2003).

Other graduate programs take a more informal approach whereby students and faculty jointly choose the match (Colón Semenza, 2005; Johnson & Huwe, 2003). Entering students may visit faculty laboratories, talk with students and the faculty member, and learn about their research. Once the student determines whom she or he would like to work with, the student is responsible for approaching the faculty member. The student and faculty jointly choose and create the match. Usually the faculty member will meet with students as a group, for example, a laboratory team, and he or she will oversee all student work. Students usually have individual meetings with the faculty member, too, though often less frequently than the group meetings. This format encourages more peer interaction among students because they meet as a team to discuss one another's projects. There is research freedom and the opportunity to choose your own projects, but overall there is less individualized research instruction and the accompanying mentorship than when mentors are assigned (Johnson & Huwe, 2003).

Many students establish more informal mentorships with faculty, practica supervisors, and advanced graduate students. There is much to learn and many people from whom you may learn. Informal mentorships are often the best kind because they develop organically and comprise professional friendships.

Mentors want the same things in graduate students as graduate students seek in mentors (Johnson & Huwe, 2003). It is a reciprocal relationship. Faculty look for students who are easy to get along with and whose personalities are compatible with their own. Qualities like emotional stability, self-esteem, and self-awareness rate highly with faculty because these qualities suggest that students will be flexible, able to regulate their emotions, and in tune with others around him or her. The ability to handle constructive criticism and use it to improve is also valued by faculty because it shows the ability to learn and benefit from feedback. Interpersonal skills indicate that the student can express him- or herself in constructive ways, communicate, and manage interpersonal relationships. Faculty seek students who are motivated and committed to their work, are conscientious, take initiative, and face challenges tenaciously.

Mentoring relationships benefit not only the student but the faculty as well (Johnson & Huwe, 2003). First, working with students increases faculty productivity. As you assist your mentor, you will earn more autonomy and take on increasing responsibility for conducting joint research, permitting the faculty member to direct his or her attention to other research tasks and other projects. Second, students offer fresh perspectives on research topics and problems. Discussions with students may lead to new ideas and alternative takes on research findings. Third, most faculty feel tremendous satisfaction in watching their students develop into psychologists. A protégé's progression from new graduate student, to research and teaching assistant, to researcher and teacher, to completing a dissertation and moving on as a professional, is rewarding to mentors because they have left their mark on the world by guiding a young professional.

CRAFT THE MENTORING RELATIONSHIP

The mentoring relationship is the bedrock of your graduate school training. Through interactions with your mentor, you will learn what it is to be a researcher and psychologist. Do not take this relationship lightly. Be deliberate in establishing this very important relationship, and you will be more likely to construct a mentorship that lasts beyond your graduate school years.

The most important part of establishing a good foundation with your mentor is knowing and communicating expectations. Good relationships come from shared expectations. Establish what your expectations are. Clarify them. Communicate them. It is hard and uncomfortable, but it must be done. Both students and faculty tend to assume that others share their expectations, but that is often not the case. Similarity in expectations predicts satisfaction and success (Johnson & Huwe, 2003). An honest discussion will let you and your mentor assess goals, interests, and expectations and evaluate compatibility. You may find that you are incompatible, just as in romantic relationships. That is okay. It is better to know that now than later. Frank discussion, though it may be uncomfortable, is what is needed. Know that this discussion will have to occur over time too, as expectations and experience may change the mentoring relationship.

Things to discuss with your mentor include the following (Johnson & Huwe, 2003):

- How long will the relationship last, for example, until the master's thesis or preliminary research project or exams are completed? Until graduation?
- How often will we meet (roughly) and for how long?
- Which projects will we work together on?
- What kinds of tasks will I do and how might those change over the course of the project as well as over the next few years?
- What do you expect from students in terms of hours, productivity, work ethic?

Despite efforts at relationship building, sometimes students' relationships with mentors become troubled. Just as in any other relationship, problems can grow and fester in mentorships. The mentorship is not working when one or both partners are not having needs met or if either is distressed or harmed by the relationship (Johnson & Huwe, 2003). Why do mentoring relationships stop working?

- Poor match of student and mentor personality, interpersonal skills, and communication styles. Sometimes people just do not get along. Both may be good at what they do, but if they have difficulty working together, there will be problems.
- Incompetence on the part of the mentor, whether he or she lacks content knowledge, methodological or applied skills, or knowledge about how to mentor.
- Emotional problems, physical or mental illness, or maladaptive traits (e.g., dependency, poor emotional regulation) on the part of the mentor or student.
- Mentor unavailability. Faculty are busy people, but some become so busy that they cannot meet with students.

- Conflict and disagreements between the protégé and mentor. Conflict is part of all relationships, but if it increases in frequency and intensity until it impedes the working relationship, it is problematic.
- Boundary issues such as exploitation or romantic/sexual attraction on the part of the student or faculty member.

How do you deal with problems in the mentoring relationship? First, do not be passive. It is easy to be paralyzed by problems, do nothing, and respond by distancing yourself. Failing to do something about it can make the problem worse until it ruins the relationship and terminates it. Do not be impulsive. In the heat of the moment, it is easy to say things that you do not mean or vent by yelling, which is not helpful. Consider the problem, how you contribute to it, and how you can resolve it. Consult with others—peers as well as a trusted faculty member. Carefully think about what you want to accomplish and how you will do it. Be assertive and direct. Be communicative, respectful, and collegial. Discuss your concerns and frustrations but also highlight what is going well. Everyone responds well to positive feedback; make part of the message positive. Offer concrete requests and examples if needed. Plan it carefully. Addressing the problem and managing conflict can strengthen the relationship. Learning how to handle these problems in positive way will be a bonus for your career growth. It will help you master an important skill because you will be sure to encounter conflict throughout your career.

Sometimes a mentorship does not work because of conflict or simply differing interests, and you will need to look for a new faculty mentor. Look up relevant departmental guidelines regarding changing mentors, and seek guidance from the department chair on how to proceed. Before deciding to make a change, consider speaking candidly with your faculty mentor. Discuss your needs and your perception of how well you and your mentor's working styles, needs, and goals match. Perhaps an agreement can be reached. Sometimes simply discussing an issue can raise each party's awareness and lead to a new working alliance. Even if you decide to seek a new faculty mentor, an honest discussion with your current mentor can prevent undue surprise and misunderstanding. Begin the mentor selection process by talking with faculty and try to line up a new mentor before you cut ties with your old mentor. Better yet, do not burn your bridges. Thank the mentor for the experiences and learning opportunities. Keep the breakup impersonal. If it is because of changing research interests, say so, because it will soften the blow. Give the mentor notice, especially if you work in his or her lab. Be sure that you are not leaving him or her in the lurch. Frame the breakup in terms of your career goals.

Tip

Document meetings with your mentor, including what was discussed and agreed on as well as any other details. It is useful to get into the habit of documenting meetings because this skill will be needed throughout your career (e.g., as a professor, you may meet with a student who is particularly contentious—documentation may be helpful later if the student complains).

Peer Relationships

Graduate school is not simply about learning from faculty but also about learning from peers. Most students establish a circle of friends in college; however, like most things, peer relationships are more complicated in graduate school.

COMPETITION AND COLLEGIALITY

The students you encounter in graduate school will be colleagues throughout your career. You may not spend much one-on-one time with some of them during graduate school or after, but your fellow graduate students are part of your cohort and are your contemporaries in the field of psychology. Establish good relationships. Over the years your peers will become leaders in the field, chairing departments, editing journals, and heading foundations and clinics. The contacts you make now may influence your career 10 or 20 years from now. It is easy to see why collegiality will be beneficial to you now (in the form of social and informational support) and later.

Collegiality is a challenge in some departments where students are competitive with each other. Competition among graduate students can range from low to high, varying by program and cohort: Graduate students in some departments or at some times are more competitive than those in other departments or at other times. At least some competition is natural. Whenever people are conducting visible work and being evaluated, some jealousy is likely to arise. Everyone feels pressure to study for the same tests, do well on the same papers, and move toward the same goals. Whether you realize it, social comparison is inevitable. Competition may be greatest among graduate students during coursework because exams and grades make comparisons easy. After completing coursework, competition may become more subtle or at least is based on different criteria. Later in graduate school, competition concerns research discoveries, conference presentations, and publications. Competition will continue, to a certain extent, after graduate school too, for prestigious internships, postdocs, academic positions, grants, and publications.

Sometimes competition among peers can escalate into conflict. Learning how to resolve peer conflicts promotes career development because conflict resolution is a skill useful in all psychology careers, academic and applied. Perhaps the most important element in managing conflict with peers is to avoid it in the first place. Self-awareness can ease problems and sometimes even avoid them. Be aware of your own triggers and biases. Everyone is sensitive to particular issues or dynamics; remember your own, and you will be better able to moderate your reactions and avoid conflict altogether.

Sometimes conflict is unavoidable. A perspective change can influence your perception of the situation and how you manage it. Consider your role. No conflict is ever completely one-sided. How do you contribute to the dynamic? Perhaps something that does not seem problematic to you troubles a peer. Sometimes people have incompatible personalities; however, that does not mean that you do not have to try to get along, especially if you are collaborating on a research project with the same mentor. Understanding your own contribution to the problem can go a long way toward rectifying it, by either changing your own behavior or having a frank discussion with the peer and making compromises.

Always give others the benefit of the doubt. Escalating conflict will help no one. If an interaction becomes heated, take a break. Go for a walk, let yourself cool down, and think carefully about the conflict. What were the antecedents? How did the conflict arise? What was your peer's role? What was your own? Consider what price you are willing to pay for being "right" and refusing to resolve the issue. What might it mean for your opportunities? Gossip spreads quickly. How might other graduate students react? Faculty? Your mentor? What is the price of saving face? When you return, take deep breaths, listen to your peer, be open to other perspectives, and try to find a workable compromise.

If faced with conflict, consult with others—peers, faculty, your mentor, and family and friends outside your program—on how to respond. Sometimes a different perspective is all that is needed to resolve a situation. However, if you seek advice from peers or faculty, be careful that you do not pull them into the conflict. Do not sling mud or attempt to make a case on your behalf against a peer. That will only make the problem worse and perhaps be divisive to your cohort as a whole.

Learn from your experiences. Consider what you have learned about working with others, yourself, and interpersonal interaction. What might you have learned that might help you prevent disagreements from escalating into full-blown conflicts? What have you learned about resolving conflicts?

PEER MENTORS

There is much to learn in graduate school and many from whom you may learn. Faculty are not the only sources of guidance; most students also look to peers for advice, information, and feedback. The more senior graduate students have more experience and technical knowledge to share. Consider them part of your mentoring network because you can learn much about research and practice by talking with peers. Do not assume that your peers are not willing to help. Of course, do not be a nuisance; seek answers to your own questions before consulting peers, but do not shy away from asking for input and perspectives.

Likewise, be a mentor to your peers. It might not seem like you have much to share, but all students enter graduate school with different experiences and skill sets. Something that seems easy to you may be a great challenge to another student. Help others when you are able. As you progress through graduate school, you will find that you have much more experience than entering students; offer them assistance. Remember all those who have mentored you, and be a mentor to others. Those whom you mentor will be colleagues throughout your career. Establish generative and reciprocal relationships now.

Department Politics

As I have discussed, relationships with faculty and peers are particularly important influences on your success as a graduate student. Relationships also become more complicated because, as a graduate student, you will be part of a family of sorts—a department. Dynamics in a nuclear family may be complex: two parents and two children all influencing and being influenced by one another. Dynamics in an academic department are exponentially more complicated. Each member of the department enters with his or her own experiences, baggage, preferences, interaction styles, level of prestige in terms of publications and grants, and need for power and control. Some faculty members have complementary styles and get along, others do not. Some faculty members like each other, others do not. Add decision-making responsibility regarding curricula, students, and budgets, and there is the potential for extreme volatility. Sometimes seemingly small issues get blown into large-scale debates because of faculty incompatibility and struggles for control.

This means that success in graduate school entails more than academics; it is important to understand the social setting and all of its players (Sumprer & Walfish, 2001). Observe interactions among the faculty. Be careful not to get involved or take sides; just observe. As you learn about which faculty seem to work well together and which do not, you will be able to make meaningful decisions that will influence your own success, such as which faculty to ask to sit on your dissertation committee and which are likely to cause problems. You will also learn that sometimes an argument is not what it seems. For example, one student described an awful dissertation committee meeting in which two faculty vigorously argued over whether a result should be depicted in one or two tables. Having observed the faculty over time, she realized that they were not really fighting over the table; the table represented something much more significant to them: control and power. In this way, an academic department is like an extended family. Aunt Martha and Aunt Brenda may argue over how much pepper to add to the soup, but there is a lifetime of history, old disputes, and power issues really at stake. Once you realize that faculty members are human, sometimes covet power, and sometimes do not get along with each other, you will be better able to carefully observe the dynamics around you and use your observations to help you progress through graduate school. Relationships influence success in graduate school; awareness of this will help you to navigate graduate school.

Recommended Reading

Johnson, W. B., & Huwe, J. M. (2003). *Getting mentored in graduate school.* Washington, DC: American Psychological Association.

O'Neill, J. M., & Wrightsman, L. S. (2001). The mentoring relationship in psychology training programs. In S. Walfish & A. K. Hess (Eds.), *Succeeding in graduate school: The career guide for psychology students* (pp. 111–128). Mahwah, NJ: Erlbaum.

Sumprer, G. F., & Walfish, S. (2001). The politics of graduate programs. In S. Walfish & A. K. Hess (Eds.), *Succeeding in graduate school: The career guide for psychology students* (pp. 77–94). Mahwah, NJ: Erlbaum.

Relationships During Graduate School 6

One aspect of graduate school that many students fail to consider is how graduate study affects their relationships with friends and family. Graduate students face not only the demands of reading, research, and writing but also the demands and needs of their loved ones. In this chapter we discuss the challenge of maintaining relationships during the graduate school years.

Relationships With Friends and Family

Perhaps the most common complaint that graduate students have about their friends and family is that no one understands what they are going through. Nongraduate-student friends and family often do not distinguish between "school" and "graduate school" and do not realize the pressures entailed by graduate study.

> "When are you going to graduate already?" teases Uncle Tony during a family get-together. "Not for a while. I have to finish my dissertation," replies Melissa. "But you finished classes a while ago," Melissa's mother adds. Later Melissa complains to her classmate, Frank, "I hate that no one gets it. My mother can't seem to wrap her head around why it takes so long to write a

> dissertation, and no one seems to understand that I'm not in college. Spring break has no meaning other than fewer interruptions to my work. And do not even get me started on the summer—no one gets that school is not in session but it does not mean that I can drop everything and act like I'm on vacation." Frank replies, "Yeah, I get the same thing. I think it is what everyone goes through."

To a certain extent, Frank is right. Unless you have experienced graduate school, it is hard to grasp the undertaking. Students can help by explaining what graduate study means and how it is different from college as well as what it will mean for their career opportunities. Regardless, not everyone will understand. Accept that and you will be much happier.

Complaints about feeling misunderstood are particularly acute among first-generation graduate students and those from working-class or disenfranchised neighborhoods whose friends and family have little experience with higher education at the undergraduate or graduate level. Ethnic minority students might be accused by family and friends of selling out or renouncing their heritage to assimilate into the larger culture. Students who are too busy to attend parties or social gatherings may be viewed as ignoring responsibilities to friends and family or as perceiving themselves as too important to make time for loved ones.

People with no graduate school or limited or no college experience may conceive of graduate school as simply "school"—a matter of attending classes and doing homework. Family and friends may not understand the nature of scientific inquiry or see its value other than as a hurdle to complete the degree; your research may not be recognized as your attempt to devise and carry out procedures to answer your own questions. Eyes may glaze over with boredom when you explain your research and what graduate study entails. Moreover, friends and family who have little familiarity with the field may assume that graduate training in psychology imparts mind-reading skills. Regardless of whether the student is in a research or applied track, friends and family may sometimes feel uncomfortable, fearing that their every move and interaction will be analyzed by you, the budding psychologist. Applied students may compound this by directing their emerging clinical skills and therapeutic capacities toward their relations with families and friends, explaining interactions and diagnosing behaviors.

It is not surprising that when students finally manage to find time to spend with friends and family, they often feel misunderstood and frustrated. What graduate students do not realize is that they contribute to some of these problems and can act to mitigate others. Immersed in coursework, research, and practice, graduate students think, breathe, and live their work and often talk incessantly about their research and applied activities despite blank and uninterested stares from listeners. It can be hard to think about or discuss anything else, but leaving work behind is essential to maintaining relationships with friends and family as well as maintaining your own mental health.

Perhaps the underlying issue to blame for the challenges graduate students face in maintaining relationships with family and friends is simply that graduate school can sometimes take over students' lives. When students work long hours and socialize mainly with graduate student peers, they lose touch with the outside world because the main topic of conversation among peers is work. Instead, take some time away from work and graduate student friends: Get distance from it all, and keep up-to-date with pop culture and other nonschool-related things that provide a common ground for conversation. As we have discussed earlier, successful students treat graduate school like a job. They put in full-time hours and sometimes work late or on weekends, but they also stop working and take time off. Do not let graduate school stop you from interacting with friends and family; nourish those relationships. You might have less time, but there is no reason to give up on relationships or to have them change radically; your family and friends are still the same people.

How do you nourish your relationships with friends and family? Take time to listen to and participate in the things your family and friends are interested in because it is good for your relationship and it is good for you. The best thing that you can do to foster and protect relationships with family and friends is to be interested in them. Many graduate students tend to become egocentric. Attend to friends and family. Listen to them and ask about them. You talk about your work all day to your colleagues and think about it nonstop. Make the time that you spend with family and friends about connecting with them, not griping about your work. Relationships with friends and family are important resources, offering support, stress relief, and opportunities to focus on the world outside of graduate school, all of which will improve your health.

Relationships With Graduate Student Friends and Lovers

Graduate school entails a great deal of work, but it also will yield fun, lifelong friendships, and perhaps even love. How will you make friends with other graduate students? Friendships with other students largely form by exposure. From the first day of graduate study you are immersed in your field, spending many hours in the department working on coursework, research, and more. You will meet other students during orientation. You will attend classes together where you will likely speak before, after, and during class. Students spend time hanging out in the department or student lounge. You will meet office mates, students whose offices are near yours, lab mates, other teaching or research assistants, and students who share your advisor. It is through contact that you will get to know the other students in your program. Be aware of this because early contacts can influence how you are perceived by others and the resulting friendships you make in graduate school. Be friendly and be accessible.

RELATIONSHIP CHALLENGES EXPERIENCED BY INTERNATIONAL STUDENTS

Friendships often come naturally to students; however, international graduate students often face the social challenge of fitting in with other students who are from a different culture (Hasan, Fouad, & Williams-Nickelson, 2008). Language difficulties can exacerbate the common graduate student feelings of alienation, incompetence, anxiety, and loneliness because even sitting in class requires effort to listen and translate, let alone that entailed in reading and writing papers. International students with strong accents may find that others have difficulty understanding them and may have to repeat themselves often, which may be embarrassing or frustrating. International students face cultural differences, unfamiliarity with the structure of U.S. institutions of higher education, and homesickness. Cultural differences are often particularly challenging for international students, who, for example, may not be used to the level of assertiveness that U.S. students demonstrate in the classroom or may feel that the institutional environment is more impersonal than that to which they are accustomed. Add the absence of familiar people and the emotional crutches of home and international students may feel lonely and homesick.

> Poonam, a graduate student from India, arrived in the United States to study experimental psychology. She spent most of her first year of study in class and her room, with little social contact. She found class excruciating because some of her professors spoke very quickly but more so because she found it difficult to formulate her ideas and express them in English quickly enough to keep up with the class discussion. She feared that her professors and classmates attributed her lack of participation to incompetence. Poonam described herself as timid, shy, and lonely. She missed her home, her family and friends. After a time she found it hard to work; her loneliness began to feel like an emptiness, a hunger. Poonam made the difficult decision to try to reach out to classmates and others at school because her loneliness would otherwise force her to return home to India.

How can international students meet people and establish a social network of graduate student friends? International students make friends in the same ways as American students: by spending time in the department, being friendly with other students, and seeking opportunities to be around other students.

- Interact with other students who work in your advisor's lab, on the same project, or in offices near yours.
- Join or create a study group to prepare for classes.

- Pay attention to social norms among your classmates: Do they socialize after class, go out for coffee, or have lunch together? Do students hang out in the lounge?
- There are many places and ways in which students interact; pay attention and tag along because generally all students are welcome at these informal gatherings, all you have to do is ask or show up.
- Always remember to be yourself. Sometimes international students may internalize pressure to assimilate to the American culture and may reject part of their own identity to do so. Psychologists value diversity: Do not relinquish yours in an effort to fit in.

Tip

Many students, even those who consider themselves proficient in English, experience difficulties with jargon. If you are having problems understanding or communicating the language, take an English as a Second Language course or a course in conversational English. That little bit of practice can make a big difference.

All students, regardless of nationality, must balance making friends and being accessible with being cautious about opening up to people too much and too quickly. Do not reveal too much about your weaknesses and fears, for example, and do not gossip. This is especially true in the first year of graduate study because you need to get a handle on who everyone is, the departmental and student politics, and social norms. It is not uncommon for students to form cliques, and it is surprising how many cliques can develop in a small cohort of students. There are all kinds of relationships to have with fellow students, from friendly to adversarial. Be aware of the relationships that you have with others and think about how you would like to shape them. This is particularly important for more competitive and adversarial relationships.

Always strive to form good working relationships. You do not have to like everyone and interact with everyone, but success lies in learning how to have functional working relationships with others, even those whom you do not like. Do not talk about others behind their backs. Gossip is a common graduate student pastime, but do not let yourself get sucked into talking badly about anyone because secrets have a way of being spilled. Your best bet in graduate school—and throughout your career—is to be pleasant. Interpersonal politics in academia are complex, and people get upset very quickly and often remain so for a long time. If you strive to work well with others and are consistently pleasant and genuine, you will be on your way to avoiding much of the fallout of academic politics.

ROMANTIC RELATIONSHIPS WITH GRADUATE STUDENTS

Sometimes graduate school friendships evolve into romantic relationships. Romantic relationships are common among graduate students because they spend a great deal of time together and experience similar highs and lows. Each member of the couple understands the pressure of graduate school and can empathize with feelings of stress, occasional burnout, and anxiety about professors, research, comps, dissertation, and finding a job after graduation. A fellow graduate student is likely to be as busy and driven as you are and so will understand the hours that you put into work.

However, some of the positive aspects of graduate student relationships have a negative side. Because a graduate student partner is as busy as you are, finding time to be alone may be difficult. A partner who is a fellow graduate student may be a motivator, encouraging you to work alongside him or her, or may be a subtle competitor with whom you compare yourself. If you are in the same department or program as your partner, he or she will likely know when things are not going right for you—with your advisor, your research, or classes. Although that may breed understanding, sometimes students do not want to bring work stresses into a relationship and do not want their partner to learn about the intimate details of their successes and failures through observation and office gossip. A graduate student is well aware of the challenges of graduate school and understands the intense pressure that you feel; at the same time, he or she feels similar pressure. Members of graduate student couples may find it difficult to provide their partners with the support that they need when they are immersed in their own graduate school dramas.

Dating in the department can be difficult. Be prepared to be the subject of gossip. All interdepartmental romantic relationships are subject to gossip, but those of gay, lesbian, bisexual, and transgender (GLBT) students may be especially prone to become the topic of gossip. GLBT students who choose to date other students may find that their relationships receive more attention than they anticipated. Psychologists are socialized to be sensitive to issues of diversity; however, beliefs do not always translate into action, and GLBT students may find that their colleagues do their fair share of gawking, at least at first. That said, all interdepartmental romantic relationships face challenges and should be considered carefully. Before you date someone in your department, consider what will happen if the relationship does not work out. Will you be able to see him or her each day? Will you be able to work together if needed? Will you withstand the gossip about the breakup? Will you be able to see him or her date someone else? If you are unsure of any of these questions, then you might consider holding off on a relationship with another graduate student. Although such relationships can be fulfilling, there is a danger that the fallout may harm your career.

ROMANTIC RELATIONSHIPS WITH PROFESSORS

One of the first differences that students may notice about graduate school is the nature of relationships among faculty and students. Graduate students work closely with faculty, as junior colleagues. They assist faculty with designing, carrying out, and interpreting research and are encouraged by faculty to devise projects of their own. Close collaboration breeds friendships. Good mentoring relationships are based on mutual respect: They are friendships. It is not uncommon for either member of the mentoring relationship to develop romantic or sexual feelings (Johnson & Huwe, 2003). Is it ever a good idea to date a professor? In short, no.

Many universities forbid graduate student–faculty relationships because they are fraught with ethical conflicts. According to the American Psychological Association's "Ethical Principles of Psychologists and Code of Conduct" (2002, p. 1065; Standard 3.05, Multiple Relationships):

> (a) A multiple relationship occurs when a psychologist is in a professional role with a person and (1) at the same time is in another role with the same person, (2) at the same time is in a relationship with a person closely associated with or related to the person with whom the psychologist has the professional relationship, or (3) promises to enter into another relationship in the future with the person or a person closely associated with or related to the person. A psychologist refrains from entering into a multiple relationship if the multiple relationship could reasonably be expected to impair the psychologist's objectivity, competence, or effectiveness in performing his or her functions as a psychologist, or otherwise risks exploitation or harm to the person with whom the professional relationship exists.

Professors instruct and evaluate students. Even professors who are not in direct supervisory roles over students have the potential to influence students' careers. A romantic relationship will likely impair a professor's objectivity and will certainly cause others to question it. Romantic or sexual relationships between faculty and students pose serious risks to both parties, especially the student. Faculty may accuse the professor of exploiting the student–mentor relationship because of the inherent power disparity. Faculty–student relationships are ripe for departmental gossip. Regardless of what you reveal, your relationship will be very visible to other department members and the subject of much speculation and discussion, some of it not very nice and nearly all of it taking place behind your back. Other graduate students may accuse the professor of favoritism and be concerned about the student's access to course materials, research equipment, and funding.

Finally, consider how such a relationship might end. Even if the relationship ends amicably, it will be a highly visible breakup. Are you ready for all of your professors and colleagues to witness the demise of your relationship? How might the relationship's end influence your working relationship with the professor? Will it affect your research? Will you have to change advisors? How might it influence your standing in the department? Will you be able to continue work toward your degree? Will gossip about your relationship follow you after graduation to your postdoc or tenure-track job? Overall, the risks of a professor–student relationship exceed the benefits. Are you willing to risk your career over a potential relationship? If the attraction is genuine, it will be there after you defend your dissertation—and then you might consider pursuing a romantic relationship.

Dating, Marriage, and Family During Graduate School

Graduate study can pose obstacles to relationships with friends and family, and even more so to romantic relationships. Some graduate students forgo dating, reasoning that their time and attention is devoted to their work. Such dedication is admirable but not necessarily healthy. People need close relationships. Friendships can fulfill many needs, but romantic relationships fulfill a different set of needs. Sometimes students ignore budding relationships or put their own needs on the back burner. Remember that you are a student, researcher, practitioner, and a person. Do not ignore your own needs or be afraid to seek out romantic relationships during the graduate school years.

DATING

Regardless of your sexual orientation, dating is hard. As a busy graduate student, finding time to meet people and date is challenging. Finding the cash to date is even more difficult. Graduate students face questions of where to meet and how to find common ground with potential dates. GLBT students who attend graduate school in small towns and rural areas may find it difficult to meet potential dates. One strategy is to get involved in the local GLBT community by participating in the GLBT organization at your institution and community organizations such as church groups. Most students find that it requires motivation and effort to maintain friendships with nongraduate student friends, and establishing romantic relationships with nongraduate student partners is even more difficult.

Many students who want to date nongraduate students look to parties as useful avenues for meeting potential dates. At parties, graduate students are often faced with the question, "What do you do?" If they are dedicated to separating work and play (and do not want to bore a potential date), they may wrestle with how much of their work to discuss with their nongraduate-student listener. Come up with a sound bite to describe your research, a 30-second explanation that very briefly explains what you do, linking it to an issue in the news if possible to help your listener relate your work to something he or she knows about. If your listener engages you in conversation, make your own decision about how to proceed, but generally err on the side of not talking too much about your work rather than "overtalking" it.

> "One of the last things I tell a person that I have just met is what I do. I feel like I have to let my potential date get to know me as a person before revealing that I'm studying for a doctorate in psychology. When I finally reveal that I'm a graduate student, I'm often met with a puzzled look," explains Natasha. "I think that I surprise people because I am well informed enough to have a conversation about pop culture and have the social skills to do so." She continues, "I think the dating situation is harder for women than men because society subtly sends the message that women should not be scholars or brilliant researchers, which influences how women are perceived by potential dates. And there seems to be a lack of eligible dates in my area, a small town, as compared to the large city where I was raised. And even when I find someone to date, it is hard to explain the amount of time and devotion I direct toward my work—that sometimes I will have to cancel dates to complete particular tasks or projects. It is frustrating."

It is common for graduate students, particularly heterosexual women, to lament the challenges posed by dating those with no experience with graduate or professional school. One reaction that many students are unprepared for is intimidation by their education. Perhaps even more intimidating than education, for some, is training in psychology. Even experimentally oriented students encounter dates who assume that because they are psychologists they can discuss topics in abnormal psychology, provide treatment recommendations, or analyze people. Graduate students who date are surprised at having to explain the differences among clinical and social or developmental psychology, for example.

Misinformation about psychology and the nature of training in psychology abounds and can be a challenge for graduate students to overcome. At the same time, the tendency of many student practitioners to unwittingly apply what they are learning and their emerging clinical skills to their relationships and interactions with others can reinforce stereotypes about dating psychology students and make establishing and maintaining romantic relationships challenging. Perhaps the best advice for dating, regardless of your psychological specialty, is to take a deep breath, forget about work, and ask about the other person. Show that you are interested in your date, attentive to his or her needs, and able to not talk about your studies, and you will have made an initial step toward establishing a new relationship.

Tip

You might also consider developing a sound bite about your work that describes it in an uninteresting way for those times when you do not want to talk about your work or when you are asked a "What do you do?" question by someone you suspect might want to engage you in an extended discussion of hot topics in psychology. Most people have a little bit of information about psychology from an undergraduate course or two, magazine articles, or simply watching *Dr. Phil.* It is not uncommon for someone who, on learning that you study psychology, wants to talk about the latest thing they heard in the news, such as debates about medicating children, postpartum depression, or whether gorillas can communicate with sign language. Think ahead if you want to avoid such conversations.

MARRIAGE AND COMMITTED RELATIONSHIPS

Graduate students who are single often describe their coupled-off classmates as lucky. No need to date, no awkward first-date conversations, and someone to provide physical and social support. Unfortunately, this is an unrealistically rosy picture because romantic relationships are just as challenging as dating, and likely more so. If you are part of a couple, understand that your relationship will change in graduate school. Be prepared. Your available time and energy will change, and so will your needs for support from your partner. Graduate study will pose serious challenges to your partnership. The strategies for protecting relationships center on being aware of the stresses posed by graduate school.

Reduce Egocentrism

Graduate students who are consumed with their work (what graduate student is not?) can spend hours talking about the theoretical basis of their work, methodological challenges, and speculations about their findings and their implications, as well as departmental politics, funding issues, how they are going to find time for all that needs to be completed, and more. Although all of this is important to your success and can occupy your mind for hours on end, your partner is not as interested in the minutiae of your work as you are. Your partner has a life, career, and stresses of his or her own. A relationship is about sharing, talking about each other's world, and finding common ground. However, remember that you and your partner will likely have very different daily experiences and may not always be able to understand what each other is experiencing. The best thing that you can do is to listen, pay attention, and ask questions with sincere interest in understanding your partner. It sounds simple, but graduate school can be so overwhelming that it is easy to forget the basics that matter so much.

Integrate Your Partner Into Your Social Life

Graduate students socialize. What better way to commiserate, share stories of trauma (which, in retrospect, are often quite funny), and blow off steam? Sometimes students who are partnered off stay away from these gatherings in favor of spending time at home with their significant other. Although alone time with your partner is very important, bonding with classmates who understand what you are undertaking is also important. What better way for your partner to feel more a part of your graduate student life than to get to know some of your friends. Bring your partner to a gathering or simply ask your partner to meet some of your classmates for coffee. Once your partner can place faces with names and get to know your classmates—and hear their stories—he or she may get a better understanding of what your day-to-day life is like at school. One caution is in order when your partner attends social gatherings: Do not talk about school all the time. Also it helps if your classmates know a little about your partner so that they have something to talk about.

Discuss Decisions, Changes, and Plans

All students begin graduate school with a general plan for what they are undertaking and how long it will take to complete the degree. That plan always changes. Sometimes the changes are inevitable, and other times they are a result of choices that one makes regarding course sequencing, research projects, and assistantships. Discuss these changes with your partner, and if you have flexibility in your decision, solicit his or her input. Open and frank discussions about what is entailed to finish with regard to time, energy, and resources will help your partner understand the process. Soliciting input on decisions will make it clearer that you are a team throughout this challenging time and that your education is something that will benefit the two of you as a couple.

Likewise, if you and your partner have children, a recurring discussion about child care and household responsibilities is in order. The division of household and child care often shifts when one member of a household enters graduate school. It may be that classes or your assistantship prevents you from picking up your child from school or that some of the housework does not get completed as often as before. Moreover, your schedule and ability to participate in child care and housework may change with each semester. Also it is important to be clear about how your work schedule and style will change over the course of graduate school. There are times, like when you are studying for comprehensive exams or writing the dissertation, that you may be less available. Communicate your needs and listen to your partner's needs to find a way to compromise so that expectations are clear and feelings are not hurt. Your partner needs to understand that your preoccupation with your work does not mean that you value him or her less. It may sound silly, but during stressful periods it is easy to forget that graduate school is only one blip in a lifelong relationship.

Protect Your Relationship

Relationship stress and problems are inevitable when one is under a great deal of pressure. It is not surprising that graduate students who are part of couples often report that their studies are a stressor in their relationship. Feelings of loneliness and rejection often arise in partners of graduate students because the quantity and quality of attention they receive from their partner can change with entry to graduate school and over the course of the semester and graduate school years. Understand this, and make a safety plan for your relationship to protect it from these common feelings. Talk about how you will set aside time to spend together, what kinds of activities you will do together, how you will connect each day, and how you will give each other time to work. Establish a consistent plan, including a plan to periodically reevaluate it so that you each have an opportunity to make changes and so that both parties do not have to feel stressed over how to tell the other person that the plan is not working. Make your partner understand that he or she is still a priority in your life.

When you are both tired and overworked, it is easy to take each other for granted and lose some of the magic of your relationship. Make time for the two of you to have fun. Date nights, ongoing plans, and timeouts from work can help you and your partner keep your connection throughout graduate school. You might be tempted to put off down time, figuring that you will take some time after your paper is completed, after your proposal is in, or after the semester ends. After you push through this batch of deadlines and projects, you will find that another batch is waiting. There will never be a good time to take off; you need to carve out down time to protect your relationship and your own sanity. All relationships require effort; graduate study does not change that.

CHILDREN

Students with children often find graduate school particularly challenging because although they have fewer economic and emotional resources, their child's needs remain constant and often increase. What can you do to integrate being a dedicated mother or father with being a busy graduate student?

Carve Out Time

Make special time for you and your child, or each of your children. Reserving special time for the two of you together will send the message that the child is special and private time is important to you. Let the child select what you will do together. Make these standing dates and do not miss any regardless of your other responsibilities. Sometimes professors might make it seem otherwise, but no paper is as important as a few hours with your child. Successful student parents find small ways to connect with their children, like using chore time as together time. For example, take advantage of time in the kitchen to chat with children, inviting them to help with cooking and setting the table.

Be Ultra-Organized

Although it is not helpful to lose a present orientation and stop living in the moment, being organized is the best thing you can do to stay on top of both of your roles as graduate student and parent. Create a schedule, monitor it, and adjust it so that the schedule keeps you on target and moving toward completing your goals for the day, week, semester, and so on. When creating a schedule, look beyond your own work; other demands in your life will influence your schedule and work habits. A schedule should include all of life's activities to permit realistic decisions about how to spend time. Work life must be considered in conjunction with home life; compromise will entail adjusting both.

Schedule time to study, do research, attend class. Parents will often find that they have to carve out special times to work, like getting up early to study for an hour before getting the kids ready, and spending a few hours on research before attending a late morning class. Parents who are successful students treat graduate school like a job, arriving at school at 8 or 9 a.m. to study, do research, complete assistantship duties, and attend class, and leaving at 5 or 6 p.m. to spend time with their children. Students who maintain this schedule consistently during the week, and who spend their work time on task, manage to spend all or part of the weekend with their families without feeling guilty.

Adjust Expectations

Adjusting expectations is essential to combining parenting with graduate study. Many graduate student parents find that it is not possible to earn As on every exam and in every course while giving their families the attention they need. Part of finding balance is accepting that Bs are not the end of the world. Once you graduate no one will look at your transcript and note that you earned only Bs; a graduate degree is a graduate degree. Likewise, make realistic expectations for your home life. It is not necessary to cook every night. The world will not end if the home is a little messy. Reduce your standards for housekeeping, and you will find some time to spend with your loved ones or yourself.

Tip

Do not wait for inspiration. Many students wait for their muse before they begin to write a paper or prepare a project. Graduate students who are parents do not have the time to wait for inspiration. Make appointments to write, and keep them by writing whatever parts of your paper flow and not waiting for inspiration to strike. Regular and reliable habits of work quickly lead to regular and reliable written products—without the need to wait for inspiration.

Seek Assistance

Graduate student parents cannot do it all. Turn to someone else for at least occasional help, whether it is your partner, a parent or other family member, or a close friend. Parents of older children might have a weekly family meeting to discuss and schedule activities and chores, listing the tasks each child agrees to do and when they will be done. Seek help at school; some universities have student-parent support groups that offer opportunities to connect and share resources with other parents. Talk with parents in your neighborhood and at your child's school. Organize a car pool to share the task of shuttling children around. Make contact with other graduate students parents: You can share tips and learn a lot. For example, perhaps you and another parent can chip in and share a babysitter on days that children are off from school.

Relationships—with friends, family, lovers, and children—are challenging regardless of graduate study; however, graduate school poses intense demands on our relationships. Managing your own time, making time for others, and directing your attention at their needs will go a long way in helping you to maintain existing relationships and establish new ones over the graduate school years.

Recommended Reading

Berzon, B. (2004). *Permanent partners: Building gay and lesbian relationships that last.* New York: Penguin Press.

Gottman, J., & DeClaire, J. (2002). *The relationship cure: A 5 step guide to strengthening your marriage, family, and friendships.* New York: Three Rivers Press.

Hasan, N. T., Fouad, N. A., & Williams-Nickelson, C. (2008). *Studying psychology in the United States: Expert guidance for international students.* Washington, DC: American Psychological Association.

Horchow, R., & Horchow, S. (2005). *The art of friendship: 70 simple rules for making meaningful connections.* New York: Quirk.

Mason, L. (2002). *The working mother's guide to life: Strategies, secrets, and solutions.* New York: Three Rivers Press.

Paul, M. (2004). *The friendship crisis: Finding, making, and keeping friends when you're not a kid anymore.* New York: Rodale Press.

Sale, J. S., Melinkoff, E., & Kollenberg, K. (1996). *The working parents handbook.* New York: Fireside.

7 The Personal Demands of Graduate Study

All first-year students find transitioning to a new place with new academic and social demands challenging. However, the pressure does not decrease as students adjust to the graduate school environment. Students' perceptions of pressure often increase as they come to understand the rigorous nature of graduate study. Managing stress effectively is essential to thriving in graduate school rather than simply surviving. In addition to coping skills, graduate students need the ability to communicate, get along with, and work productively with others to succeed in their academic and professional careers. In this chapter we discuss these basic but essential skills entailed in managing stress, interpersonal relationships, and conflict.

Understanding and Managing Stress

Students who attend graduate school are used to excelling; they were the top students in their programs and classes. However, graduate school is a different and surprising story because students find that their classmates are just like them—ambitious, intelligent, and talented. This alone, moving from being a big fish in a small pond to a school of similar fish in a larger pond, is stressful. Graduate school and stress go hand-in-hand. Although some stress acts as a motivator, pushing students to excel, high levels of stress can immobilize students and impede their functioning. Students intuitively understand this, yet knowledge does not always lead to appropriate action. Moreover, students' knowledge of psychological concepts and emerging competence in applied skills may prevent them from recognizing and treating the symptoms of stress, assuming that they "know better." Everyone tends to lack objective insight into their behavior at one time or another, but stress is so inherent to graduate study that they may be unable to determine when stress levels exceed their capacities to cope.

SOURCES OF STRESS IN GRADUATE SCHOOL

The first step in addressing stress is to identify the source. The easy answer—graduate school—is not so simple. What are the factors that contribute to the stress of graduate school? Graduate study entails several life changes: the transition to the academic world within the first few months of graduate school, a move to a new town or city, and new work demands and habits, for example. Graduate students must adapt to a heavy workload of reading, research, writing, and coursework in addition to activities to enhance and fund their education, such as assistantships, seminars, and study groups. Students who lack funding work jobs that eat into their study and research time or take out loans that they must pay after graduation, the knowledge of which is often a source of stress.

Other stressful experiences inherent to graduate study include comprehensive examinations, writing the thesis, preparing the dissertation proposal, dissertation proposal defense, dissertation defense, applying for internship, and the first few months as an intern (Goplerud, 2001). Ambiguity is another source of stress because graduate students receive structured feedback less often than when they were undergraduate students. Soliciting faculty perspectives on one's progress toward coursework and research goals is its own stressor. Applied students face many challenges, including developing an identity as a practitioner, managing professional roles and dealing with role ambiguity (e.g., balancing the student, researcher, and clinician roles), and learning to cope with clinical work that can be academically, professionally, and emotionally demanding (Goplerud, 2001). Multiple activities, job demands, and supervisors may conflict, such as demands for work and time made by course instructors, assistantship supervisors, practicum supervisors, and mentors. Students have multiple bosses—many faculty (who may or may not get along with one another)—who can influence students' careers for better or worse. Managing each relationship and their overlap is a source of stress on its own.

Aside from these specific threats, the ambiguous nature of training underlies much of the anxiety that students experience (Pica, 1998). Student clinicians face especially threatening challenges, such as assessing suicidality in patients or deciding when to warn third parties of potential violence; even run-of-the-mill therapy poses risks to the patient and student. Training is hands-on. Students learn in class but they also learn by doing; there is no other way to learn clinical skills. That said, it is anxiety provoking to begin practice because one does not yet have the experience or knowledge needed to make good and confident decisions about how to handle situations and treatment decisions (Pica, 1998). It is only by conducting intake interviews, testing, assessments, and therapy sessions that students begin to acquire the practical skills that accompany their book knowledge and begin to feel more competent and confident. Even fully trained psychotherapists report high levels of distress with the pressures that come with providing mental health services to others (Dearing, Maddux, & Tangney, 2005).

Graduate students are also faced with nonacademic stressors, such as maintaining relationships with friends and family despite limited time and energy; managing the multiple roles of student, parent, partner, friend, and family member; nurturing romantic relationships; maintaining long-distance romantic relationships; and finding free time. Uncertainty about the future is a common stressor: uncertainty about how long it will take to complete the dissertation, geographic location of an internship, and what will happen after graduation, whether one will find a job, be offered a postdoc, or land the elusive academic position.

Moreover, the characteristics of good graduate students are the same ones that may place them at risk for burnout from stress. For example, graduate students tend to show perfectionist tendencies, they place high expectations on themselves, and they do not accept failure. Although these tendencies influence their drive and promote success, they also make burnout more likely because there is no room for mistake, and students often have unrealistic expectations for their performance. The self-reliance, high levels of motivation, and independence characteristics of successful graduate students may prohibit them from identifying and admitting when stressors are impairing their functioning and from soliciting help.

SYMPTOMS AND OUTCOMES OF STRESS

Although some stress is useful, for example, motivating students to study for an exam, high levels of stress impair their ability to function. The first step in managing stress is learning to recognize it. Exhibit 7.1 illustrates cognitive, physical, and emotional symptoms of stress.

Some symptoms of stress also increase the experience of stress. Inadequate sleep, higher levels of alcohol use, depression, and susceptibility

EXHIBIT 7.1

Symptoms of Stress

Cognitive symptoms
- Memory difficulties
- Difficulty making decisions
- Difficulty attending and concentrating
- Rumination
- Racing thoughts; feeling like you cannot slow down
- Desire to escape or run away
- Sense of being overwhelmed or swamped

Physical symptoms
- Headaches
- Digestive disorders
- Muscle tension and pain
- Chest pain
- Shortness of breath
- Acne and other skin problems
- Skin rashes
- Frequent illness
- Fatigue
- Sleep disturbances
- Significant weight gain or loss
- High blood pressure
- Increased use of tobacco, alcohol, drugs, caffeine
- Restless activity and habits such as nail biting, hair twisting, pacing

Emotional symptoms
- Mood swings
- Fear of failure
- Frustration
- Anger
- Irritability
- Overreaction to unexpected situations or events
- Feeling anxious
- Feeling inadequate, reduced confidence
- Feeling depressed

Note. From Aldwin (2005), Charlesworth and Nathan (2004), Goplerud (2001), Lazarus (2000), Lovallo (2004), and Tubesing (1981).

to illness are symptoms of stress, but they also increase the subjective experience of stress (Goplerud, 2001).

Sleep

In recent years people have begun sleeping less and spending more time watching television and surfing the Internet, making sleep seem like an expendable luxury to most (Institute of Medicine of the National Academies, 2006). The pressure to produce—to complete assignments, come up with ideas for research projects, and meet other academic demands while maintaining some semblance of a personal life—can lead many students to forgo sleep. Other students do not choose to go without sleep; they simply cannot get a full night's sleep and find themselves staring at the ceiling and thinking about work at 3 a.m. Insomnia is a common indicator of excess stress.

As psychology students know, sleep is a necessity, restoring people's minds and bodies, preserving health, and aiding in consolidating memories. Most people need about 7 to 8 hours of sleep, although some need as little as 5 or more than 9; a loss of 90 minutes of sleep a night reduces daytime alertness by one third (Institute of Medicine of the National Academies, 2006). Deficits in sleep accumulate and extract physical and emotional tolls. Symptoms of sleep deprivation include sleepiness, irritability, depressed mood, lack of motivation, poor attention and memory, interpersonal conflicts, work dissatisfaction, and anxiety (Levine, 2006; Schindler et al., 2006). The very skills that make a graduate student successful—cognitive capacities for attention, memory, and problem solving as well as interpersonal skills to communicate well and avoid and manage conflict—are what are impaired by sleep deprivation. It is easy to see how the correlates of sleep deprivation worsen a person's subjective feelings of stress.

Tip

Most graduate students acknowledge that sleep is important, but they are not able to sleep well consistently. Follow these guidelines to increase your odds of sleeping well.

- Get up at the same time every day.
- Do not sleep in.
- Exercise regularly.
- Sleep in a cool room free of disturbing light and noise.
- Do not go to bed right after you eat and do not go to bed hungry.
- Avoid caffeine in the afternoon and evening.
- Avoid excessive alcohol use.
- Do not work in bed.
- Write down your to-do list and any worries at least half an hour before going to bed.

Alcohol Use

Long days of classes, research, and working with clients pose challenges for graduate students. A common way to unwind after a difficult day is with a beer or glass of wine, often with other students. Many graduate students describe alcohol use as pervasive in academic circles, with most students drinking regularly and some every day (Levine, 2005). Alcohol is sometimes part of the academic culture. Some departments sponsor wine and cheese events weekly, before seminars, for example. End-of-the-semester formal and informal parties with faculty and graduate students are commonly held in on-campus and off-campus bars.

The ubiquity of alcohol use in graduate departments poses a danger to students who are saddled with more stress than they can effectively manage. Calming down over drinks at the end of the day may be an enjoyable way to unwind with friends or alone, but the challenge is distinguishing safe from problematic drinking, which interferes with functioning and leads to problems at work and in interpersonal relationships. One of the cardinal qualities of alcohol dependence is the inability to appreciate the problem and seek help (i.e., to deny the problem). What is safe drinking, then? The U.S. government quantifies "safe" as 1 standard drink per day for women and 2 standard drinks per day for men; more than 7 drinks per week for women or 14 drinks per week for men may be a sign of a problem (National Institute on Alcohol Abuse and Alcoholism, 2008). A standard drink is defined as 12 ounces of beer, 5 ounces of wine, or 1.5 ounces of 80-proof distilled spirits. Determining what is a safe level is a personal decision; a safe level does not impair your functioning as student, professional, parent, and friend.

Depression

Students of psychology, even undergraduate students, *know* depression. Many can recite the *Diagnostic and Statistical Manual of Mental Disorders* (4th ed., text revision; American Psychiatric Association, 2000) criteria by heart and easily identify depression in clients and even other students. Recognizing depression in themselves is not as easy. Despite professional training, depression is somewhat of a dirty word in most academic departments. Graduate students are expected to tough it out and grit their teeth as they jump through the hoops. Some may feel numb, tired, and irritable for weeks; assume that it is part of the grind; and never consider seeking help. Aside from emotional discomfort, depression impairs one's cognitive functioning, slowing thought and memory.

Some "classic" graduate student behaviors are also common indicators of depression. For example, consider the following graduate student manifestations of criteria for major depressive episode (American Psychiatric Association, 2000):

- Persistent sad, numb mood, feeling hopeless: "I don't know why I'm even doing this experiment, it won't work."

- Diminished interest or pleasure in activities: "I hate everything. I don't want to go hiking. It's no fun because I have so many more important things to worry about."
- Significant weight loss or weight gain: "I'm too busy to eat." "My stomach is killing me so I can't eat." "I cannot stop eating—I'll go to the vending machine and take a break."
- Insomnia or hypersomnia: "I'm so tired but I can't sleep." "All I want to do is sleep."
- Fatigue: "I'm so exhausted." "I feel like a walking zombie."
- Psychomotor agitation or retardation: "I can't keep still. Maybe pacing will help me use up this nervous energy." "I don't want to move. I feel so slow. Just want to sit and stare at a wall."
- Feelings of worthlessness or excessive/inappropriate guilt: "I'm a lousy teacher because my students did so poorly on that test." "I should have been able to make that experiment work; if I were a better researcher it would have worked." "I'm a terrible psychologist, I don't work hard enough."
- Problems concentrating, thinking, making decisions: "I keep thinking about this experiment but I can't figure it out. Other stuff keeps intruding." "I don't know how to organize my day—what should I do first? I'm afraid that if I make the wrong decision I'll ruin the day."

Depression may be sparked by a variety of graduate school experiences, such as moving to a new place, the transition to graduate school, heavy workloads, relationships with mentors, and the challenge of maintaining personal relationships. Specific milestones in graduate school can also mark the beginning of depressive episodes, such as completing coursework, taking comprehensive exams, completing the dissertation proposal, and defending the dissertation.

Illness

Stress is associated with physical illness, including common colds, obesity, hypertension, and more (Billings & Moos, 1982; Miller & Thoresen, 2003).

> "Ouch! My back!," Amy cried as she coughed. "Are you okay?" asked her office mate, Cyanne.
> "I think I threw my back out. Maybe it's all this coughing."
> "But your back was bad last semester too, well before this cold."
> "You're right. I guess I'm just getting old too fast."
> "Maybe you should go to a doctor. You've had a cold all semester—not the same one, but still, you're sick almost all the time."
> "You're not one to talk given your digestive problems. And Cyanne, you get sick right after every exam."
> "Yeah, Amy, my stomach is eating itself. I blame that on my advisor though."

"Maybe we both just need time off, Cyanne. I know I do. I've been so stressed. I really think the stress makes a difference. You know that rash I get on my leg?"

"Yeah, it's gross."

"Thanks. Well, it's been there since our first year of graduate school. I went to a dermatologist and everything. The medicine works sort of, but the rash is still here. It's been years with it getting better and worse. When my advisor went on sabbatical, it went away completely, the itchiness, redness, and icky dryness."

"It's a Dr. Folger rash!"

"I think so because when she came back from sabbatical, my rash came with her."

Many students, like Amy and Cyanne, find that stress influences their health and makes them more susceptible to colds. Many graduate students can predict when they will experience colds and illnesses. Most will not use this information to prevent illness but may instead note, "I always seem to get sick during finals week." Coping effectively with stress is a critical way of protecting yourself against illness and other harmful effects of stress.

COPING WITH STRESS

Understanding the common symptoms and effects of stress is an important first step toward reducing its impact. However, knowledge about stress is not enough to change its effect on you. Managing stress entails taking an active role in identifying your stress triggers, what stress looks like for you, and what coping techniques work for you. There is no one-size-fits-all solution for dealing with stress.

Become Informed

Being informed and knowing what to expect during the graduate years can help to prevent and reduce stress. What are the rites of passage in your program, key transition points when you are likely to experience elevated levels of stress? Are particular courses thought to be more challenging and serve greater risks than others? What other rites of passage exist? Some programs include a second-year research project or thesis, particular applied experience, and comprehensive exams. Knowing what to expect will help you to plan ahead and will reduce anxiety; knowing little is as stressful as the unknown.

Identify sources of information about your program—trusted peers, advanced students, support staff, and faculty—and learn as much as you can about departmental mores, critical hurdles, informal rules, and common mistakes made by graduate students as they complete program requirements (Goplerud, 2001). Contacts who are aware of departmental and program history are especially helpful. They can normalize stress reactions by providing you with a history and an overview of common reactions that students have to program hurdles such as comprehensive exams. They can provide advice on juggling the multiple demands of graduate school, avoiding common pitfalls, and preparing ahead for particularly challenging phases of graduate study (e.g., studying for comprehensive exams or the proposal preparation phase of the dissertation).

Assess and Adjust Your Expectations

An important stressor for graduate students is the pressure of social comparison. For the very first time in their education, most students are faced with not being the best, the smartest, the most articulate and literate student in their program. Graduate students are natural perfectionists. The quality that drove them to excel during college and win admittance to graduate school is also a great source of stress. Much of this stress is unnecessary. Are you being too hard on yourself? Are your expectations realistic? In graduate school you will be surrounded by overachievers; that is the nature of graduate study because only the best students are admitted. In graduate school, good is often enough. There is no need to be the best at everything; it is not possible. Adjust your expectations; make them more realistic. Strive to be a competent and responsible professional, but accept that it is not necessary to earn the highest grades in every class, for example.

Reexamine your goals. Why did you attend graduate school? What do you seek to learn? Who do you hope to become? What is important to you? Once you enter graduate school and are faced with peers who are similar to you in ambition and ability, it is easy to forget about your goals and get caught up in social comparison and competition. Knowing your goals and reviewing them periodically will help you to keep your perspective and concentrate on what is important to you rather than being caught up in the social comparison cycle (Goplerud, 2001).

Look for student and faculty role models who balance professionalism with a well-rounded nature. Understand who you are and learn to love that person. Everyone has positive qualities in their professional selves as well as in their personal selves. Sometimes people ignore their personal development during their quest for professional achievement. Keeping personal development goals in mind may help keep your expectations for your professional achievement in more realistic territory.

Understand and Monitor Your Stress Indicators

Students of psychology are aware of the ways in which stress harms one's health. Although it is easy to assess stress in other people and advise them to maintain their health, one is often less objective when considering one's own stress levels. What are the signs that you are wound up? How do you know that you are under stress? Everyone experiences stress in different ways, so it is important to understand what stress looks like for you. Identify indicators of stress, including physical symptoms such as headaches, tight muscles, and insomnia, and psychosocial indictors, such as irritability, feeling like you are getting nothing done, working long hours, and avoiding people. Once you have identified your stress indicators, your job is to be aware and alert to early warning signs that stress is building up (Goplerud, 2001). When your stress response increases, release stress by making time for yourself, engaging in physical activity, eating well, and spending time socializing with friends and family.

Although the demands of graduate study are automatic stressors, some sources of stress are more unexpected. Sometimes interacting with particular people is a source of stress (Goplerud, 2001). Monitor your feelings while talking with others. You might notice that regular contact with a particular person makes you anxious; for example, he or she focuses on talking about negative things, like arguments within the department, or about anxiety-provoking things, such as speculating who will fail comprehensive exams. If you find that conversing with a person consistently increases your anxiety, then avoid that person or limit interactions to particular activities, such as sharing information.

Remember That Life Continues

During the graduate school years, some students feel like they are living in a bubble, where time stops in the outside world while they struggle through the hoops of earning their graduate degrees. However, the stresses of life will, and should, intrude on the graduate school bubble. It is impossible to put life on hold for the next few years; to do so would be unhealthy because social connections are vital to your emotional and physical health. Find time for life; schedule time away from your work. It is challenging, but view your training within the broader context of your life and your life plans (Goplerud, 2001). Treat graduate study like a job. There will always be more work to complete; there is not always a second opportunity to experience life events. Set your work priorities but also set your personal priorities; schedule your time in light of both.

Stress can pose risks to your physical, emotional, and intellectual health. It is particularly important that you care for yourself by eating well and getting regular exercise. Physical activity is one of the best ways to manage stress because it gives your body an opportunity to release pent-up energy and work through muscle tension. Exercise also has positive effects on your subjective experience and your emotions. Take regular time off from work. Have a life outside of school. Maintain hobbies and interests outside of work. Make time for social activities. Spend time with family and friends.

Seek Support

When you are stressed and feeling the accompanying negative feelings of anxiety and depression, the last thing that you want to do is to be with other people. Why waste time socializing when you can be completing your assignments and making headway on your research? It is when you are feeling stressed that social activity, such as conversing with others, becomes most important. Social support—the quality and size of your support networks—helps to buffer the negative effects of stress (Dunkley, Blankstein, Halsall, Williams, & Winkworth, 2000). Interacting with other students can validate your feelings and help you see that it is normal to feel stressed. At the same time, socializing can help you to relieve tension; laughter is invigorating.

Exert Control

One of the best ways to reduce and avoid high stress is to increase your sense of personal control. The sooner you figure out how to manage the daily stresses of graduate school, the happier you will feel. Some sources of stress, such as tests, advisors, and milestone events (e.g., comps, dissertation proposals, internship interviews), are unavoidable. The trick to dealing with these unavoidable stresses is to control what you can: your thoughts and behavior. How do you increase your sense of personal control?

Change your thinking. Consider the thoughts that accompany particular stressors. If your advisor is overly critical or difficult to get along with, for example, a common response is to internalize the criticism and, in extreme cases, feel like a hopeless failure who is unlikely to become a psychologist. Instead, you can learn to manage your response to criticism by anticipating it, interpreting it as helpful advice, and learning not to take it personally. This will not happen overnight, but you can train yourself to change how you think about criticism. It may not be possible to change the source of stress, but you can change your response to it.

Learn to relax. Much of graduate school is challenging and stressful. To maintain a sense of balance and control over the myriad events that influence how you spend the days and years ahead of you, learn relaxation techniques to help you relax after a long day, and more important, when you are faced with stressful events. Some of the suggested readings at the end of this chapter discuss relaxation techniques in detail.

Tip

Try this "relaxation response," a form of meditation. Find a quiet environment where you can be alone without distractions. Get into a comfortable position, preferably with your spine straight. Try sitting down cross-legged or in the lotus position. Do not lie down or you might fall asleep during the relaxation session. Focus your concentration on a word or phrase. This is your point of focus. Begin to breathe deeply and slowly. Inhale through your nose. As you exhale through your mouth, repeat your chosen word or phrase. Concentrate on your point of focus and do not worry about your thought processes. It is difficult to eliminate distracting thoughts. Instead concentrate on your point of focus. Try not to dwell on your distracting thoughts; let them slip away. Continue for 10 minutes, and you will feel much more relaxed. It will take time to build up to 10 minutes comfortably. Aim to build to 20.

Create a sense of order. Perhaps the most challenging aspect of graduate study is the relative lack of control. Tasks and deadlines are handed down to students, who must arrange their work habits accordingly. Organize your time and your environment efficiently, and the stress that accompanies assignments and deadlines will decrease. Use the techniques described in chapter 4 to schedule time for work and play and to create a work space that suits your needs and maximizes your efficiency.

One part of organizing your work habits is to assess your activities. In deciding how to allocate your time, consider how each obligation and activity complements your goals. Some obligations, such as sitting in on a class in a related but nonessential area or tutoring undergraduates to supplement your income, may consume many resources for little gain. Seminars, workshops, and other training opportunities abound. Although you should take advantage of such opportunities and be active and visible in your department, participating in them all will drain your time and energy, making your life more stressful. Make choices about how to structure and spend your time to maximize your returns (Goplerud, 2001; Peters, 1997).

Getting Along With Others and Managing Conflict

Success in graduate school entails more than academic ability; book smarts is not enough. "People smarts" (i.e., interpersonal skills) are critical tools for graduate students and essential for clinicians. Professional success in graduate school and beyond depends on your ability to build and maintain relationships with others, including advisors, other professors, dissertation committee, supervisors, peers, and clients. Successful psychologists are effective communicators. Communication does not come easily to everyone and certainly is not easy all the time for anyone; you must put in the time and effort required to understand others and be understood by them.

UNDERSTAND YOURSELF

Before you can communicate your message to others, you must understand yourself: What are your wants, needs, goals, and motives? Understanding yourself also entails being aware of your communication strengths and weaknesses. Is it easy for you to approach others? Express your needs? Grasp other people's perspectives? What are your pet peeves, the quirks, characteristics, comments, and activities that annoy you? Everyone finds something irksome; it is important to know your triggers so that you can keep them from hampering your communication and preventing your needs from being met.

RECOGNIZE DIFFERENCES AND DO NOT ASSUME

> "I asked if he needed help creating the data file, and Jeff said he didn't. And yet the file is not right! He should know how to put together a data file by now," complained Ann. "Well, the file is not exactly wrong, just not set up to run the analyses you planned," corrected Dan. "He should have known that I wanted to run those analyses—they're in the proposal. Anyone would know to set up the data file in order to run those analyses," Ann countered. "Did you explain this to Jeff? Did you talk about the analyses you planned?" asked Dan. "He said he knew how to set up data files. I didn't think I'd have to show him," explained Ann.

It is clear Ann and Jeff were not on the same page. There are lots of things Ann could have done to prevent the ensuing frustration and hurt feelings that she and Jeff share, but perhaps the most simple is to remember that people are different. They have different working styles, are motivated by different things, and have different interests and sensitivities. Understand and appreciate people's differences, and you will be better able to interact with them and meet your own (and their) needs. Try to understand other people's perspectives and, regardless of whether you agree, respect their views. Do not assume that others share your own sensitivities.

One often gets upset with colleagues because one assumes that they *should know better*—and know what behaviors are unacceptable, that is, in one's view. For example, washing the coffee pot in the student lounge is simply good manners. It is easy to forget that everyone, graduate students included, operates from a different base of experience and perspective. What seems obvious to you is not necessarily so for others. Confront the problem by identifying it, explaining the difference, and suggesting a solution. Alternatively, make a conscious decision to live with it and create a plan for managing and eliminating the resulting annoyance. Without mentioning it, the problem will reoccur. Without changing your reaction to it, you will remain unhappy and your irritation is likely to grow, strain relations, and make an unwanted explosive reaction more likely.

Recognizing differences is not enough. Respect them. The basics of protecting and nurturing your personal relationships also apply to professional relationships. Cultivating relationships with peers, advisors, and supervisors is about treating them with respect. This is true whether or not you like the person. You may not like everyone with whom you work, but you must get along with them to work effectively. Give credit where it is due. Acknowledge others for their help and contributions. Thank them. Offer assistance and return favors. Respect colleagues' advice, assistance, and expertise. If you are at fault, apologize. In short, the rules of the sandbox also apply at work.

Another aspect of recognizing and respecting differences entails understanding that people have their own needs and desires. Most people, students and faculty alike, have their own agenda that is designed to meet their own needs. Your agendas do not always match those of the people around you. For example, a desire to present a piece of research at an upcoming conference may conflict with a mentor's desire to wait to gather more data. A student who plans to take the lead in collecting data for her advisor's research may be surprised at the advisor's choice of another student to lead or colead data collection. Everyone has their own agenda designed to fulfill their goals and needs. That is part of life and is not inherently bad because it promotes your achievement and protects you. Remember that not everyone has the same agenda, and no one will know yours unless you share it.

LISTEN

Good communicators know that people want to feel heard. It is not necessary to agree with them, just listen. Show that you are listening by giving your complete attention. In daily conversation, reflect back what a person has said, adding questions and points of clarification. When dealing with a crisis or confrontation, ask the person to tell you about the issue at hand, his or her concerns, what about the issue concerns him or her, and what would make the person feel better. The important part is to not react, simply listen.

What someone says and what one hears are often very different. One's experiences, perspectives, attitudes, biases, and desires can filter what gets through and influence one's interpretation. Repeating or summarizing what you have heard gives the other person a chance to correct miscommunication and provides an accurate message for you to consider. Good listeners clear their minds and focus on what the other person is saying, stopping to reflect on their understanding, reflecting back what they hear, and asking whether their understanding is accurate before compiling their response.

RESPOND, NOT REACT

Sometimes people are overwhelmed by emotional reactions and react on those feelings. Effective communicators pause after receiving a message to separate their feelings from their thoughts. Gut reactions—emotional responses—without considering the message, whether the response is appropriate, and the potential consequences of one's response can harm relationships with others. Graduate school is very much about relationships, so firing from the hip without considering the cause and consequences can be harmful to a student's career. Recognize that you are a participant in communication with others; sometimes your own personal reactions influence your communications with others and may even be the cause of the problem. Step back and evaluate your role. Recognizing that some of the blame for poor communication and its consequences lies with you is often discomfiting and painful, but becoming an effective communicator—a critical task for psychology students—relies on it.

Just as your own emotional reactions influence your responses to others, their gut reactions influence how they interpret and respond to you. Remember that your listeners also struggle with separating emotional from reasoned reactions. Do not take another's emotional reaction—anger or attack—personally because their response is likely about their own anxieties and frustrations. Step back from the situation to let the person cool. If you cannot remove yourself, take a deep breath, count, and let the person vent. Eventually he or she will be ready to talk. Above all, remain rational, difficult as that may be, and do not let your emotional reactions take over. Before speaking or acting, stop and consider your message, its purpose, and potential consequence. People often reply to attacks quickly, feeling that they must defend their view or themselves immediately. Resist the urge. You can always respond to the comment or issue later. Take the time to ensure that you are communicating the message you intend.

KEEP IT IN PERSPECTIVE AND STAY POSITIVE

Students who have good people skills know how to step back from a situation and objectively evaluate its importance. Effective communicators keep issues in perspective and do not get lost in the argument. Sometimes students become consumed with being right, so much so that they lose the message and the purpose of the communication itself.

It is not always necessary to be right, to win an argument, or to have things your way. Choose your battles wisely because you cannot win every one and will lose important contacts in the fight. Moreover, not only do effective communicators keep issues in perspective, but they also work to retain a positive perspective. Graduate students are known for complaining. They have much to complain about; there are lots of demands placed on them and little to no control over their plight. Successful students work to keep a positive attitude and communicate that attitude to others. When confronted with challenges they stop to ask themselves, "What's the positive side of this? What can I learn? Is there some good in this situation?" Communicate these positive, active views and others—peers and faculty—will enjoy interacting with you and will view you positively, both of which influence effective communication.

Good communication skills do not come easy. Communication, exchanging ideas with others, requires effort and practice. Listening to others demands attention, concentration, and the ability to reflect back what you have heard. Recognizing your own and others' needs entails a great deal of awareness and perspective. Successfully navigating conflict demands the ability to differentiate emotional reactions from reasoned responses and to carry out communication that is based on reason. These skills often do not come naturally, but they are essential tools for psychologists.

Discussions about graduate school tend to focus on the academic, juggling coursework with research, assistantships, and practica. Managing multiple demands exacts a personal toll on students. Stress is inevitable and a part of graduate study. However, students can learn to change their experience of and reaction to stress to promote psychological health and adaptive functioning. Interpersonal skills are an important tool for cultivating the relationships that are essential to success in graduate school and ensuring that one's needs are met.

These personal demands of graduate study—dealing with stress and learning how to get along with others—are challenging for all students, but some seek assistance in managing it all. About half of graduate students in clinical and counseling psychology programs enter therapy (Dearing et al., 2005). Short-term issue-focused therapy and training can help students develop coping skills to aid their transition from students to professionals. Practitioners may also find therapy particularly from a professional perspective; experiencing therapy may offer insight into the role of client and a personal perspective of characteristics of effective therapists (Dearing et al., 2005). On-campus counseling centers and low-cost community centers, such as mental health clinic and women's centers, are sources of confidential mental health services to assist students with managing stress and the resulting anxiety and depression as well as develop skills for reducing stress and improving interpersonal relationships.

Remember that competent professionals are aware of their own functioning, both personal and professional, and seek to enhance their functioning and improve their professional capacities through whatever means necessary, academic or personal, including seeking therapy when needed. Self-awareness is not simply a goal to which to strive; it is a necessary part of professional development.

Recommended Reading

Addis, M. E., & Martell, C. R. (2004). *Overcoming depression one step at a time: The new behavioral activation approach to getting your life back.* Oakland, CA: New Harbinger.

Bolton, R. (1986). *People skills: How to assert yourself, listen to others, and resolve conflicts.* New York: Touchstone.

Bourne, E. J., & Garano, L. (2003). *Coping with anxiety: 10 simple ways to relieve anxiety, fear and worry.* Oakland, CA: New Harbinger.

Budjac Corvette, B. A. (2006). *Conflict management: A practical guide to developing negotiation strategies.* Upper Saddle River, NJ: Prentice Hall.

Burnard, P. (1991). *Coping with stress in the health professions: A practical guide (Therapy in practice series).* London: Chapman & Hall.

Charlesworth, E. A., & Nathan, R. G. (2004). *Stress management: A comprehensive guide to wellness.* New York: Ballantine Books.

Health Care Communication Group, Barnard, S., Hughes, K. T., & St. James, D. (2001). *Writing, speaking, and communication skills for health professionals.* New Haven, CT: Yale University Press.

Knaus, W. J., & Ellis, A. (2006). *The cognitive behavioral workbook for depression: A step-by-step program.* Oakland, CA: New Harbinger.

Lazarus, J. (2000). *Stress relief and relaxation techniques.* New York: McGraw-Hill.

Luciani, J. J. (2006). *Self-coaching: The powerful program to beat anxiety and depression* (2nd ed.). Hoboken, NJ: Wiley.

Tubesing, D. A. (1981). *Kicking your stress habits: A do-it-yourself guide for coping with stress.* Duluth, MN: Whole Person Associates.

8 Thriving in Practicum and Internship

The road to becoming a competent clinician begins with a solid base of knowledge and general skills that are further developed and refined through opportunities to provide therapeutic services in supervised settings. For many graduate students the practicum experience is the first supervised practice experience. Most students will complete more than one practicum. The internship is another supervised experience that affords students increasing autonomy. Most students will complete an internship as doctoral candidates and a second after earning the doctoral degree. In this chapter the practicum and internship experience for graduate students in psychology are explored.

Practicum

All graduate training programs in clinical, counseling, and school psychology accredited by the American Psychological Associational (APA) require that students complete practicum training (Gross, 2005). The practicum, also known as an externship, serves as the foundation for much of clinical training because it is the first supervised practice experience that most students have. The practicum is a supervised context for training that offers students the opportunity to learn by doing, consider career options, and begin to form a professional identity (Gross, 2005). Over the 2 to 3 years of practice, students accrue about as many hours as in internship.

Practicum sites include all of the settings in which psychologists work, including military, Veterans Affairs, public, and private hospitals; university clinics and counseling centers; correctional institutions; social service agencies; schools; and community mental health clinics (Lewis, Hatcher, & Pate, 2005). Practicum training activities include the range of tasks that compose the professional role of psychologists, such as clinical assessments, program development, evaluation, research, community consultation, advocacy, supervision, teaching, and administration (Lewis et al., 2005). Take advantage of these varied practice opportunities by seeking experience with as many populations, presenting problems, and life circumstances as possible (Katell, Levant, & Loonstra, 2003). Seek the greatest breadth of experience your practicum setting affords to fill in gaps and round out your training. Exposure to clients of all ages, ethnic groups, and social backgrounds (e.g., religion, socioeconomic status, and worldview), as well as to frequently occurring, challenging, and long-term illnesses and diagnoses will be beneficial (Katell et al., 2003). Supervised experience in test administration, scoring, and report preparation, especially integrated report writing, will make you competitive for internship because many graduate programs have not included such experiences (Clemence & Handler, 2001).

Many students begin practicum very early in graduate school, sometimes just as they are becoming oriented to the program and field. Most students feel anxious when beginning their first practicum experience. Anxiety is normal, but you need to move beyond it. Clinical experiences are cumulative, building on each other, and the accumulated skills follow you, so a good start is important not only to your practicum experience but also to your career as a psychologist (Rosen, n.d.). As you begin your practicum, remember that although you are not being paid for your services, you should aspire to the highest levels of professionalism because this learning opportunity is a gift that will advance your professional development.

KNOW AGENCY POLICIES AND PROCEDURES

Stay on top of agency policies and procedures. Clinical work is accompanied by a great deal of paperwork and policies. Students must learn these and act in accord with them; policies exist for a reason. Questioning a policy is permissible, but be respectful and understand that the policy likely will not change. Instead, the purpose of asking questions is to understand the policy. Sometimes understanding the basis of a policy helps students buy into it. Regardless of whether they "buy into" the policy, students are obligated to abide by agency rules because the clients' best interests and safety must always come first.

UNDERSTAND THE ROLE OF SUPERVISION

Many students are apprehensive about supervision; they view it as criticism.

> "I wish she'd just get off my back," said Jane. "I'm tired of the constant criticism. Everything I do could be improved. That's true of everything everyone does! I cannot wait until this placement ends. The constant scrutiny is making me anxious about my every decision and move. And when we meet to talk about my work, my supervisor complains about what I have not brought and what I have not done. Why do I have to bring all of my reports, especially those on patients we've already discussed? No one is perfect; why hold me up to an unrealistic and unattainable standard?"

Jane's perspective on supervision reflects a lack of understanding of the purpose of supervision and the role of supervisors. Supervision is the greatest tool for learning how to be a psychologist. There is something to learn from every supervisor (usually many, many things!). Approach supervisory relationships with the attitude that you would like to learn all that you can and benefit from your supervisor's experience (Rosen, n.d.).

Make supervision work by communicating with your supervisor and clarifying expectations. How often will you meet, and how should you prepare? How far in advance do you have to send tapes of your sessions to your supervisor? What written materials or forms should you bring? Clarifying expectations and then being prepared for your meetings communicate the message that you are responsible and care about your work.

What happens to your clients is ultimately your supervisor's responsibility because he or she is liable for your activities. Your supervisor will be responsible for your errors and is at higher risk for being involved in litigation. Supervisors stick their necks out to aid students' professional development. Accordingly, supervisors are obligated to give you feedback, both positive and negative. Take any feedback given and use it. Feedback is a gift not to be squandered.

BE PLANFUL, RELIABLE, AND PROACTIVE

When planning your practicum, keep all of your obligations and responsibilities in perspective. Carefully plan your coursework, even taking fewer classes if possible because practicum—providing your clients with effective services—will take more energy and effort, both intellectual and emotional, than you anticipate or realize (Rosen, n.d.). On a daily and weekly basis, think about how to schedule your time to balance agency rules about scheduling clients with your own needs. What works for you with regard to your own energy level and alertness? How many clients can you realistically see in a day, and how much time do you need between appointments? Remember that attendance at practicum is not optional. Be there and be on time. Tardiness and missed appointments harm clients. Your job is to help, not harm. Also make time for the administrative activities and thought work that accompany practice, including paperwork, questions, phone calls, reflection, and reviewing tapes of sessions (Rosen, n.d.). The resources in chapter 4 will help.

Competent professionals are reliable. Do not blindly agree to requests without thinking about whether and how you will complete them. Keep promises and obligations. Graduate students and professionals often have a tendency to say yes to all requests. Only agree to a task if you can complete it because your word is all that you have (Rosen, n.d.). If you consistently say yes and make promises that you cannot keep, others will stop asking, and it will harm your career because you will be labeled as unreliable and be offered fewer opportunities.

In addition to being planful and reliable, competent professionals are proactive in managing their work and needs. Determine what will help you do your job to the best of your ability and request it. If you foresee scheduling problems, for example, seek assistance well in advance to keep it from becoming a problem (Rosen, n.d.). Carefully consider your work and needs. If you need something—more supervision, assistance with a particular client, or help with your own personal or professional problems—ask for it. Having the resources to do your job well is not just about making things easy for you, it is about providing clients with the best care possible.

Overall, practica are limited-time engagements. Keep that in mind. If your setting, supervisor, or clients are not what you expected and are more or less challenging than you would prefer, remember that the practicum will pass soon enough. Learn what you can, and aim to do good through your work with clients and relationships with staff (Rosen, n.d.). Although the practicum is temporary, its effects on your career are long lasting. Your behavior reflects not only on you but also on your department, so poor performance will follow you. Finally, remember that practicum provides experiences that form the basis for internship and that your practicum supervisors are in the best position to write your letters of recommendation for internship. Take advantage of this knowledge and work to develop strong relationships with direct supervisors who can speak to your therapeutic skills (Rosen, n.d.).

Internship

Internship bridges graduate training and professional practice (Katell et al., 2003). The internship experience is one in which students integrate their research and applied experiences with their scientific, professional, and ethical knowledge and attitudes to engage in professional practice (Stedman, 2006). Internship offers training in a variety of skills as well as opportunities to develop skills in specialized areas or with specialized populations. During the internship year, students practice under supervision, become socialized as psychologists, and develop a sense of professional identity. Internship training is designed to help students learn to become autonomous and responsible professionals.

All APA-accredited training programs require an internship as part of doctoral training. The APA's Committee on Accreditation stipulates the requirements for an adequate internship training program and evaluates internship programs. Programs that meet its criteria are listed as APA accredited. Note that not all internships are APA accredited; however, many states require the completion of an APA-accredited internship for licensure, so it is in your best interest to seek an APA-accredited internship (Megargee, 2001). The internship is a structured training experience. Each internship site is headed by a doctoral-level director who is responsible for the training experience and is on site at least 20 hours each week (Hall & Hsu, 2000). Full-time, licensed doctoral-level staff supervise interns, providing at least 2 hours of individual supervision each week.

The activities of interns are also highly structured; they must work at least 1,500 hours over a 9- to 24-month period with at least one quarter of the hours allocated to face-to-face work with clients. At least 2 hours each week must be spent on training such as conferences and seminars. Internship settings include all of the settings in which psychologists practice, including Veterans Affairs hospitals and medical centers, public and private hospitals and psychiatric facilities, community mental health centers, state institutions, and a variety of other facilities. Internship activities include all activities performed by practicing psychologists, such as clinical assessment, program development, evaluation, research, community consultation, advocacy, training, teaching, supervision, and administration.

In 2007, much like any other year, nearly 3,700 students applied to internships at the approximately 600 Association of Psychology Postdoctoral and Internship Center (APPIC) training member programs (APPIC Board of Directors, 2007). Twenty-five percent of applicants were not assigned to internship programs on Match Day, the day when internship assignments are announced. Many unmatched students successfully obtain internships in the same application year, as discussed later in this chapter. However, the takeaway message is clear: There are not enough internship slots to accommodate all applicants.

PREPARING FOR INTERNSHIP

The shortage of internship slots means that competition is fierce (Madson, Aten, & Leach, 2007). Think ahead and plan early to ensure that you obtain needed training experiences and fill gaps in your skill base. Every graduate program has basic requirements that must be fulfilled before students can apply for internships (Megargee, 2001). Learn about these requirements early in your graduate school career so that you can make sure that you satisfy them and are not delayed. Departments usually require that students have completed all coursework, a specified number of practicum hours, and doctoral comprehensive exams (Megargee, 2001). Some departments require students to have completed and defended their dissertation. Know departmental requirements so that you are not surprised to learn that you have not satisfied them and cannot apply for internship. Even if your department does not require that you complete doctoral comprehensive exams, it is a good idea to plan on completing your comps before applying to internship because nearly all internships listed in the APPIC directory specify that applicants must be doctoral candidates (Hall & Hsu, 1999).

Students who are competitive for internship opportunities have broad training. Seek to develop general knowledge and skill in as many areas of clinical training as possible (Katell et al., 2003; Madson et al., 2007; Rodolfa et al., 1999). Internship directors expect a great deal of professional experience, usually including more practicum hours than academic departments require, and most internship directors rate clinical experience as more important than academic achievement (Megargee, 2001; Stedman, 2006). The APA *Accreditation Handbook* (American Psychological Association, 1986) requires a minimum of 400 hours, with at least 150 hours in direct service and 75 hours in scheduled supervision before a student is eligible for internship. Many departments require that students obtain more than the 400-hour minimum (Megargee, 2001). Internships vary in their requirements, with 600 as the average minimum number of hours required (Kaslow, Pate, & Thorn, 2005), but some internships require as many as 1,200 hours (Katell et al., 2003). Although many students complete 1,500 hours or more in an attempt to increase their attractiveness to internship directors under the belief that the number of practicum hours completed is the best indicator of competence (Gloria, Castillo, Choi-Pearson, & Rangel, 1997; Kaslow et al., 2005), the number of practicum hours completed is not a particularly good predictor of internship placement (Boggs & Douce, 2000).

Once students reach the minimum number of practice hours, competencies become important in securing an internship (Katell et al., 2003). Supervised experiences in assessment, clinical diagnosis, intervention, research, and program evaluation are valuable to your application (Katell et al., 2003; Stedman, 2006). Also important is the match between the applicant and internship program—how well the applicant's academic and applied training, practicum experiences, and goals fit the internship training opportunities and objectives (Katell et al., 2003; Rodolfa et al., 1999). Internship directors also expect students to have completed their coursework and doctoral comprehensive exams (Rodolfa et al., 1999).

Tip

Prepare for internship by keeping in touch with more advanced students as they begin their internship year. What skills were they expected to have? What would they have done differently? Advanced students' advice is very helpful in preparing for and making decisions about internship.

APPLYING TO INTERNSHIP

The internship process is a rite of passage—a capstone experience to the doctoral degree—that all psychologists in applied fields complete (Keilin & Constantine, 2001). Remember that you are not the first to struggle with constructing an application and navigating the internship process from application to completion. Anxiety about internship begins early, often during the first year of graduate education when students first begin to learn about the internship process, listen to more advanced students gripe about the process, and consider internship preferences as well as strategies for improving their potential to secure preferred placements (Prinstein, Lopez, & Rasmussen, 2003). Without doubt, applying for internship is a stressful process, but it also offers students an important opportunity to evaluate their skills, consider and refine career goals, develop job application and interviewing skills, and begin to establish a professional identity (Megargee, 2001; Williams-Nickelson & Keilin, 2007).

Internship applications entail multiple components: the application, essays, letters of recommendation, and interview, as well as a curriculum vitae (see chapter 13 for discussion of the curriculum vitae). The following sections discuss choosing and applying to internship sites.

Tip

Begin planning for internship as early as possible. The internship application requires that you document all of your clinical experience. Maintain these records as you progress through graduate school. Attempting to recollect this information likely will entail a great deal of time and result in omissions. Keep a detailed record of all of your practicum and supervision hours, including information about the client populations, activities, and assessment devices encountered. Keep a list of the names, contact information, and credentials of supervisors.

Selecting Internship Sites

Before you review materials for any internship site, consider and set your goals for internship and your career. To what kind of career do you aspire? What clinical experiences have you had? What activities, populations, and settings do you have experience with? How do your experiences compare with your career aspirations? What gaps in training exist? Consider your career and training goals to guide your choice of internship sites to which to apply. What kind of internship experience (e.g., populations, treatment modalities, orientations) will help you attain your career goals? It is not uncommon for graduate students not to have resolved these questions. Graduate study is an enormous undertaking. Very often students focus on the task at hand but lose the big picture. Now it is time to consider the big picture. A thorough consideration of your short- and long-term goals and evaluation of your experiences, competencies, and deficits will help you select an appropriate internship and will help you construct a successful application (Prinstein et al., 2003).

Learn about internship sites by searching the APPIC Web site (http://appic.org). The Web site permits you to search the internship directory and read descriptions of internship sites that match your search criteria. Many internship site descriptions include Web links that will enable you to learn more about the site and download or request applications. Gather as much material as possible and read it carefully because many sites sound similar on paper. Through careful study, you can begin to discern differences among sites and how well they match your goals (Williams-Nickelson & Keilin, 2007). Rule out sites that do not match your needs. How many training opportunities, such as seminars, are available? What is the theoretical orientation? It is better to be in a setting that encourages or at least respects and tolerates practice from multiple theoretical perspectives because it will give you exposure to multiple ways to consider and solve problems in therapy (Megargee, 2001). What research opportunities exist, if any? Internship sites vary in their commitment to research support and training. Select sites that match your interest in obtaining research training.

Many students spend a great deal of time trying to find the perfect internship. There is no such thing. No one site will be able to satisfy all of your training desires (Megargee, 2001). All programs will satisfy the minimum training requirements and your basic training needs. Many programs will provide specialized experiences that will prepare you to work with the populations, settings, and issues of your choice. Professional development is career-long; you will not learn all there is to know during your internship, but you will learn *something.* Aim to secure an internship site that moves you closer to your goals.

How many sites should you apply to? Do not overapply. In 2006, the mean number of internship sites applicants applied to was 12.9; from 1999 to 2005 mean applications submitted by applicants ranged from 12.1 to 13.8 (APPIC Board of Directors, 2006). Applying to 15 or more internship sites does not increase your chances for a successful match (Prinstein et al., 2003; Williams-Nickelson & Keilin, 2007). Completing this many applications is a tremendous task, and attending all interviews extended is virtually impossible. Never apply to a site that you would not seriously consider selecting; do not apply to safety sites. Discuss your selections and decision process with your mentor and other trusted faculty members as well as peers, especially more advanced peers who have internship experience (Lopez & Draper, 1997). Aim to compile a list of internships to apply to by September of your application year.

After you have selected sites to which you will apply, get organized to reduce your stress and to ensure that you stay on top of this demanding process and avoid being surprised by looming (or even missed!) deadlines. Gather essential information from each internship site application and add a cover sheet that prominently lists the deadline and helpful organizing information like site preferences and activities (i.e., material that helps you to differentiate the site from others as well as rank the site with regard to your interest; Williams-Nickelson & Keilin, 2007). Organize internship site applications by deadline date. Sites vary in their application deadlines; you do not want to miss one.

Applying to internship is a time-consuming, expensive, and stressful process. Completing the application and responses to application questions, writing application essays, and soliciting reference letters take time. Applying to internship is expensive; costs for ordering transcripts, traveling, and hotel stays quickly add up. In 2006, the average applicant spent \$1,508 on applying to internship (median = \$1,120, *SD* = \$1,348; APPIC Board of Directors, 2006). Many students find the competition for internship slots and the pressure of being evaluated stressful. One thing to understand is that rejection is almost certain: You will get rejected by at least one program to which you apply. The trick is to apply to several programs to which you are a good match. The lack of control over the process and uncertainty about the outcome are sources of stress for nearly all students. Create a sense of order by controlling what you can: your timeline for completing applications. Give yourself the time to carefully consider your application and compile applications at your own pace.

The Application

The APPIC Application for Psychology Internship (AAPI) is a lengthy document that was created by soliciting questions for inclusion from hundreds of APPIC internship sites. Not all questions will be relevant for all internship sites or all applicants. Applicants sometimes become anxious because their training does not match all of the areas inquired about in the AAPI. Applicants are not expected to have experience in all of the areas of competence included in the application, but they are expected to show some competencies and be trainable and able to learn (Prinstein et al., 2003). Internship training directors look for indicators of students' ability to adapt and learn because it is impossible for any applicant to be competent in all areas of training.

Perhaps the most challenging part of completing the AAPI application is compiling all of the information required to address the highly specific and complicated questions. Applicants are asked to report all clinical experiences:

- number of hours of direct service contact;
- hours spent preparing and organizing case material;
- supervision hours;
- experience administering, scoring, and interpreting assessments (including specific instruments); and
- client characteristics, including age, complaint, diagnosis, and intervention applied.

It is easy to see why it is often suggested that students record this information throughout graduate training because it is very hard to organize it retrospectively (Prinstein et al., 2003). A few hours spent recording training information each semester will save you many hours later on.

Admissions Essay

Many students dread the essay component of the internship application. However, the essays are your chance to discuss your background, training, interests, and goals and to convince internship directors that you are the right person for their position. Each essay focuses on a specific topic, such as research interests or experiences with diversity, but applicants should approach each essay question as an opportunity to state their interests and match with the particular internship site (Prinstein et al., 2003).

The self-evaluation that you completed to select internship sites that match your skills, interests, and needs will help you to construct essays that articulate your background, abilities, and training needs while addressing the topics identified in each of the assigned essays. Carefully plan your essays so that you can distribute information about your experiences, competencies, interests, goals, and fit to the internship across the five essays. As you construct your essays, remember to be concise and to-the-point because internship admissions committees will read hundreds of applications. Make it easy for training directors to identify your competencies and fit to the program by carefully articulating them in your essay.

The first essay requests an autobiographical statement. The ambiguity entailed in this assignment often befuddles applicants, who then might write about childhood memories, tell their life story, or restate the material in their curriculum vitae (Prinstein et al., 2003). None of these approaches is effective. The autobiographical essay is an opportunity to discuss your goals for training and your career, factors that led to your pursuing graduate study, and how your experiences have shaped your career goals. Highlight how the training site complements your goals. There is no way to predict exactly what the internship admissions committee is looking for in the autobiographical essay because committees vary in their emphases. Some are interested in the personal and seek to learn about you as a person. Others focus on the professional and want a review of your experiences and goals for training and your career. Committees often consider both of these, as well as trying to get a feel for your personality and how you would act during social interactions with patients, peers, and supervisors (Lopez & Prinstein, 2007). Rather than attempting to divine the admission committee's vision of the perfect candidate, explain how your educational and applied experiences have influenced your goals for internship training and how these goals match the opportunities offered by the site (Prinstein et al., 2003). What additional training do you seek to make progress on your professional development and career goals?

The second essay asks applicants to discuss how they think about cases. It is an opportunity to illustrate how you conceptualize cases, how your theoretical orientation informs your work, and your approach to assessment, diagnosis, and treatment (Lopez & Prinstein, 2007). Your discussion of the theoretical orientation with which you approach cases, your view of assessment, and the types of information you seek (e.g., how you consider the client's own perspective or the role of his or her relationships) reveal your approach to practice, which reveals your fit to the training site. What are your goals regarding case conceptualization? What experiences do you seek to strengthen your weaknesses?

The third essay, on diversity, inquires about applicants' experiences with diverse populations within the context of clinical training. Discuss your experiences working with clients who are diverse with regard to ethnicity, socioeconomic status, or background. What if you do not have such experience? Many applicants who have little clinical experience with diverse clients wonder how to address this question (Prinstein et al., 2003). Be honest. Discuss your weaknesses briefly, then turn it around and move on to an in-depth discussion of your thoughts about diversity and how it applies to clinical work (Lopez & Prinstein, 2007). What does diversity mean to you? How do you or will you consider diversity issues in your work, both research and applied? What training goals do you have with regard to diversity, and how can the internship site fit these training needs?

Research is addressed in the fourth essay. Internship sites vary in their orientation toward research, so this essay will be more or less important depending on the particular internship site's orientation. Students with research interests should take advantage of this essay as an opportunity to discuss their planned program of research. Discuss your work thus far, your contributions to papers with coauthors, and specific responsibilities you have held in research projects. It is understood that, as a student, you are still working out the details in your program of research, that it is not all planned but is a work in progress. How might your experiences at the internship contribute to your research goals? Can you identity ways that you can contribute to current projects at the internship site? Here is where you may discuss your dissertation, its topic, current status, and expected completion date.

In the final essay, you are to discuss your training experiences and goals relative to the opportunities offered by the internship site. Use this as a summative essay. Reiterate the points you have made in the earlier essays with regard to how the internship site matches your overall training goals (Essay 1); clinical experiences and training goals (Essay 2); perspective on diversity and related training goals (Essay 3); and research orientation, if relevant (Essay 4; Prinstein et al., 2003). This final essay is to be written specifically for a given internship site because you are to discuss how the opportunities offered at the specific site fit with your competencies and are essential to achieving your training and career goals (Lopez & Prinstein, 2007). Demonstrate enthusiasm for the site and how your professional development will benefit from the training offered.

Letters of Recommendation

Letters of recommendation are not just for admission to graduate study. They are an important component of applications for internship. Choose referrers who can offer you a very strong and enthusiastic recommendation. This is important because all letters of recommendation are highly positive. A letter that is lukewarm is the kiss of death to an application. Advice for soliciting letters of recommendation for graduate study also applies here (Prinstein et al., 2003). Ask early to give referrers enough time to do a good job (a minimum of 2 weeks, but preferably at least 1 month), and provide them with all your relevant information (including curriculum vitae, transcript, overview of clinical experiences, copies of essays, and any other relevant information such as copies of papers or article submissions). Solicit recommendations only from doctoral-level psychologists, professors, mentors, and supervisors who know you well and have positively evaluated your clinical skills. Note that the emphasis is on their evaluation of your *clin-*

ical skills, so only choose referrers who can write informed and positive letters evaluating your clinical competencies.

INTERNSHIP INTERVIEWS

After submitting applications, the waiting begins. Although it may seem like an eternity, you will soon begin to receive letters and e-mails inviting you to interview at some, or all, of the internship training programs to which you applied. Students will often spend part of December and nearly all of January planning and traveling to interviews. Most students are overwhelmed with the task of squeezing in multiple interviews in different states into such a short time frame. Although it may seem like a good idea to schedule interviews back to back, it is better to schedule one day between each interview to rest and recuperate from the demanding experience (Prinstein, 2007; Prinstein et al., 2003). Once you have heard from some sites, it is acceptable to call others to determine your status and whether you should plan for additional interviews. That said, be respectful of an internship director's time and do not be a pest.

Interviews vary. Some interviews will be conducted by phone, and many more will be in person. Some sites will offer large group interviews, bringing all candidates in at once, which can make it difficult to schedule one-on-one meetings with potential supervisors (Prinstein, 2007). Others will offer small group interviews, with a subset of applicants, or even one-on-one interviews. Most sites will offer a tour of the facility and an informational session. Afterward you can expect individual and group interviews with faculty, interns, and staff. Internship sites vary in their overall approach toward interviews; at some sites applicants can expect challenging questions and standardized questions that are asked of all applicants, others may emphasize collegial chitchat, and others may ask no questions but rather solicit applicant questions about the training site. Exhibit 8.1 illustrates questions that you may be asked.

Recognize that if you are invited for an interview, you have met the basic criteria set by the internship site. The interview entails determining the overall fit of the applicant and site on the basis of stated goals, personality and social skills, and interpersonal factors. Now it is your opportunity to evaluate the internship site. Pay attention to the overall response you receive during the interview because this may offer a good idea of what it might be like to be an intern. Are you treated with courtesy and respect? Pay attention to the interns you see. Do they look happy? Does it seem that they are treated well? Respected? Exhibit 8.2 lists sample questions that can help you to learn more about the internship site and position. Make notes on your impressions and observations; these will inform your choices in the match.

EXHIBIT 8.1

Questions to Expect in an Internship Interview

- Discuss your theoretical approach to psychotherapy.
- Present a case study that illustrates your theoretical approach.
- What are your strengths and weaknesses as a therapist?
- What kinds of clients do you prefer working with?
- What types of clients are most challenging?
- How do you hope to grow over the internship year?
- What are your experiences with supervision?
- Discuss positive and negative experiences you have had with supervision.
- What supervision are you looking for in your internship?
- Describe an ethical issue that you have encountered. How did you handle it?
- Describe a conflict that you have experienced in supervision. How did you resolve it?
- Why did you apply to this internship?
- Tell me about yourself.
- What are your goals for internship training?
- What research do you want to pursue during your internship?
- Is your dissertation complete? What is the status?
- Why did you choose to be a psychologist?
- What are the strengths and weaknesses of your graduate program and training?
- Why should you be selected for this internship?
- Discuss your experience with assessment.
- Discuss your research experience.
- If you were not a psychologist, what would you do?
- What does diversity mean to you? How do you address it in your clinical work?
- What is your experience with diverse groups?

Note. From Keilin and Constantine (2001) and Prinstein (2007).

EXHIBIT 8.2

Questions You Should Ask During an Internship Interview

- What are you looking for in an internship?
- Describe the typical work week for an intern.
- How would interns describe the program's strengths and weaknesses? What do you think are the strengths and weaknesses of this program?
- What kinds of treatment opportunities are available?
- How are supervisors assigned?
- How strong an emphasis is placed on research?
- What kinds of assessment opportunities are available?
- What is the theoretical orientation of supervisors?
- What types of training are available for interns?
- How is this position funded? Do you have concerns about the stability of funding?
- What changes do you expect in this agency over the next few years?
- What kinds of jobs have previous interns obtained?
- What assistance does the program offer interns with regard to the job search process?

Note. From Keilin and Constantine (2001) and Prinstein (2007).

Tip

Not asking questions implies that you are not interested, which is not the message you want to send (Megargee, 2001). Ask educated questions. Do not ask for information that you should already know, such as a general description of the program. Ask similar questions with different interviewers to get multiple perspectives on issues and cross-check data.

THE MATCH

Ultimately, applicants and internship sites are matched by a computerized service called the Match, instituted by the APPIC in 1999 as a way of streamlining the internship application process, which was prone to pressure tactics and game playing on the part of internship sites and applicants (Keilin, 2007). It is not an easy process, but the computer Match makes it more likely that applicants get their preferred internship sites and internship directors get their preferred applicants.

After completing your last interview, review your notes for all internship sites that you have visited. Evaluate the programs and rank order the internships by preference. Include only sites that you would like to attend because the results of the match are binding. Submit your rank-ordered preferences to the Match. The Match timeline is straightforward: (a) From September to October applicants submit their match registrations; (b) during January and February, as applicants complete interviews, they construct a rank-ordered list of internship sites; and (c) results are released in late February.

Match Day is usually the fourth Monday in February. On the Friday before Match Day, students are notified as to whether they have been successfully matched to a program and accepted to an internship program on their list. In 2007, 75% of applicants were successfully matched to internship sites, with 45% matching their first-choice site and about 80% securing a slot with their top three choices (APPIC Board of Directors, 2007). Students who are notified that they are not matched have the weekend to work through their anger and disappointment, and then consider alternative internship sites. On Monday, Match Day, unmatched applicants can pursue internships at sites that are also unmatched and are listed in the APPIC Clearinghouse. Of the roughly 20% of students who are not matched on Match Day, 65% to 70% secure a slot within the same application year (Keilin, Thorn, Rodolfa, Constantine, & Kaslow, 2000).

Students who receive word that they are successfully matched on the Friday prior to Match Day can relax over the weekend. On Match Day,

Monday, they learn the name of their internship site. Internship programs and applicants learn of the match simultaneously. The internship training director will often contact their new interns by phone after receiving Match results. Internship training directors are required to send new interns letters confirming the details of their appointment, including information about the stipend, fringe benefits, and starting and ending dates.

Tip

Enter your rankings online early, well before the deadline, in case you experience Internet problems or the Web site is down. Do not let technological mishaps prevent you from submitting your rankings and securing an internship.

EMBARKING ON INTERNSHIP

Many students are surprised to learn that having made an internship match does not reduce the stress they feel. The excitement of beginning internship is similar to that of entering graduate school: new surroundings, moving, getting settled in a new home and place, new colleagues, and a new role. Transitions are stressful, but the transition to internship entails more than starting fresh. Students also must complete what they have started (e.g., dissertations), identify existing professional development needs, determine how to fulfill those needs, and adapt to their increasingly sophisticated role as practitioner. Aid your transition by carefully planning your internship year. Conduct a self-assessment and talk to your mentor, supervisors, faculty, and peers about strengths and weaknesses in your training (Denicola & Furze, 2001). What do you hope to learn during your internship year? How much time will you spend filling in gaps and rounding out your training versus seeking expertise in a new area?

Perhaps one of the best things that you can do before beginning internship is to complete your dissertation. Students who have not finished dissertations or try to finish them while on internship may feel distracted, preoccupied, and pressured (Keilin & Constantine, 2001). Strive to complete your dissertation prior to beginning internship, and you can devote your attention to the learning opportunity before you, have more time and energy to devote to internship training, and feel less stressed (Keilin & Constantine, 2001). Students who complete the dissertation before beginning internship report finding the internship year more enjoyable than do students who have not completed their dissertation (Keilin & Constantine, 2001).

Although it may not be possible to complete your dissertation, work diligently to at least defend your proposal before beginning internship. Students who begin internship with a completed dissertation proposal tend to make more progress on their dissertations during internship year than do students who have not defended their dissertation proposal (Krieshok, Lopez, Somberg, & Cantrell, 2000). While it is possible to make progress on your dissertation during internship, most students overestimate what they can accomplish (Krieshok et al., 2000). If, like most students, you plan to work on your dissertation during your internship year, carefully carve out time to work on your dissertation; ultimately, the number of hours that students put in predicts dissertation completion (Krieshok et al., 2000).

As you begin internship, remember that the most important component of internship training is supervision. Take advantage of the structure, guidance, and support offered by your supervisors. Supervisory relationships change over the course of internship as interns' competence grows, and these relationships influence interns' professional development and identity (Stedman, 2006). Early interactions with clients often are accompanied by uneasiness and overwhelm. Supervisors provide support to new interns by assisting in planning and implementing interventions, permitting interns to focus on developing basic skills and establishing relationships with clients (Katell et al., 2003).

As interns internalize new skills and develop confidence, they are able to take on increasing responsibilities in managing the therapeutic relationship and look to supervisors for knowledge and consultation rather than hands-on guidance (Maki & Delworth, 1995). Supervisors expect interns to implement more complex therapeutic techniques and will assign them more difficult clients. At the same time, interns may experience ambivalence, struggle with motivation, and experience some countertransference and overidentification with clients. Psychotherapy can help interns progress through challenging stages of professional development.

Once interns have progressed through the turmoil and motivational issues that commonly accompany early advances in therapeutic competence, they continue to learn new skills and consolidate existing skills and move toward autonomy in therapeutic functioning and supervisory relationships (Katell et al., 2003; Stedman, 2006). During this latter phase of internship, the focus is on refining skills and therapeutic techniques and increasing autonomy from supervisors. Throughout your training and professional development, it is critical that you learn to systematically monitor and examine yourself and how your new skills and interactions with clients influence your well-being and functioning.

Making the transition from student to professional is a long, bumpy ride through academic preparation, years of practicum, and the internship. New interns are faced with many stressors, including demanding full-time work, new levels of autonomy in clinical practice, performance evaluations, and advances in professional identity (Turner et al., 2005). The task for interns is to be aware, take responsibility for and address self-care needs, and understand how they can use strategies to combat stress and promote optimal functioning (Norcross, 2000). All of these are essential to becoming a competent psychologist.

Recommended Reading

Denicola, J. A., & Furze, C. T. (2001). The internship year: The transition from student to professional. In S. Walfish & A. K. Hess (Eds.), *Succeeding in graduate school: The career guide for psychology students* (pp. 335–349). Mahwah, NJ: Erlbaum.

Katell, A. D., Levant, R. F., & Loonstra, A. S. (2003). Gaining clinical experience in and after graduate school. In M. J. Prinstein & M. D. Patterson (Eds.), *The portable mentor: Expert guide to a successful career in psychology* (pp. 135–143). New York: Kluwer Academic/Plenum Publishers.

Keilin, W. G., & Constantine, M. G. (2001). Applying to professional psychology internship programs. In S. Walfish & A. K. Hess (Eds.), *Succeeding in graduate school: The career guide for psychology students* (pp. 319–333). Mahwah, NJ: Erlbaum.

Madson, M. B., Chapman, L. K., Wood-Barclaw, N. L., & Williams-Nickelson, C. (2005). *Succeeding in practicum: An APAGS resource guide.* Washington, DC: American Psychological Association of Graduate Students.

Matthews, J. R., & Walker, C. E. (2006). *Your practicum in psychology: A guide for maximizing knowledge and competence.* Washington, DC: American Psychological Association.

Megargee, E. I. (2001). *Megargee's guide to obtaining a psychology internship* (4th ed.). New York: Brunner-Routledge.

Prinstein, M. J., Lopez, S. J., & Rasmussen, H. N. (2003). Navigating the internship application process. In M. J. Prinstein & M. D. Patterson (Eds.), *The portable mentor: Expert guide to a successful career in psychology* (pp. 157–169). New York: Kluwer Academic/Plenum Publishers.

Stedman, J. M. (2006). What we know about predoctoral internship training: A review. *Training and Education in Professional Psychology, 2,* 80–95.

Vaughn, T. J. (2006). *Psychology licensure and certification: What students need to know.* Washington, DC: American Psychological Association.

Williams-Nickelson, C., & Prinstein, M. J. (Eds.). (2007). *Internships in psychology: The APAGS workbook for writing successful applications and finding the right match.* Washington, DC: American Psychological Association.

Zammit, G. K., & Hull, J. W. (1995). *Guidebook for clinical psychology interns.* New York: Plenum Press.

Teaching 9

Teaching offers many rewards, but it also is a great responsibility that entails much effort. As an instructor, you will have the opportunity to touch the lives of many students, observe their advances in learning, and feel that you have made a difference. As much as it is rewarding, teaching is also challenging. Sometimes classes go wrong, students seem ambivalent, or the ongoing learning that is part of good teaching becomes overwhelming.

Most graduate students gain at least some teaching experience in graduate school. Some obtain early experience through teaching assistantships whereby they assist a faculty member in teaching a course and engage in various teaching activities, including leading discussion groups, teaching lab sections, grading assignments and exams, and interacting with students. Other graduate students find themselves immersed in teaching without having early experiences as teaching assistants.

Attitudes about teaching vary among graduate students (Mitchell, 1996). Some complain that it takes time away from their research and applied work. Other students view opportunities to teach as a benefit of graduate training. Universities vary in the preparation that they offer graduate students who wish to teach (Korn, 2001; Rando & Rozenblit, 2003). Some offer formal teaching programs, whereas others provide only superficial preparation with an orientation day or a departmental teaching handbook. When departments provide minimal or no training in teaching, it sends a message that teaching is not important and that research and clinical training are what matter (Meyers & Prieto, 2000).

If your graduate program does not provide adequate training in teaching, you are not doomed. Many universities have centers dedicated to fostering teaching, often with names like Center for Excellence in Teaching, that offer workshops and disseminate materials on best practices in teaching (Rando & Rozenblit, 2003). With initiative and hard work, you can learn how to teach and how to improve your teaching. Many universities publish extensive teaching handbooks on the Internet that are available to teachers everywhere. The following are some examples:

- Streichler, R. (2005). *Graduate teaching assistant handbook.* San Diego: University of California, San Diego, Office of Graduate Studies and Research. Retrieved November 30, 2007, from http://www-ctd.ucsd.edu/resources/tahandbook.pdf
- University of Massachusetts Amherst. (2000). *Handbook for teaching assistants.* Retrieved November 30, 2007, from http://umass.edu/cft/handbook/Handbook_06-07.pdf
- Hadwyn, A., & Wilcox, S. (2006). *A handbook for teaching assistants.* Kingston, Ontario, Canada: Queen's University, Center for Teaching and Learning. Retrieved November 30, 2007, from http://www.queensu.ca/ctl/resources/files/pdf/handbook2006.pdf

The advice and resources in this chapter will guide you in learning about teaching: how to teach and how to integrate teaching, preparation, and grading into your already packed schedule.

Preparing Your Course

One of the most important secrets to good teaching is preparation. As soon as you are assigned a class, begin preparing. Preparation is an ongoing activity, beginning well before the start of the semester and continuing throughout the semester. Nearly all graduate students—and many faculty—agree that teaching takes more time than they anticipate. Reis (1997) noted that a good rule of thumb is to estimate how long you think it will take to teach a course well (i.e., choose reading assignments, choose class activities, prepare lectures and discussion questions, write exams and assignments, grade exams and assignments, and interact with students), and then double or triple your estimate. Teaching gets easier and takes less time as you gain experience, but good teaching will always require preparation. Teaching your first class is stressful; even many experienced professors find teaching stressful. Minimize your stress with careful planning and preparation for the semester ahead.

CLARIFY DEPARTMENT AND UNIVERSITY EXPECTATIONS AND POLICIES

Although instructors generally act with autonomy, selecting the methods that they deem most appropriate in their classes, all departments and universities have policies and expectations for instructor behavior (Mitchell, 1996). Know the answers to the following:

- What does your department expect from you?
- How many office hours are you required to hold and over how many days?
- If you do not already have an office, where should you hold office hours?
- Has a textbook been assigned to the course or must you select and order one?
- What is the deadline for textbook orders?
- Is there a standard outline for the course?
- Has a syllabus been prepared or do you write it?
- What are departmental and university policies regarding attendance (i.e., must you record attendance)?
- What is the maximum number of students to expect in class?
- What are department and university policies about academic honesty?
- What is the protocol for dealing with instances of plagiarism or cheating?

Read the university catalog to learn more about policies that apply to students. Many departments and universities publish handbooks describing instructional policies and procedures.

IDENTIFY OBJECTIVES

Planning your course entails much more than learning about policies and regulations. Most new instructors are simultaneously excited and anxious about teaching their course. No matter how early one begins to plan, it never feels like there is enough time. There is strong temptation to rush into a course; replicate the textbook; or plan on a class-to-class basis, constructing lectures, activities, and assignments as you go.

What is your philosophy of teaching? Your teaching philosophy expresses your beliefs and values about teaching (Korn, 2001): What does good teaching entail? What is your style of teaching? How do people learn? What does it mean to teach? Your philosophy of teaching should inform the objectives you set for your class (Korn, 2001). Your objectives will guide your decisions about teaching methods and what will happen day to day in your class: whether, how often, and for what kinds of content you will lecture, use class discussion, small groups, and so on (Korn, 2001). Your objectives also will influence your choice of assessment methods.

Once you have begun to consider your teaching philosophy, consider the course you are assigned to teach. Identify your objectives (McKeachie, 1994). What do you want to accomplish? What do you want students to learn; what topics are most important? What should a student walk out of your course knowing? These course goals will help you make choices about what content to include, emphasize, and skip (Vesilind, 2000). Use your teaching philosophy and course objectives to organize your course planning. Your philosophy of teaching will help you make decisions about how to best help students grasp information and then design experiences and assignments to achieve that goal (Vesilind, 2000).

Tip

Do not overstuff your course. On average you will have 45 contact hours with students over the entire semester. Those hours go very quickly. It is not possible to cover everything that you believe is important. Make choices: What is the fundamental, essential knowledge that a student must walk away with? What are the themes of your course? Take everything you think students should know from a course, and cut it in half. Then teach that half well. All instructors want to show students the latest, neatest stuff, but it is more important that students grasp the fundamentals. You can always add the neat stuff back as icing on the cake if you have time.

SYLLABUS

New instructors are often surprised by the time and care required in crafting a syllabus. The course syllabus is a contract that discusses expectations: your goals for student learning; what students can expect with regard to course content, assignments, and course policies; and what you expect from students (Korn, 2001). Your syllabus should spell out as many details about your course as possible, such as the following (Curzan & Damour, 2000; Korn, 2001; Vesilind, 2000):

- basic information such as the course name and number, meeting time and place, and your name;
- your contact information, including office hours, e-mail, and phone number;

- textbooks and articles, and if articles are on library or electronic reserve, how to obtain them;
- goals (i.e., what students will learn and be able to do at the end of the course);
- course schedule with due dates for reading assignments and topics to be covered each day;
- late-work policy (i.e., whether it is accepted, whether points are deducted for late work, how many points are deducted each day, and at what point late work will not be accepted);
- attendance policy;
- academic dishonesty policy;
- grading policy (i.e., how students' work will be evaluated and how final grades will be computed);
- test dates;
- makeup policy;
- explanation of what you mean by participation and how it will be graded;
- instructions for how papers and assignments should be formatted (e.g., double spaced, in 12-point Times New Roman font, 1-inch margins, in accordance with American Psychological Association style); and
- support services (e.g., student learning centers, tutoring centers).

Although it might seem like a lot of work to plan how to handle the wide range of issues that may arise, careful consideration now will save you much time and aggravation later, and it will help you to be clear and fair in interactions with students.

> Timothy sits back and puts his feet up on the desk, "I just let a student take an exam early. She asked very early in the semester and my policy is that students can take exams early but cannot make up missed exams. She approached me and explained that it was personal. I didn't push it. I just realized that I should have because it turns out that the exam is scheduled for the day after her birthday. She didn't want to take it with a hangover—so I've just enabled binge drinking!" Lena laughs, "You should have asked for more information. That's OK. I'm in my own policy-related quagmire. My policy is no late work. Ever. Except a student experienced a death in the family and asked if he could submit his paper late. OK. Another student was in the emergency room, so I accepted the late assignment. Then other requests to submit late work began trickling in: car problems, sick children, computer viruses, and so on. I do not know how to stop all of these requests and still be fair."

A clearly documented set of course policies articulates how you will handle the myriad situations and requests that arise regarding absences, late or missing work, and formatting of assignments. Creating policies is not enough; you must apply them consistently. Your course policies will provide a guideline to follow when issues arise and will help you to make decisions that are consistent over time and across students; in other words, applying your course policies unwaveringly will help you to make decisions that are fair. One of your tasks as instructor is to establish authority in the classroom; a clearly defined and enforced set of policies provides a sense of structure to the class that communicates that authority (Curzan & Damour, 2000).

Tip

Consider your syllabus a work in progress. As the semester advances, you may encounter issues not addressed in your syllabus (e.g., cell phone use in the classroom). Take notes on these incidents and incorporate what you have learned into the following semester's syllabus.

CHARACTERISTICS OF EFFECTIVE TEACHERS

Any discussion of teaching methods and strategies, such as that within this chapter, is best framed by considering what is entailed in teaching well. Effective teachers

- *Are knowledgeable.* It is impossible to be an effective teacher if you do not have a grasp of the course content (Korn, 2001). Prepare for classes by reading the text and especially by staying on top of the current literature. As a new teacher, it is common to fear that you will not be able to address students' questions. Undoubtedly you will have more knowledge about the course content than your students, but there will come a time when you do not have an answer to a student's question. When it occurs, say so. And promise to get the information for the next class (and do it!).
- *Are organized.* Effective teachers take care in constructing and organizing the course and each class, making learning objectives and methods used to achieve those objectives transparent to all. Good teachers also maintain organized files whereby they can track their lecture notes, source material, and student papers and grades. Organized instructors return student papers in a timely fashion with comments that are appropriate to the course content and specific assignment at hand.
- *Are clear.* Effective teachers are understood by students. They are excellent communicators and can express ideas in a way that students understand. Clarity of expression applies not just to speaking skills but also to the use of examples, exercises, technology, and visuals.

- *Are enthusiastic.* Instructor enthusiasm carries a great deal of weight with students. Instructors' excitement about the subject matter is contagious, motivating students and maintaining their interest.
- *Develop rapport with students.* Instructors are sensitive to student interests, concerned with their learning, and willing to provide help outside of class. Effective instructors make students feel respected and want students to feel comfortable approaching them.

Teaching Your Course

There is no substitute for preparation in increasing feelings of competence; however, even the most prepared instructors encounter surprises each semester. Be aware that it is impossible to prepare for every possibility. Do what you can, but remember to be flexible, accept that things do not always go as planned, and be prepared to modify your class plan.

MEETING YOUR CLASS

On the first day of class it is normal for new (and even experienced) instructors to feel nervous. It goes with the territory. Introducing yourself to a roomful of undergraduate students, spelling out your plan for the semester, and subtly establishing your authority is quite a challenge. Yet, the first class sets the tone for the semester, so it is important to carefully plan and prepare for this initial meeting.

Tip

Arrive at class early. Write your name and the course number and title on the board. As you wait for the class to begin, engage a few students in conversation. If you are too nervous to engage in chitchat, organize your materials and make friendly eye contact with students as they enter. Your goal is to make yourself and your students feel more comfortable.

Plan your first class meeting with the knowledge that students usually are nervous too. They want to learn about the instructor: Is he or she competent, fair, knowledgeable, interesting? Student want instructors who are enthusiastic and sympathetic to their concerns (Mitchell, 1996). Your goal in this first class is to ease student anxiety by interesting them in the material, introducing yourself, and covering course policies.

Many instructors begin the class by distributing the syllabus. There is nothing wrong with starting with the essentials. However, one of your tasks for the first class is to spark students' interest. Spend a few minutes discussing a case, problem, or current event that is relevant to course content. For example, a quiz discussing common misconceptions about psychology can give students a chance to see what will be covered in Introductory Psychology. Similarly, a case portraying a mental disorder, parenting style, or another psychological concept can engage students and increase their interest in the course matter. This initial activity is an opportunity to encourage students to participate and demonstrates that you are interested in what they have to say, can lead a discussion, and can respond to student comments with enthusiasm and fairness. As you conclude the activity, explain that this is a brief taste of the content that will be covered this semester.

Once you have engaged students and given them an idea of what to expect in the course, distribute the syllabus. Discuss your contact information, office hours, and when you are available at other times. Go over the syllabus line by line. Encourage students to ask questions. Students often will not read the syllabus, so draw their attention to essential information (Curzan & Damour, 2000). Discuss how the assignments fulfill course goals. Review dates of tests and other deadlines. Discuss policies on grading, attendance, late work, and makeup tests.

Make interpersonal contact. Tell students a little bit about your professional self, such as your educational background, area of research or practice, or an interesting professional experience that you have had (Mitchell, 1996). Learn a little bit about your students. Students will be shy, but try to engage them. Students do not want to be anonymous—they want you to learn their names (Vesilind, 2000). Try your best to learn student names. If possible, go around and have each student introduce him- or herself, and have students say something about themselves and why they are taking the course. Another way is to have students interview each other and then introduce each other. This helps students get to know each other, which will aid in discussions and group work later.

Tip

A noninvasive way of learning about students is to ask them to write responses on an index card. Ask that they record basic personal information such as their major, classes, personal interests, contact information, and something that they hope to learn in the class. Note that you might use these index cards throughout the semester to quickly take attendance by sorting them into piles of students who are in attendance or are missing.

PLANNING AND TEACHING CLASS

As instructor, your job is to impart information to students, but more important, to help them learn how to think. A college education teaches a student how to think. As an instructor, your job is to help students learn to think in more sophisticated ways; specifically, as an instructor of psychology courses, your job is to help students learn how to think like psychologists. How do you do this? In small steps. Within each class period, you might impart new information, help students analyze previously learned material and think about it in new ways, or help students consider how the course content can be applied to solve real-world problems and what additional information or research is needed to do so (Curzan & Damour, 2000). That is a big task. It is no wonder that most instructors, especially new instructors, overprepare for classes. Overpreparation tends to result in too much material to cover in a given class period, which can lead an instructor to rush through material, presenting it too quickly to permit student discussion and participation and leading to poor comprehension and anxious, displeased students.

Instead, make class preparation an ongoing activity rather than a single lengthy session each week. Experts on faculty development recommend that instructors prepare for about 1½ and no more than 2 hours for each hour spent in class (Boice, 2000). Prepare in several 20- to 30-minute sessions throughout the week rather than in a single marathon session. This keeps your teaching in mind all week, permitting you to add examples as they come to you rather than struggling. It also encourages you to consider various ways of presenting information because you are working with it all week.

Perhaps one of the most challenging aspects of class planning is to exert restraint. It is not possible to cover all of the material in the assigned readings. Select what is most important: a critical concept, a topic that students are likely to find difficult, update of a topic by discussing the most recently published literature, or a concept not covered in the assignment. Explain your strategy to students—that you will not repeat all of the material in the assigned readings and that their job is to read carefully and critically, identifying questions to bring to class.

Once you have decided on your goals for a particular class, create a lesson plan, which is your strategy for the class: what you will cover, how you will cover it, and how you will involve students (Curzan & Damour, 2000). Your lesson plan should address the following:

- How much talking will you do?
- How much do you expect students to participate?
- How will you get students to participate?
- What activities, discussion topics, or examples will you use to make your point?

- In what ways must students prepare beforehand?
- What materials do you need during class? (Curzan & Damour, 2000)

Write the plan down. Add time frames to keep yourself on track. It is easy to get sidetracked when you are in front of 20, 40, or more students. Instructors have two general choices in how to present information: lecture and discussion.

Tip

Begin and end class on time. Waiting until the last few stragglers enter the room reinforces their tardiness, and students will come later and later. Reward students for being on time by starting on time. Likewise, end class on time. Keep track of time so that you do not run over.

Lecture Method

Lectures get a bad rap; some argue that they encourage passive learning because students listen to the material. However, lectures can be effective and efficient ways of conveying information (Vesilind, 2000). They can be updated with new information on the go, can be modified even in mid-lecture on the basis of student responses, and are familiar to students; there is live contact between the student and instructor (Vesilind, 2000).

A good lecture is well planned. Your lecture should present no more than three or four major issues, with time for examples and questions. Anything more than a few points and your students will be overwhelmed. Determine the critical message of your lecture and then remove the adornments to present the bare bones in a succinct story. Students will absorb the salient points easily if they are few in number, clear, and coupled with examples. Emphasize the fundamentals during class time. Students need concrete, well-organized information in class. Out-of-class assignments, papers, and activities allow students to explore unresolved issues in the field and illustrate the true complexity of psychological science.

You can enhance the quality of your lectures by remembering some simple rules. First and foremost is the importance of enthusiasm (Vesilind, 2000). Your mood will rub off on your students, and their response will influence your mood. If you lack excitement, your students will reflect boredom back to you, and any enthusiasm you had will likely plummet. Fake enthusiasm if you must, and you may begin to believe yourself and truly become enthusiastic. Other rules of lecturing:

- There is no substitute for preparation (Vesilind, 2000). Consider how you will present information, what examples you will use, and how you will inflect your voice to draw attention to a particular point.
- Run short. Always prepare lectures that are a bit shorter than you intend (Vesilind, 2000). Lectures are nearly always longer than instructors intend. Beginning-of-class announcements, chatter, student questions, distributing assignments, and so on all eat into class time.
- Talk loudly—louder and a bit slower than you think you should (Korn, 2001; Vesilind, 2000). Ask students in the back of the room if they can hear you. Sometimes students who cannot hear you will not speak up on their own and instead strain to hear throughout class (or give up trying and doodle or read). Vary your pitch and volume to stress points.
- Try not to fidget. Some lecturers inadvertently adjust and readjust their sleeve, tie, hair, jewelry, and so on. Others pace the room as they lecture. Fidgeting and pacing are distracting (Korn, 2001; Vesilind, 2000).
- Use the lectern. Stand still most of the time, not drooping over it.
- Use movement to emphasize a point, thumping a fist on the lectern, drawing arms wide, or stepping away.
- Be confident. Do not reveal that you have not had time to prep, or that you have a cold, or that it is a lousy lecture, and so on. Students will not notice these things unless you draw attention to them.
- Do not talk to yourself. Sometimes, mid-lecture, an instructor will stop and ask him- or herself a question, "Where should I go now?" "Should I cover this next?" Remember where you are, and think but do not speak your thoughts. Talking to yourself distracts students and gives the impression that you are making it up as you go (Vesilind, 2000).
- Use visual aids, but use them well (Korn, 2001; Vesilind, 2000). PowerPoint slides and handouts can display an outline of your presentation as well as illustrate concepts. Effective slides are concise. Never read from your slides. Instead, use them as an outline and note-taking tool for your students. Your lecture should provide the details omitted from your slides. Other media, such as videos, illustrate concepts that lectures leave wanting (e.g., illustrations of infant motor development). Include media in your classroom when relevant. Work to help students see the connection between course content and media; links that seem obvious to an instructor often are not obvious to students.
- Summarize major points at the end of each section of your lecture and at the end of class.

Do not write out your lecture (Korn, 2001; Vesilind, 2000). Outline your major points and add examples, discussion questions, and activities, but leave room for flexibility and to think on your feet. Students do not want to sit in on a lecture that is simply read from a sheaf of pages. Outlining your ideas will enable you to craft your lecture on the go and make changes, additions, or deletions, based on your audience.

Lecture is best combined with other teaching methods. Break up your lectures so that they are presented in 20-minute chunks. What is wrong with a 1- or 2-hour lecture? Research shows that students remember the first and the last 10 minutes of lectures but little of the intervening time (Hartley & Davies, 1978). Undergraduate students have a limited attention span, so take advantage of it to structure your class. Switch gears after each 20-minute minilecture and do something different: Pose a discussion question, a short in-class writing assignment, small group discussion, or problem-solving activity.

Tip

Allow sufficient time for students to respond to questions. After posing a question, wait 20 to 30 seconds before rephrasing it, offering a follow-up, or answering it yourself. Students need time to think about the question and consider responses. All too often instructors do not wait long enough for students to respond. At first it may feel agonizing, but slowly count to yourself to 20 or 30, and someone likely will respond before you are through. If not, rephrase the question.

Discussion Method

A second method of instruction is through the use of discussion—full class discussions as well as small group discussions—often in response to a case, problem, or set of questions. Advocates point out that learning is an active process; when students manipulate and apply the content to be learned, they are more likely to understand and retain it and to make it their own. As instructor, your choice of whether to rely on lecture or discussion represents a false dichotomy because the two are most effective when they accompany each other.

Discussion questions, group exercises, brainstorming, and problem-posing and problem-solving sessions can be used to illustrate the points of your lecture in a meaningful and memorable way. The success of discussion relies on all students being active (Korn, 2001). Plan your discussion and include it in your lesson plan (Curzan & Damour, 2000). Will you divide students into groups? How? How long will students work together before participating in a class discussion? What information will you give students and what problem will you pose? How will you record and summarize information? What is the takeaway message for students and how will you convey it? There are many ways to improve your discussions:

- *Ask reflective questions.* Reflective questions are not yes or no questions but those that require students to think (e.g., What would you do in this situation? Why do you think the researchers chose this particular methodology?).
- *Respond to students with care.* Your response to students—their answers as well as the questions that they ask—will largely determine how much participation you can expect from students. Take their comments seriously and provide positive feedback for comments by finding something in the students' comment that is interesting or accurate (Curzan & Damour, 2000). Take care to ensure that a student is never sorry for speaking.
- *Use prewriting* (Curzan & Damour, 2000; Mitchell, 1996). Ask students to write about the question first for 3 to 5 minutes, then solicit their responses. The benefit of asking students to consider the question in writing is that they will have time to think through their response and feel more comfortable discussing their views without fear of forgetting their point.
- *Consider discussion groups.* Break the class down into pairs or small groups to work through a problem or case. Later, as a class, discuss each group's perspective and contribution.
- *Be flexible.* Discussions often flow to places instructors do not predict; that is often a very good thing. As long as the discussion is content related, encourage it and let it wander where it will because flexibility permits students to discuss the material in ways that they see as relevant, which facilitates learning (Curzan & Damour, 2000).
- *Facilitate discussion* (Korn, 2001). Your role is to help students talk about a topic. Let students take the lead and do not talk too much. Guide the discussion by probing with additional questions, drawing attention to relevant points, and summarizing the discussion. Do not respond to every student comment yourself; encourage students to talk with each other. If the discussion becomes lopsided, play devil's advocate (Curzan & Damour, 2000).
- *Tell students how to prepare.* If you plan to devote a significant portion of an entire class to discussion, tell your students how to prepare (e.g., what to read, how to review and summarize, and whether to prepare discussion questions).

- *Summarize points made in discussion.* Ensure that students understand the message that you wish for them to take away (Mitchell, 1996).

Tip

It is inevitable: Every instructor finds him- or herself unprepared for class at one time or another. How can you keep from admitting to your students that you are unprepared?

- Pose discussion questions to guide students through the material.
- Ask students to spend the first 5 minutes reviewing the assignment and previous lecture notes before writing down the one question they would most like you to address. Collect the questions, sort them, and answer them.
- Ask the class to spend the first 10 minutes reviewing a particular part of the assignment so that they have it clearly in mind. While they are reviewing it, think of a discussion problem involving the material they are reviewing. Break the class into groups to discuss the problem. Get reports from the groups or ask groups to evaluate each other's responses.

Interacting With Students

Professors interact with students, some of whom are very different from them, inside the classroom but also outside of class during office hours and by e-mail. Interactions with students are the most rewarding aspects of teaching but also the most challenging.

EXPECT AND RESPECT DIVERSITY

Expect diversity in your classroom and understand that diversity comes in many forms, including but not limited to gender, ethnic background, sexual orientation, and age (McKeachie, 1994). Be aware of your use of language. Avoid gender and ethnic stereotyping. Because your students come from all different backgrounds, it is helpful to draw on a broad range of examples to illustrate your points; try not to focus on examples that are drawn from only one culture (Mitchell, 1996).

Many students are surprised to encounter so-called nontraditional students in their classes. Many universities define nontraditional student as one who is 24 years of age or older. These students are adults, often with jobs and families. It is common for new instructors to feel awkward when their students are older than they are (Mitchell, 1996). In these cases, however, it is important to remember that students are in class to learn. Instructors impart knowledge and are the experts in class; age is not a good predictor of capacity. Take nontraditional students seriously, and as with other students, solicit their input. Nontraditional students offer real-world experience that can be valuable in illustrating concepts and grounding class discussions (Korn, 2001).

One of the challenges in helping diverse students feel welcome in the classroom is that such students may feel alone and singled out (McKeachie, 1994). Underrepresented students may feel lost or hesitant to speak out on issues, especially when their views differ from those held by the majority of classmates. Students who may feel like outsiders need special assistance in getting involved in class discussions and activities.

OFFICE HOURS AND E-MAIL

Contact with students is not limited to the classroom. Office hours are specific times that are set aside for interacting with students. Sometimes no one will come to your office during these hours; other times you will be visited by several students. These are times to answer questions, get to know students, and provide guidance to help students meet course requirements. Some students, however, might be better at attending your office hours than class. Office hours are not for lecturing or teaching all of the content covered in class; they are for assisting students with specific questions or who need individual guidance in addition to what is provided in class.

E-mail is a common way for students to make contact with you. Check your e-mail regularly. Answer e-mails from students as quickly as possible. Be sure to proofread your e-mails to students and check for inconsistencies, errors, and appropriateness of tone. Use a professional and respectful tone in e-mails with students. If answering a student's question requires a lengthy email, ask the student to come see you during office hours rather than spend a great deal of time composing a lengthy response.

Some instructors complain that student e-mails are overly familiar and informal, addressing the instructor by first name, not addressing the instructor at all, using Internet slang (e.g., "u" for you), or using accusatory language (e.g., a one-sentence e-mail such as "Why did you give me a C?" or "Why did you give me an F when I did everything you told me to do?"). When you receive such e-mails, use a more formal tone than usual, addressing the student and his or her request or comment and then providing your response. If the issue seems antagonistic, or if the student's e-mail comes across as difficult or challenging, send yourself a copy (i.e., cc) on all of your correspondence with him or her. Always have a record of interactions with students who may challenge your teaching or their grades. If possible, cc all e-mails to students to yourself. Save all student e-mails for at least a semester after the course ends, or at least until the period in which students can request reviews and changes of grades ends (Curzan & Damour, 2000).

Tip

Instructors often encounter a student who is in need of psychological assistance. He or she might come to you after class or during office hours or might send an e-mail. Many instructors find it challenging to maintain their professional boundaries and not offer the student counseling. However, offering counseling to the student oversteps your professional boundary as instructor. Encourage the student to visit the campus counseling center or offer to accompany him or her there.

Balancing Professional and Personal Development

Preparing and teaching a course is an exercise in professional development: choosing course goals, designing a plan, selecting assignments and activities, and carrying out the course plan. Many graduate students fret over a critical aspect of teaching: establishing authority in the classroom. What they often do not realize is that good teaching is a performance and that a part of establishing authority in the classroom entails acting out the role of "professor"; over time it will feel less like acting and you will believe that you are in charge of the classroom (Curzan & Damour, 2000). With experience, you will become more confident in your role.

REFLECTIVE TEACHING

Good teachers are reflective teachers. They consider their day-to-day classroom experiences and continually seek improvement. Teaching is a skill that is constantly refined and honed. When you acknowledge that there is always room for improvement and you are always learning, it will be easier to view those times when class does not seem to gel or when things do not go right as learning opportunities (Curzan & Damour, 2000). After each class take brief notes on what seems to work in the classroom and what does not, and then consider why an activity or lecture did or did not work. What went well, and what could have gone better? How would you change your lesson plan given what you know now? What worked? Were your examples effective? Did your group activity engage students? Did your discussion questions begin the discussion you had anticipated? Always remember that a bad class session does not ruin the course and that there are many reasons for a bad class: student or instructor fatigue, being overwhelmed, lack of preparation, challenging reading assignments, and more. None of these mean that you are a bad instructor—if you reflect and learn from them.

One way to help you to reflect on what students are learning and make changes to help them learn more is the 1-minute paper. During the last few minutes of class, ask students to write a short paper on the most important thing they learned today and what important question remains unanswered. By looking over the papers, you can get a sense of what students learn. If it seems that they share misunderstandings or lack information, you can correct it next time (Vesilind, 2000). Refer to these papers in the next class to help students to understand that you read them and are taking their feedback into account.

Another version of the 1-minute paper is to solicit student feedback about the course. Do it during the semester rather than waiting until it is too late to make changes. Sure, feedback can bruise the ego, but there is much to learn from student feedback. How do you obtain it? Use 1-minute papers. At the end of class, ask students to write for about a minute on a topic you assign. You might ask: How is the class going? Is there anything you want to tell me about or ask regarding instruction? This can be painful but very helpful because you are gathering information about what works and what does not work during the semester so that you can make changes. Ask stud [illegible] anonymously list and explain two or three things that work re[illegible] two or three things that they would change about the co[illegible]on. It takes a strong stomach, but you can learn much, and [illegible] kind.

SCHEDULE AND LIMIT P[illegible] AND GRADING TIME

Instructors who take their teaching seriously [illegible] it can become an all-consuming activity. Class prepara[illegible], will encompass as much time as you let them (Curzan & D[illegible]0). Set aside time each week to prepare your classes, and do not wo[illegible]yond the allotted time. Be sure to prepare a day or two ahead of class so that you have time to create and copy handouts and other materials. In addition, plan your work ahead of time; consider your own schedule as you write the class syllabus and plan assignments. Schedule papers and exams for times when you are not working on papers of your own. Try your best to align the class deadlines with your needs to avoid receiving too many incoming tasks at once.

MAINTAIN PERSPECTIVE

Keep things in perspective. Although you spend a great deal of time planning each class and fret over the details of how to present information, start discussions, and engage students, your students are not observing how you teach; they are focused on absorbing the information. Students have lives—lots of other things are on their minds, like other classes, jobs, friends, and more.

Some instructors find it difficult to separate their sense of self from their work in the classroom, so that their mood changes in relation to their teaching day. A good day in class makes them feel great, and a troubled teaching day puts them on a low (Curzan & Damour, 2000). Enjoy your successes and accept that classes will not always go well. Even the best teachers have bad teaching days or bad courses. Do not let your sense of competence and self-esteem skyrocket and plummet along with the day's class.

Many instructors wonder why some students are so bored by material that is, at least to the instructor, fascinating. Remember that your experience of college is likely very different from that of your students. You enrolled in graduate study because you love learning. However, only a small percentage of your students will go on to graduate school. Your best students will learn regardless of what you do. The other 90% will vary. In general education courses that are taken by nonmajors, you may find that some students do not seem to care and may earn an F no matter what you do. In general education elective courses, you are teaching the mass of students, and they are quite varied and often very different from you. Although you must attempt to engage students, recognize that your enthusiasm may convince some of your students that at least some aspects of your field are interesting, but you will not be able to sway all of your students. Do not let it depress you.

Remember that there are places where you can turn for help. Turn to your mentor and other faculty in the department who teach well, and pick their brains. Ask other instructors for copies of their syllabi and for suggestions on how to structure classes and create course policies. Most universities have centers for teaching effectiveness or instructional development; take advantage of these resources. Even if your institution is short of teaching-related resources, there are plenty of books and Web sites that can help you improve your teaching (see the Recommended Reading). Finally, remember that good teaching develops over many years. Practice moderation in class preparation and teaching activities, and you will find that balancing teaching and an active research program is challenging but not impossible.

Recommended Reading

Boice, R. (2000). *Advice for new faculty members.* Boston: Allyn & Bacon.

Curzan, A., & Damour, L. (2000). *First day to final grade: A graduate student's guide to teaching.* Ann Arbor: University of Michigan Press.

Davis, B. G. (1993). *Tools for teaching.* San Francisco: Jossey-Bass.

Korn, J. H. (2001). Developing teaching skills. In S. Walfish & A. K. Hess (Eds.), *Succeeding in graduate school: The career guide for psychology students* (pp. 221–232). Mahwah, NJ: Erlbaum.

Lucas, S. G., & Bernstein, D. A. (2005). *Teaching psychology: A step by step guide.* Mahwah, NJ: Erlbaum.

McKeachie, W. J. (1994). *Teaching tips: Strategies, research, and theory for college and university teachers* (9th ed.). Lexington, MA: D.C. Heath.

Perlman, B., McCann, L. I., & McFadden, S. H. (Eds.). (1999). *Lessons learned: Practical advice for the teaching of psychology.* Washington, DC: American Psychological Society.

Vesilind, P. A. (2000). *So you want to be a professor?* Thousand Oaks, CA: Sage.

Writing the Dissertation 10

Once students reach ABD ("all but dissertation") status, the end of graduate study is in sight. Or is it? The final hurdle, the dissertation, is a monumental one indeed. Although graduate study is often likened to a marathon, the dissertation is a marathon unto itself.

A doctoral dissertation in psychology typically entails conducting an original empirical study; however, some practitioner-oriented programs also accept a lengthy literature review paper that applies theoretical and empirical literature to a real-world problem. In either case, the resulting dissertation typically encompasses more than 100 written pages and can run to 300 pages in length. The thesis, the culminating project for the master's degree, is similar to a dissertation, though smaller in scope and entailing about 50 to 100 written pages. Completing the dissertation itself is less a test of aptitude than one of organization, motivation, endurance, and willpower (Mitchell, 1996). Graduate students are a smart bunch; those who pass comprehensive exams and become doctoral candidates have the intellect to design and carry out a dissertation. Intellect, however, is not enough. Just as it is helpful to envision graduate study as a step-by-step process, the dissertation is best conceived of as a process rather than an event.

The Dissertation Proposal

The dissertation proposal does not simply happen. Many students are surprised at the amount of work that occurs before the proposal is even written. Perhaps the most challenging part of the dissertation is finding a topic.

CHOOSE A TOPIC

It is not uncommon for doctoral candidates to find themselves at a loss for a topic. Choice of research topic is a big deal because 1 to 2 years or even more will be spent conducting the dissertation, and the dissertation may serve as a foundation for constructing a program of research after graduation.

> After reading Sam's abstract, Eric comments, "Looks like a good idea. Bring it to your mentor and see what she thinks." "I don't know. It's not ready yet. I'm not sure that another study on depression will contribute to the literature. I want to work on a new and exciting problem," Sam replies. "This is the fourth idea you've honed and thrown out. How long did it take you to do this? A month? How about all of the others? You've probably spent the last 6 months playing with ideas, four of which would be great for a dissertation. Are you ever going to settle on one?" asks Eric. Sam replies, "Yeah, I know. My mentor also is pushing me to make a decision. How do I know which topic is the right one—one that I can do and will take me somewhere, careerwise? It's such an important decision."

Sam is right: Choosing a topic for the dissertation is a big deal. It should not be taken lightly, but do not become paralyzed by the decision. Keep in mind the following:

- *Your dissertation does not have to change the world.* It must represent an original study but it need not be earth-shattering or revolutionary (Mitchell, 1996). It is not unusual for students to approach the dissertation by considering the biggest problems in their field. Scholars spend their lives studying these questions. The dissertation is a project that must be finite. Choose a manageable project that you can complete in a reasonable amount of time. No one wants to stay ABD forever.
- *Plan your dissertation with your career in mind.* If you are seeking a practitioner career, then select a project that will have relevance to your clinical work and real-world practice (Malley-Morrison, Patterson, & Yap, 2003). If you aim for an academic career, choose

a topic that will serve as a base for future work and that will have the potential to make a significant contribution to the field (Malley-Morrison et al., 2003). Making a significant contribution is not the same as changing the field entirely, however; do not bite off more than you can chew.

- *Choose a topic that you are passionate about.* Your dissertation will consume nearly every waking thought for the next 1 to 2 or more years of your life. Choose a topic that will retain your interest because you will become tired of your project, regardless of how excited you are at its inception. The intensity of dissertation research can make even the most interesting project tedious at least for a time, so it is essential to choose a topic that you find fascinating.
- *Do not choose a topic that is too close to home.* Although researchers often turn to their own experience for research ideas, be careful to choose problems that do not touch on intimate personal issues that may impede your progress. Sometimes research breakthroughs may spur personal insights that may be detrimental to motivation, delaying dissertation completion.
- *Choose a topic that is practical.* As you consider ideas, ask yourself whether you have the experience and equipment needed to conduct the study you plan. What will your project cost? What physical resources are required (e.g., lab space, computer software, measures, equipment, copying expenses). How much time will the project take?

Choosing a dissertation project is a decision that combines intellectual, emotional, and practical considerations. The ideal topic evokes fascination and passion, does not touch on emotional or personal hot spots, and is practical given the resources at hand. Once you have a potential topic, begin discussing your ideas with your advisor, who will chair your dissertation committee.

WRITE THE PREPROPOSAL

Some departments require that graduate students submit a preproposal to their advisor and committee. Regardless of whether it is required, it is a good idea to prepare a preproposal. A preproposal is a miniproposal, just a few pages in length, that explains the problem under study and outlines the proposed project, explaining the purpose, method, data analysis techniques, and anticipated findings (Malley-Morrison et al., 2003; Peters, 1997; Rossman, 2002).

"I am not able to sit on your committee," Dr. Flanagan said. "It isn't clear to me that you have narrowed down your research

> question and determined how to study it." "But I've thought it all through," replied Robin. "Tell you what," said Dr. Flanagan, "why don't you send me a write-up, a brief overview of your study including how you will operationalize and measure the constructs, and I'll think about it."

Dr. Flanagan is asking Robin to create a preproposal. Constructing a preproposal, a concise yet detailed outline of your proposed dissertation research, will force you to refine your ideas and think about your project concretely. Only after you have considered the rationale underlying your research and pondered the specifics of how you will answer your question can you write the proposal. Consider how you will obtain participants, characteristics of participants, what measures or apparatus you will construct and use, what you will do with the data you collect, and what analyses you will conduct. Answering these questions is challenging but necessary to ensure that you have considered all aspects of your project and that your time, effort, and resources are not expended pursing dead ends.

The resulting document will help your advisor evaluate the merits of the proposed research and make suggestions for revisions. The preproposal is also valuable in approaching potential committee members and soliciting feedback to ensure that you and your dissertation committee are on the same page before you write the dissertation proposal. The preproposal is a useful tool because it demonstrates that you have considered your project, and it gives you a basis for communicating with faculty who may become members of your committee. The document permits committee members to make informed decisions about whether to participate in your dissertation committee and confidence that you are ready to begin writing the dissertation proposal.

SELECT THE COMMITTEE

The ease with which you complete your dissertation is closely related to the functioning of your dissertation committee. The committee's charge is to evaluate and approve your dissertation proposal and judge the quality of the resulting dissertation and defense (Peters, 1997). Your advisor has the responsibility of guiding your research; committee members will vary in their involvement depending on their research interests, your relationship with them, and their personalities (e.g., some faculty may have a high need for involvement and control). Dissertation committees typically consist of four to five members, including the advisor, who chairs the committee. Committee members hold a great deal of sway in whether and how quickly you complete your dissertation. Take care and be strategic in selecting committee members.

Tip

Begin considering potential committee members early in your graduate school career. Note which faculty are good communicators and teachers. Consider their availability and openness to interacting with students. Some faculty are more student oriented than others. Pay attention to personality traits and whether the faculty member's personal characteristics and style mesh with your own. Attend to these details throughout graduate school and you will find that you have a good idea of which faculty to approach for your dissertation committee.

Choose committee members in consultation with your advisor. Before approaching your advisor, construct a list of potential committee members. Consider faculty with whom you work well and who have similar research interests. Talk to other students about their experiences with faculty as committee members. Did the committee members read their work beforehand? Was there animosity among particular faculty? Did some committee members appear to show off to others? Were some too busy to read drafts or meet? Do the same type of homework that you would do to select an advisor (see chap. 5) because your committee will hold a great deal of sway over the success of your dissertation.

Once you have formed some ideas about potential faculty, solicit your advisor's suggestions on committee members. You want committee members who will work well together. Your advisor is likely to have insight into relations among faculty—which faculty get along well and which do not. Interpersonal dynamics among committee members will influence how smooth the dissertation process is. Above all, select faculty with whom your advisor can work amicably (Mitchell, 1996). If your advisor suggests faculty who do not cover the range of expertise you feel is needed, make alternative suggestions and pay attention to your advisor's response. Any hesitation or lukewarm praise may indicate that your advisor thinks the professor is not a good choice: Your advisor may feel that he or she cannot work well with the professor, disagree about the relevance of his or her expertise, or have another concern about the professor (Mitchell, 1996). Take these concerns seriously.

As you consider potential committee members, attempt to create a committee composed of faculty who (Cone & Foster, 2006; Frank & Stein, 2004; Malley-Morrison et al., 2003; Rossman, 2002)

- hold differing backgrounds on your topic to encourage consideration of diverse perspectives,

- have expertise in your topic area (suggestions about literature to review, methodologies to use or avoid, and advice concerning what studies have and have not been conducted can save you time),
- have methodological expertise in your area,
- have statistical expertise,
- get along well with each other,
- respect each other's point of view,
- have time to read and consult,
- are interested in your topic,
- are fair and trustworthy,
- are well respected,
- communicate well,
- are good listeners,
- are enthusiastic,
- are available, and
- are organized.

No one faculty member will have all of these qualities and areas of expertise. Aim to put together a committee that collectively represents these areas of expertise and whose faculty are good-willed, bright, and helpful. Their criticisms and objections should be motivated by a desire to help you to write the best dissertation that you can, not to show off or rival other committee members. Sometimes committee members try to look brilliant in front of their colleagues at the student's expense. This may be more common among junior faculty who may feel that they have something to prove and therefore judge the student harshly, but some senior faculty also are blowhards (Peters, 1997).

In approaching potential committee members, remember that it is their choice whether to sit on your committee (Cone & Foster, 2006). Provide the faculty member with enough information so that he or she can make a reasoned decision about whether to participate on your dissertation committee. Provide the preproposal, which will give a overview of your project. Explain what expertise you think the faculty can provide (e.g., statistical expertise or content expertise). Discuss your timetable for writing the proposal and for conducting the study assuming that it is approved. The timetable is essential so that faculty can determine their availability. You do not want to discover that you have to postpone your proposal meeting because a committee member is away on sabbatical and cannot meet.

Simply asking a faculty member to sit on your committee does not guarantee that he or she will. Faculty members do not have to sit on your committee. Some may not have time or interest. Some may suspect that helping you will require too much time. Others may be uncertain of your ability. This is where relationships with faculty established over the graduate school years come into play. Faculty who know and think highly of you are more likely to want to help you and to participate in your dissertation committee. Remember that by approving your dissertation, committee members are in effect telling the world that you are a competent and independent scholar; they must have faith in your abilities to take part in the process.

Tip

If a change is needed in the composition of your dissertation committee, be sure that you know the department or university policy. Discuss the change with your advisor, who may do the legwork for you. Make the change as informally and discreetly as possible. Emphasize nonpersonal reasons for the change, such as research differences or needs. Usually the faculty member will be relieved by the change.

WRITE AND DEFEND THE PROPOSAL

Once you have prepared the preproposal, your advisor has approved it, and you have selected committee members, you are ready to begin writing the dissertation proposal. The dissertation proposal is a complete plan and template for the dissertation. The exact format of the dissertation proposal varies by department and university, but the content is consistent (Malley-Morrison et al., 2003). The dissertation proposal explains the purpose of your study and discusses it within the context of classic and current research (Cone & Foster, 2006; Mitchell, 1996; Peters, 1997). After an extensive Review of the Literature and Statement of the Problem (preliminary versions of what will become chapters 1 and 2 of the dissertation), the Methodology chapter explains how your research project will be completed, with the accompanying rationale for your choices in participants, measures, apparatuses, and procedures. The final chapter in most dissertation proposals discusses data analysis: what statistical techniques will be used to test the hypotheses. Many of the resources listed at the end of this chapter describe the elements of dissertation proposals in detail.

Once the proposal is complete and deemed acceptable by the dissertation advisor, it must be approved by the dissertation committee before data collection can begin. For most students, the dissertation proposal meeting is the first formal meeting they have with their advisor and committee members (Cone & Foster, 2006). Departments vary in how proposal meetings are scheduled; usually the student and advisor consult about dates and either the student or advisor approaches committee members to schedule the meeting. Sometimes department

Tip

Save your work early, often, and in multiple locations. Losing your dissertation proposal is a catastrophic event. Fortunately, this event happens relatively rarely, but most graduate students have heard of the friend-of-a-friend who lost the hard and electronic copy of his or her dissertation in a fire. This urban legend has other variants, like the student's laptop was in his or her car, which was then stolen, and so on. Regardless of whether these stories are true, there is one clear message: Back up your work. Save computer files periodically as you work. Back up the modified files onto a flash drive every day. You might consider keeping your files in several places, especially a place outside of your home such as on university servers. Another option is to e-mail files to yourself so that they are archived on your e-mail server. There are many ways to back up your work. Choose one or two and use them without fail.

secretaries or staff will contact all parties to schedule the proposal meeting.

Proposal meetings take two general styles, varying by department and committee composition: process oriented and evaluation oriented (Cone & Foster, 2006). The process-oriented meeting is a collaborative model in which committee members ask questions to clarify their understanding of the proposal, discuss potential problems, and suggest alternatives. The emphasis is on committee members collaborating with the student to strengthen the dissertation. Alternatively, proposal meetings that are evaluation oriented require that the student defend the proposal. The emphasis is on the student's ability to explain the theoretical and empirical rationale for the proposed study and the methodologies chosen. Evaluation-oriented meetings are conducted similarly to dissertation defense meetings. Many committees combine elements of both approaches so that proposal meetings entail collaborative and evaluative components (Cone & Foster, 2006).

Prepare for your proposal meeting by getting as much information about this meeting from your advisor as you can. How long can you expect it to last? What can you expect? What kinds of questions will you be asked? What issues does he or she expect to be raised? Review your proposal so that it is fresh in your mind and you recall its details. Arrive early to give yourself time to acclimate and feel comfortable. Generally you can expect to begin the meeting by providing a brief formal overview that explains the rationale for your study and the methodology you plan to use (Cone & Foster, 2006). Afterward, committee members will ask you questions about the rationale for your choices, for example, why you decided to use a particular measure and not another. Committee members might discuss a potential problem and ask your thoughts or whether you have considered it. Questions might center on your choice of measures, design, or procedures. Expect to be asked to explain why the topic is important, discuss statistical issues, the contribution of your work to the literature, or the applied and policy implications of your work (Cone & Foster, 2006).

This is an important opportunity for you to establish yourself as a colleague. You—and not your chair—should address the committee members' questions. Consider the range of potential questions well in advance because your responses will determine whether you pass the dissertation proposal meeting and are permitted to collect data. It is not a race. Take your time in responding to questions. If you are stumped, restate the question to give yourself time to think. It is permissible to say that you do not know once or twice during the meeting. You might add that, if they prefer, you will find the answer and get back to the committee.

Expect criticism. Your job is to think carefully to determine whether the suggestions will help your project. Committee members' suggestions vary in quality, feasibility, and ease of implementation (Cone & Foster, 2006). Consider each suggestion carefully. Take your time and think; there is no need to respond immediately. Say, "That's an interesting suggestion. I need to think about that for a moment." Sometimes another committee member may jump in with a comment or another question. Other times the room may grow still waiting for your response. First consider whether the suggestion would improve the proposed study. If the answer is yes, weigh the amount of improvement expected against the amount of work entailed. Discuss the pros and cons with your committee members. The fact that a suggestion entails a great deal of work is not a good rationale for dismissing it (Cone & Foster, 2006).

Every proposal is modified somewhat during the proposal meeting. Take notes on the discussion and whatever changes are agreed on, as well as the rationale for the changes. Your chairperson might offer to take notes, but it is always a good idea to keep your own set of notes as well. Reread the agreed-on changes to ensure that you and your committee are on the same page.

At the end of the meeting, it is common for students to be asked to leave the room while the committee discusses the proposal. When you return to the room, you will learn the fate of your proposal. Some are approved without changes. More commonly, the proposal is approved pending the agreed-on revisions. Sometimes committees will require that students revise and resubmit proposals before they are approved, sometimes entailing a second meeting, Finally, a proposal may be rejected. Outright rejection is uncommon but may occur if a project is methodologically flawed or lacks sophistication. The student is then asked to prepare another proposal. This illustrates the importance of involving your committee early in the proposal process so that you can discuss your project, get their input, and avoid nasty surprises.

The Dissertation

Selecting a committee and managing it effectively are important to your success in completing your dissertation, but the real task is in conducting the work and writing the dissertation itself. Once your dissertation proposal is approved, you are free to conduct your study. Carry out the procedures you have planned and described, and collect your data. Once you have collected your data, the fun begins: Enter the data, analyze it, and determine your findings. As a graduate student you likely have already obtained experience in conducting research. Carrying out a research study should feel somewhat familiar, if not routine. The list of suggested readings at the end of this chapter presents several resources that discuss the nuts and bolts of conducting dissertation research. Many students view conducting research as concrete, a series of challenging tasks that must be completed. Writing, however, may not come as naturally to students.

The dissertation is the largest document that a graduate student ever has written, and likely will be the largest document he or she ever will write. Many students who write papers easily are surprised to discover that the dissertation is much more difficult than any paper they have written. It is often during the writing stage of the dissertation that students find themselves adrift. The dissertation is comprehensive and entails much more than simply writing a paper. The literature review itself is very comprehensive, more so than students have encountered, and entails more variables. However, the dissertation also entails an empirical component, and students generally are not prepared for the challenges that arise in conducting independent research, many of which are not under one's control (Malley-Morrison et al., 2003). Moreover, the dissertation is a lengthy process. It will most certainly take longer than you anticipate (Malley-Morrison et al., 2003). Create a timeline for completing the dissertation in a timely fashion and stick to it.

A common error that students make in writing is that they wait until they have read everything about their topic before beginning to write. Do not try to read everything on the subject first (Peters, 1997). Read in spurts. Gather information, apply it to your project, and return to read more. It is more important that you develop your idea and plan your methodology than cover every reference (Peters, 1997). Of course, you must read to choose methodologies, but do not fall into the trap of not beginning writing because you have more to read. That will certainly prolong the dissertation.

Perfectionism is another way of prolonging the dissertation. Bury the fantasy of creating the ideal dissertation and simply write. No dissertation is ideal, nor is any journal article or book. Write well, but write for your audience—your dissertation committee—and no one else. Your sole intent is to communicate your project to your committee in a way they approve. Keep that intent in mind and do not be swayed by ambitions of perfection. Just write.

Expect to go through many drafts. Even after you feel satisfied with what you have written, your committee will request changes. If you let your work sit for a week, you will find that even a chapter you thought you were satisfied with requires revision. Also, do not expect your later drafts to take less time than your earlier drafts, because in the final stages of writing you will incorporate committee comments, proofread, and likely find many small revisions that you would like to make. These later drafts will take more time than you anticipate. Seek input as you write to ensure that you and your committee members are on the same page.

Prepare a progress report to keep the committee informed of your work. The progress report often is not a formal meeting or document; it is not a recognized step in most departments. But creating an interim report is a useful informal task. After analyzing data, write it up as a Results chapter, and include a preliminary Discussion chapter that explains your findings within the context of the literature and your hypotheses, as well as strengths and limitations of your findings. Note that *preliminary* does not mean rough. Compose a polished report and submit it to your advisor for feedback on your findings and interpretations. Once you and your advisor agree on the content, submit the progress report to the committee and seek one-on-one meetings with each committee member. Obtaining early feedback will help you to revise your project and prepare for the dissertation defense. Because the reputation of the department and university is at stake with every dissertation, expect your dissertation to be rigorously reviewed (Malley-Morrison et al., 2003). The more that your committee members know about your project and the more that you know about their concerns, the less likely you will be surprised at your dissertation defense.

MANAGE THE DISSERTATION COMMITTEE

The most effective way of managing your dissertation committee and minimizing problems is to understand their expectations of you (Peters, 1997). The committee expects that you will develop the capacity to do independent work because the dissertation is an independent project. Although the committee consults and oversees your work, the ultimate responsibility for decision making and carrying out decisions lies with you. As an independent scholar, you will be expected to act without being prodded by your committee to make timely progress, to maintain contact and inform them of your progress, and to be honest about your progress (Peters, 1997). If you are experiencing difficulty, your committee will expect you to be forthcoming, explain it, and ask for help.

Dissertation committees expect students to be responsive to their advice (Peters, 1997). Most people find it very frustrating to make carefully considered suggestions and comments that are ignored. Whether to take the committee's suggestions is obviously your call, but regardless of your decision, you must give evidence of having considered the advice—and be able to explain and defend your choice. It is a process of give and take. Give in on what does not harm your study. If you give some then, you are likely to encounter less resistance if you dig in your heels on something that you think is important. Committees expect students to be friendly, cheerful, and, above all else, motivated to get the job done. Losing motivation will alienate your committee and will make them wonder why they agreed to help.

In addition to understanding what is expected of you, a proactive way of managing your committee early on is to adopt a professional stance, keeping your committee involved and informed as colleagues. One of the most important ways of ensuring that you are not surprised by committee members' suggestions and evaluations of your work is to involve them early on. Draw committee members into the dissertation process as soon as you can; you want them to understand your dissertation and provide input so that they feel part of the process and identify with your success (Peters, 1997). This makes the dissertation a collaborative process—all have a stake—which ensures that the dissertation proceeds smoothly (Martin, 2001). Present your dissertation as you go along (Peters, 1997). Distribute a polished copy of each chapter as you complete it and solicit early input and feedback.

Throughout the dissertation phase, keep in contact with committee members. Schedule regular meetings with each committee member to provide updates on your progress, describe challenges that you are facing, and solicit their input (Mitchell, 1996). The purpose of these meetings is to build a relationship within which problems can be resolved as they arise (Peters, 1997). No dissertation runs completely smoothly from beginning to end because no research project is that clear-cut. Even faculty projects meet challenges and sometimes completely derail. Aim to meet with committee members regularly, sometimes one more regularly than others. For example, you might meet with the statistics expert more often while you are conducting analyses and you might meet with the general expert every other month. The meeting schedule will vary by your needs and the committee member's availability.

Tip

Maintain contact with all of your committee members even if you or they are not on campus by periodically sending a short e-mail to the faculty member, to "say hello and touch base," give a brief update on your progress (a couple of sentences on your current activities), ask a quick question, and so on.

Document everything and circulate reports to keep everyone informed of the project and your progress. Keep detailed notes for all of your meetings, including topics discussed, decisions reached, and drafts submitted or returned (Mitchell, 1996). Detailed notes will protect you from misrecollections, misunderstandings, and forgotten comments. Whenever you meet with your advisor or committee, take notes and write a memo that reflects your understanding of the meeting and action to take. After individual meetings, send the committee member your memo and ask for input or corrections. Then ask whether you can distribute it to the rest of the committee. Do not distribute the memo without speaking with the committee member and obtaining corrections so as to not misrepresent his or her comments and alienate him or her. Be sure that any decisions made at full committee meetings are spelled out clearly and agreed to by all. In addition, make regular written progress reports to your committee every month or so (Peters, 1997) to keep them in the loop and prevent them from forgetting about you or your project.

Recognize that you will sometimes have conflicting suggestions to reconcile. It is common for committee members to offer very different suggestions on how to improve the study. One strategy is to respond to those suggestions that you can that do not entail major changes in the study and that do not conflict with each other (Mitchell, 1996). Sometimes if faculty see some changes—their changes—they forget about others. If none of the suggestions radically improves your project, be prepared to explain your decision. Remember that generally, the more that you fight your committee, the longer it will take you to complete your dissertation and graduate (Mitchell, 1996). So pick your battles.

DEFEND THE DISSERTATION

Before you can defend your dissertation, you must produce the complete and final draft of the dissertation. Once you have completed the progress report, much of your dissertation is already written. Update the Review of the Literature and Statement of the Problem to include recent research, comments from committee members, and your findings (e.g., update the

Tip

Sometimes conflict and animosity among committee members will be unstated but instead expressed through comments on your project. Faculty might express conflicting suggestions, argue about aspects of the proposal, and engage in a tug of war with your proposal as the rope (Peters, 1997). In many cases you can proceed through the meeting and dissertation process without hassles other than a bruised ego and extra frustration. If the conflicts are preventing your progress, in unusual circumstances, that is, consult your advisor. He or she may be able to contact the committee members and resolve the issue. If your advisor cannot resolve the issue informally, then perhaps a full committee meeting is in order, based on your advisor's suggestion, and perhaps the committee can find a way around academic differences.

Participants section of the Methodology chapter). Revise the Results and Discussion chapters in accordance with the comments you received from committee members in response to the progress report. Most departments require a Conclusions chapter in which the student draws broad conclusions about the work at hand and considers the larger implications of the work for the field, application, and policy. Update appendixes and references. Finally, write the summary abstract. Take care to include as many relevant details as you can so that a reader may grasp the work and findings by reading the summary alone. Sometimes dissertation committee members or visitors enter the dissertation defense meeting after having read only the summary.

The dissertation defense, sometimes called an *oral defense* or *oral exam,* occurs after you have analyzed your data and written your dissertation. During the dissertation defense, you defend your choice of topic, design, methodology, and statistical analyses; your implementation of the study and analyses; and your interpretation of the results and write-up of the project. The dissertation defense is often a very formal meeting because it is the last hurdle to completing the doctorate (Cone & Foster, 2006). It is a coming-out rite of passage in which students join the community of scholars (Rudestam & Newton, 2007).

First, expect to present your dissertation to your committee. Often students present their dissertations as a colloquium to the department, lasting up to 45 minutes (Rudestam & Newton, 2007). Alternatively, or in addition, you may present a 15-minute summary of your work to the committee. Chapter 11 discusses some of the nuts and bolts of presentations. The summary is followed by questions and comments from committee members designed to determine whether you understand

and can articulate your findings and can discuss them from a scientific perspective. The committee will expect you to discuss your work within the context of other research and to do so intelligently.

As with the proposal meeting, committee members are likely to ask challenging questions. If so, stick to your position and respectfully refute the argument (Peters, 1997). Again, if someone asks a question that you cannot answer, say that you do not know, and if the answer later comes to you, relay it (Peters, 1997). Another tactic is to give a partial answer and then ask another committee member for his or her thoughts on the issue, which can buy you time or take the conversation in a whole other direction (Peters, 1997).

Most students approach the dissertation defense with at least some anxiety. The best antidote for anxiety is preparation. How do you prepare for the dissertation defense? The strategies for preparing for the proposal defense, described earlier, also apply here. In addition, consider the following:

- *Play devil's advocate with yourself.* Know your study inside and out, and identify as many weaknesses as possible and develop points to counter them (Rossman, 2002). Consider potential arguments and prepare counterarguments. Consider different theoretical explanations, weaknesses of measures, alternative designs, threats to validity, and alternative statistical analyses and interpretations. What are the potential holes in your work?
- *Hold a mock defense.* Assemble a group of graduate students and perhaps a faculty member to act as a mock committee to judge how well you defend your dissertation. Often questions that arise from student mock defense committees are more challenging than those from the dissertation committee (Rossman, 2002).
- *Attend dissertation defense meetings.* Observe the process firsthand for pointers on how to handle yourself.
- *Change your perspective.* Take control of the meeting psychologically by remembering that you are being socialized into the world of scholars (Cone & Foster, 2006). View the meeting as a discussion among peers rather than a formal examination. Remember that you know more about your project than anyone. Focus on ways of communicating that knowledge.

If you have kept your committee members in the loop and consulted with them throughout the process, there should be no big surprises. Take notes at the defense meeting; your advisor may offer to, but regardless, take your own set of notes about comments and suggested revisions. The most probable outcome is a pass with minor revisions. Most students have to complete at least minor revisions in response to comments from committee members (Rudestam & Newton, 2007), including clarifications of methodological details, adding references, and so on. If so, complete these as soon as possible. Once the revisions are complete, you will need to prepare several copies of your dissertation for submission to the graduate school and library.

The dissertation is a very large project that can seem insurmountable. Completing the dissertation—moving from preproposal to proposal to carrying out the research and analyzing the findings to constructing the progress report to writing the complete dissertation—is a lengthy process that requires regular and consistent effort. You will make progress on the dissertation if you apply the general principles of writing and working efficiently discussed in chapter 4. Aim to write for at least a short period daily and for more sustained periods regularly. Write to a schedule so that you learn to flex your writing muscles at will. A modest and steady pace will sustain your progress in dissertation writing over the duration of your work and ensure that you make consistent and reliable progress on your dissertation. Remember that your goal is to complete something that satisfies the graduate program's requirements in as little time as possible. In the case of the doctoral dissertation, perfection is not possible, but *good* is enough.

Recommended Reading

Bolker, J. (1998). *Writing your dissertation in fifteen minutes a day: A guide to starting, revising, and finishing your doctoral thesis.* New York: Owl Books.

Cone, J. D., & Foster, S. L. (2006). *Dissertations and theses from start to finish: Psychology and related fields* (2nd ed.). Washington, DC: American Psychological Association.

Heppner, P. P., & Heppner, M. J. (2003). *Writing and publishing your thesis, dissertation, and research: A guide for students in the helping professions.* Belmont, CA: Wadsworth.

Leong, F. T. (2007). *The psychology research handbook: A guide for graduate students and research assistants.* Thousand Oaks, CA: Sage.

Locke, L. F. (1999). *Proposals that work: A guide for planning dissertations and grant proposals.* Thousand Oaks, CA: Sage.

Rudestam, K. E., & Newton, R. R. (2007). *Surviving your dissertation: A comprehensive guide to content and process* (3rd ed.). Thousand Oaks, CA: Sage.

Finding Your Professional Voice

11

During the graduate school years students are socialized as psychologists and thereby learn and internalize the norms and culture of the discipline. The next step in professional socialization requires that students interact with others outside of their department and university, with members of the profession as a whole. It is only by interacting with other psychologists that they begin to find their own professional voice as practitioners and scholars.

Professional Associations and Societies

One of the simplest steps in cultivating a professional voice is to become an active member of a professional organization. Since psychology's inception, psychologists have organized into professional associations that promote the clinical, research, and personal interests of psychologists (Dodgen, Fowler, & Williams-Nickelson, 2003). Professional associations seek to further knowledge in their fields, keep members informed about such advances, provide members with professional development resources and opportunities, and offer a range of services to members and the public (Fowler, 1999).

Participating in these organizations offers many opportunities for personal and professional development. There are a great many psychological associations; Exhibit 11.1 lists a sampling of professional associations in psychology (Dodgen et al., 2003).

All psychological associations have a mission statement that guides their activities. For example, consider the missions of the American Psychological Association (APA) and the Association for Psychological Science (APS). The mission of the APA (http://www.apa.org) is to advance the science and profession of psychology, promote psychologists' professional development, and disseminate the findings of psychological research and practice as a means of promoting health and human welfare. Similarly, the APS (http://www.psychologicalscience.org) seeks to "promote, protect, and advance the interests of scientifically oriented psychology in research, application, teaching, and the improvement of human welfare." Most psychological associations are oriented toward one or more of these goals (Dodgen et al., 2003). These goals are achieved in a variety of ways as described in the next section.

BENEFITS OF PARTICIPATING IN PROFESSIONAL ASSOCIATIONS

Psychological associations fulfill their mission to advance knowledge about the science and profession of psychology through information sharing (Dodgen et al., 2003). Most professional organizations sponsor annual or biennial conferences that permit psychologists to disseminate and learn about recent findings in practice and research. Many psychological organizations contribute to the literature within the discipline by publishing journals wherein psychologists may share their expertise in

EXHIBIT 11.1

Professional Associations in Psychology: An Incomplete Listing

American Psychological Association
Association for Psychological Science
Canadian Psychological Association
Regional psychological associations (Eastern, New England, Southeastern, Southwestern, and Western Psychological Association)
U.S. state psychological associations for all 50 states
International Psychological Association
International Council of Psychologists
International Association of Applied Psychology
American Psychological Association of Graduate Students
Psychometric Society
National Association of School Psychologists
Association of Practicing Psychologists
International Union of Psychological Science

research and applied activities, disseminate research findings, and benefit from the expertise of others. Most professional organizations publish newsletters containing information about the organization's activities, news items, and articles on practical topics of interest to members. For example, recent issues of the *APA Monitor*, the monthly magazine of the APA, contains articles on topics related to current events, new research, and professional development issues for psychologists of all ages. Professional associations also award fellowships, scholarships, and grants to members to advance their professional development.

In addition to providing opportunities for psychologists to remain current in the field, professional associations provide a means of helping psychologists develop and maintain a sense of professional identity through contact with other psychologists (Dodgen et al., 2003). Opportunities for professional and personal development through interaction with colleagues abound in graduate school but are less common afterward, especially for practitioners who are no longer immersed in academia. Many early career psychologists express the feeling of being isolated from the field at large after graduation. Professional associations provide opportunities for practicing psychologists to come together, consider issues of relevance to them, and network with psychologists who live and work nearby or have topical interests. Interacting with colleagues helps early career psychologists develop bonds with other psychologists and develop their own professional identity (Dodgen et al., 2003). Networking opportunities advance careers because it is through connections with other professionals that the early career psychologist will receive invitations to present research, serve as a reviewer for conferences and journals, and participate in committees that oversee the work of professional associations.

HOW TO GET INVOLVED IN PROFESSIONAL ASSOCIATIONS

Although the benefits of joining a professional organization are great, there is much more to be gained. There are many ways for you to get involved in the leadership of professional organizations. Most organizations have multiple boards, committees, and councils that govern their activities. All of these are leadership positions; some are elected by members, others are elected by a subgroup within the organization, and others are appointed by leaders of the organization (Dodgen et al., 2003). For example, the APA has many committees and subcommittees that govern the association and its activities, such as the Board of Convention Affairs, Board of Educational Affairs, Elections Committee, Ethics Committee, Finance Committee, Membership Committee, Committee on Accreditation, Committee on Professional Practice and Standards, and more. Many committees have slots designated for graduate students, so it is never too early to get involved in professional associations. For example, many APA divisions (oriented toward a content area or activity of psychology; e.g., Society of Clinical Psychology, Society for the Psychological Study of Men and Masculinity, and the Society for the Teaching of Psychology) place increasing emphasis on student representation; at least 23 divisions have student representatives, and some hold voting power in the division's executive committee. These are opportunities for students to develop unique skill sets, such as conference planning, organizational management, and organizational finance.

Many professional associations also have graduate student organizations. For example, the American Psychological Association of Graduate Students (APAGS) is a graduate student organization within the APA that is a governance body that assists in shaping APA policy. Graduate students may seek involvement in the graduate student divisions and organizations of various organizations; despite the "student" label, many graduate student divisions, committees, and organizations wield power within the larger organization. For example, the APAGS was founded in 1988 and over the past 2 decades has become the largest organization within the APA, larger than any of the 52 APA divisions (Dodgen et al., 2003).

As the APAGS has grown, its activities have expanded and it has become well integrated into the APA. The APAGS offers many opportunities to get involved, develop leadership skills, network, and carve out an identity as an emerging psychologist. Some positions within the APAGS are appointed (typically by the current APAGS president). Students may run for any elected position on any of the APAGS committees, which largely parallel the committee structure of the APA. The APAGS also appoint students to participate in a variety of APA committees, including the important governing bodies of the APA, the Board of Directors and the Council of Representatives, which gives students the opportunity to work alongside psychologists who are leaders in the field.

Professional Conferences

Most professional associations within psychology sponsor conferences, either yearly or every other year. The two largest of these conferences are held annually by the APA and APS. Attending a professional conference is something that every graduate should experience, ideally more than once, because it is another method of socialization into the discipline.

WHY ATTEND PROFESSIONAL CONFERENCES?

There is much to learn and observe at a conference. Conferences are the place to learn about cutting-edge research before it is published in journals. Conferences are places to find out what's hot and what's not in your field. At conferences you will observe the various debates and controversies firsthand: see major scholars discuss their work and rival scholars comment on each other's work. Conferences offer excellent opportunities to network with faculty as well as other students (Reis, 1997). Attending conferences is an efficient way to meet interesting people—some of the best minds in the field—and participate in discussions that shape the field. Multiple components of your professional preparation and socialization can be carried out at conferences, including learning, discussing, and presenting (Reis, 1997).

As much as there is to gain from conferences, they often are expensive. They entail travel to a different city and involve the expenses of airfare or a road trip, lodging, registration, and meals. All of these can add up quickly, but these challenges should not keep students from attending conferences. Most graduate students save money by attending conferences together, sharing rooms, and researching affordable menu options. Many departments offer at least modest funding to support student travel, and many universities offer additional sources of funding through offices of student life, graduate associations, and more. Ask around and you may locate funding for part or even all of your trip.

HOW TO ATTEND A CONFERENCE

Conferences can range from as few as a hundred or so attendees at very specialized or local events, such as a rural state's psychological association meeting, to thousands of attendees at large meetings, such as the APA's annual convention, which can host up to 20,000 attendees. Large conferences can seem overwhelming because it is easy to be intimidated by well-known speakers and attendees (Reis, 1997), but they also offer tremendous opportunities for professional development.

As Reis (1997) explained, one way of managing being overwhelmed is to play a game with yourself, asking yourself various questions as you sit in on talks and observe the interactions around you:

- What can I learn during this conference?
- What learning opportunities are unique to this conference?
- If I were giving this talk, what would I do differently?
- Can I do this? What can I do to make myself ready to give talks at professional conferences?
- What professors' behaviors should I emulate?
- What are the characteristics of effective presentations?
- How do presenters deal with hostile questions? Is there a better way that they could have addressed the questioner?
- Are there recent alumni at this conference whom I can network with?

- How does politics influence career success? How are faculty gathering and what is happing in these interactions? What are possible benefits of such interactions?

At the end of every lecture or panel discussion, questions are solicited from the audience. If you have a relevant question, ask it. Many students wonder how the audience members think up such interesting questions and how they remember the details of the talk. It requires strategy. Keep notes. Jot questions and comments as you think of them during the talk. Sometimes at particularly large meetings you might feel like you can only speak if you are a leader in the field or have a brilliant comment or question to share. Many bright but wary students do not ask questions. Fight the fear and shyness and jump into the discussion. Do this, however, only if you have concentrated throughout the presentation and are certain that your question was not already answered (Arney, 2003). You might find that a big-shot psychologist asks your question before you have the chance. Rather than get bummed at being scooped, revel in the fact that you thought of the same question as Dr. Big Shot.

> As one student recalls, "When I attended my first conference, the American Psychological Association Annual Convention, I was amazed. Thousand of psychologists attended presentations, and it was great to feel like I was part of the profession. It made me remember what I went to graduate school for and helped me see what I'm striving to be."

At social gatherings, talk with others who share your research interests. If you see a speaker whose work you find interesting, briefly introduce yourself and ask a question. Describe your work briefly (in 2 minutes or less). Listen to others explain their work and ask relevant questions. Do not restrict your interactions to faculty; talk with graduate students because they will be your colleagues as early career psychologists within the next few years. Think before you speak: Be kind and complimentary, and avoid negative comments about anyone, especially those with whom you are not personally acquainted. Although the conference may be large, the world of psychology is a small one. Finally, it goes without saying that you will be hypervigilant of your alcohol consumption at social events to avoid the slightest tipsiness.

Networking

Throughout this book I have discussed how other people can have an impact on your success in graduate school. Guess what? Relationships with others will influence your success throughout your professional career as well. Good scholarly or practitioner work is not sufficient to guarantee your employment and success after graduate school. When employment positions or other professional opportunities open up, such as practicum, internship, and research collaboration opportunities, decision makers are more likely to choose known entities—friends, acquaintances, and other contacts—over others, all things being equal (Bloom, Karp, & Cohen, 1998).

NETWORKING OPPORTUNITIES

Your first important networking source is your mentor. Develop close ties with your mentor and you will become privy to his or her network. Graduate students are often seen as progeny of their mentors (Bloom et al., 1998), so take advantage of the relationships that your mentor has worked hard to establish (but be careful to do no harm!). Faculty within your department are another part of your network. Establish collaborative and well-functioning relationships with faculty in your department. When opportunities arise, they will be more likely to keep you in mind and pass your name along. Also remember that faculty gossip among themselves, so poor interactions with one faculty member are likely to be communicated to others in his or her network.

Most departments and universities periodically invite scholars to give colloquia addresses or seminars. These are opportunities to get to know experts in the field. Read the visiting scholar's work beforehand, and if you are interested, then try to talk with him or her after the seminar or during the social hour that usually accompanies it.

Conferences are a wonderful opportunity to network, as I have discussed. The atmosphere at most conferences is congenial and supportive of chitchat. It is easy to start conversations while waiting in line, after a talk, or during a social hour. Do not stand in a corner by yourself between sessions—mingle. Visit poster sessions and talk with researchers about their work. Ask a question, share a comment: Everyone wants to talk about their research. Do not confine your networking to established psychologists; talk with graduate students too because they will be the new wave of early career psychologists to emerge. Establish contacts now, and you will find them to be useful later in your career with regard to collaborations, recommendations, and other forms of assistance.

There are other ways in which you can interact with the scientific community (Bloom et al., 1998). If you read a particularly interesting article, write an e-mail to the authors with comments or questions (remember to keep such e-mails short as most professionals are quite busy). If your work intersects with that of a psychologist whom you admire, send a reprint to him or her. Ask questions when they arise. However, be sincere in your questions and comments. When others contact you—and they will—offer the same assistance that you would expect.

NETWORKING STRATEGIES

It may not come easily, but networking is not necessarily difficult. I have already discussed several approaches. The gist of networking is simple: Talk with people. Many students find networking challenging because it entails a certain amount of self-promotion, which goes against the grain of many scientists and practitioners (Bloom et al., 1998). Part of succeeding as a professional is becoming an assertive promoter of your work. Training directors, grant directors, and job search committees need to know who you are and what you do—and, especially, what you do well. Successful professionals are go-getters who learn how to network with confidence (Bloom et al., 1998). Easier said than done. Try these strategies to ensure relatively pain-free networking:

- Create a 15- to 20-second networking speech that says something about your work, experience, or interests. Do not introduce yourself as simply a graduate student without saying something more that expresses something interesting and memorable about yourself and may spur a conversation with the other person. Instead of introducing yourself as, "Joe Smith, a graduate student," for example, include more, such as, "I'm Joe Smith and I'm a graduate student of personality development at XU. I'm interested in how personality changes in adulthood."
- Turn the attention on the other person. People love to talk about themselves, so asking what they do will start a conversation. One approach is to ask people how they got into their line of work.
- Never put others down or gossip. It can be easy to fall into a conversation in which you talk negatively about someone. Avoid it at all costs because it will always come back to haunt you and will affect your listener's perception of you.
- Maintain connections by following up with an e-mail or call every few months. Congratulate them on their accomplishments, sending an e-mail on seeing a new article published, for example.

Contributing to the Scholarly Literature

Publications and presentations are the currency of academia. Your scholarly reputation rests on the quality of your scholarly work. Publications influence career opportunities, invitations to collaborate with other scholars, and funding opportunities (McCabe & McCabe, 2000). Most research projects are disseminated to the world in two steps: They are presented at professional conferences, and they are then written up and submitted to journals. Both of these forms of scholarship are subject to peer review, examination by several experts who review its merits.

PARTICIPATING IN PEER REVIEW

An important way to develop a sense of professional identity is to get involved in the peer review process for conference and journal article submissions. Some journals, such as the *Journal of Social Issues, Cultural Diversity and Ethnic Minority Psychology, Political Psychology,* and *Representative Social Research in Psychology* (Dingfelder, 2005) reserve slots on their editorial boards for students. Editors often advertise the availability of editorial slots or review opportunities in the first few or last few pages of each journal. Most of these editorial positions require that students formally apply or be nominated. However, you do not need to be member of an editorial board to get peer review experience.

There are many informal routes to becoming a reviewer for a journal or conference. Consult with your mentor. Offer to assist your mentor with his or her reviews; with the journal editor's permission, your mentor might pass along reviewing tasks. Your mentor may be able to put you in contact with a conference organizer who needs help reviewing proposals.

If you have the opportunity to review a paper, do it well and return the review in a timely fashion. If you are unsure what your review should look like (a common question), ask for sample reviews. A journal editor or your mentor may be willing to provide students with sections of reviews that exemplify particularly helpful or unhelpful comments. Seek feedback from your mentor about reviews to ensure that you are balancing criticism with collegiality.

In assessing the paper in question, consider the following (McKarney, 2001):

- What is the purpose and conclusion of the paper? Is the work original?
- Is the research of high quality?
- Are the findings enough to justify publication (i.e., is there enough new information)?
- What are strengths of the paper?
- What are weaknesses and limitations of the paper?
- Did the study achieve its stated goals?
- Is the methodology clear and pertinent to the question at hand?
- Do the statistical analyses make sense given the question?
- Can you follow the results, tables, and illustrations?
- Do you have any editorial/presentation suggestions? Is there a way to improve the paper?
- Are all the references pertinent? Any additions?

Be fair to authors by keeping your own strengths and weaknesses in mind. For example, avoid making comments on statistical analyses that you do not understand, especially if you are not strong in statistics. Sometimes, however, not understanding a section of an article, statistics or otherwise, is the author's fault. Always offer constructive comments. Critique specific aspects of the paper and be as constructive as possible. Be honest and try to help the author by making specific questions, comments, and suggestions. Write the review that you, yourself, would find most helpful.

CONFERENCE PRESENTATIONS

Conference presentations permit you to disseminate your findings to groups of professionals, receive their questions and feedback, and then incorporate that feedback into your work before preparing the final paper to submit to a journal (Cone & Foster, 2006). Conference presentations provide opportunities for feedback as well as exposure.

There are many presentation outlets ranging in formality from informal discussions with colleagues over coffee to departmental colloquia to presentations at state, national, and international conferences (Cone & Foster, 2006). Where you submit your research depends on a variety of practical and professional factors, including the location of the conference, cost of attending, whether it is general or specific to a given subfield of psychology, prestige, and range of conference attendees (e.g., academics, practitioners; McCabe & McCabe, 2000). If you are inclined toward an academic career, submit your work to national conferences such as the annual conventions of the APS and APA or to meetings held by discipline-specific groups such as the Society for Research in Child Development (SRCD). You can learn about the timing of these conferences by examining the publications of each organization. Information about conferences typically appears in newsletters. The Web sites of professional organizations usually list conference dates and locations as well as provide information about how to submit papers for review.

Submitting an Abstract

An important rule to remember regarding submitting work to conferences is that submissions are due long before the conference. For example, the APA holds its convention in August each year, yet submissions must be received by early December. Plan ahead if you choose to present your research at a national conference. Most conferences adopt a variety of presentation formats. The most common are the poster presentation and paper/symposium.

Poster presentations are best for disseminating preliminary or pilot findings (Cohen & Greco, 2003). Present your project on poster board: The purpose, method, results, and conclusions are summarized clearly and succinctly on a poster board. Poster sessions vary in duration from 1 to 2 hours. The researcher must be present at the poster to discuss the work with interested parties. Poster presentations are less formal presentations than others because the discussion comprises one-on-one conversations. Posters sessions usually are themed, so that all posters displayed have a common theme, such as personality psychology or biological psychology, and posters are displayed in a large room. The audience walks through and talks one-on-one with researchers. Conference reviewers accept more poster presentations than oral presentations.

Most conferences consider oral presentations only as part of a larger package, a symposium. The symposium is the most common format for oral presentation, in which several researchers present on a common topic. All of the oral presentations within a symposium are submitted together; all of the presentations that compose the symposium are collectively accepted or rejected. Symposia vary in format, but typically each presentation is allotted 12 to 20 minutes depending on time constraints. Each paper represents a different viewpoint or facet of the topic. The chair of the symposium is responsible for compiling submissions and submitting the symposium abstract to the conference. During the symposium, the chair introduces speakers, might conduct a presentation, and, at the end, may summarize the symposium and moderate as the audience asks questions. Sometimes the symposium will include a discussant who offers remarks on each paper, discusses how the symposium presentations intersect with the overall literature, and draws broad-based conclusions.

Preparing a good conference submission is challenging because only an abstract is submitted, not the entire paper. Good abstracts are clear and easily comprehended by someone who is not familiar with your work. The cardinal rule is to adhere to the instructions for submissions, including format, content, and word limit (Cohen & Greco, 2003; McCabe & McCabe, 2000). The abstract, typically 300 to 500 words, explains the research study in one or two pages, including a rationale for your research, the methodology, results, and reference to the implications of the work. About 60% of the space should be allocated toward describing methods and results because these are the elements that the program committee will focus on in evaluating the merit of the abstract (Cone & Foster, 2006). Sometimes experienced researchers will submit an abstract that includes only preliminary data, stating that additional data are being collected and will be presented. Submitting research prior to analyzing the data, however, is risky. What if the results are contrary to those predicted (Cohen & Greco, 2003)? Never take this route because it is better to not present than to present work that is of low quality (Cohen & Greco, 2003)

Allow time to write the abstract. The short length can be deceptive. Composing an effective abstract is difficult. It goes without saying to not wait until the day the abstract is due to begin writing. If you have coauthors, allow time for multiple drafts that includes time for them to review the abstract and add comments and revisions. Follow the instructions for submitting your abstract; failing to do so might result in rejection. Most conferences use electronic submission. Learn about how to submit your abstract well before the deadline. Remember that Web pages and submission systems might be overloaded with submissions on the day of the deadline, so submit your work ahead of time to avoid problems with the server as well as prevent potential problems with your own system from interfering with your submission (McCabe & McCabe, 2000).

Poster Presentations

The task in preparing a poster is to clearly represent a research project in a concise visual format. The poster parallels the organization of formal journal articles, including the title, abstract, introduction and purpose, methods, results, discussion and conclusion, and references (Cone & Foster, 2006). Material organized by bullet points (brief phrases rather than lengthy sentences) is often easy to read and quickly comprehend (Cohen & Greco, 2003). Allocate a page to your abstract; one to two to the introduction and rationale; two pages for the method; one or two pages for the results, supplemented by no more than three tables and figures; and one to two pages for discussion. Use a consistent large font (visible from 3 feet away) throughout. The low-tech approach to preparing a poster is to print these pages and attach each to a colored poster board or even construction paper that permits a one-half- or three-quarter-inch border around each page and attach to the large conference poster board (typically 4 feet × 8 feet). If funds and resources are available, print your presentation out as a poster.

Tip Bring plenty of tacks and other materials to hang your poster just in case there are not enough supplies.

Poster presentations are grouped by theme so that numerous projects on a given theme (e.g., health psychology) are presented at once within a 1-hour or 1½-hour period. Sessions are booked back to back, so you will have about 10 minutes or less to hang your poster. Arrive early to find your designated poster area. Bring tacks to hang your poster in case your stand does not have enough. Have handouts available—at least 50 for a national conference—as well as paper to record contact information for audience members who would like more information.

Presenters are expected to stand by their posters throughout the session and discuss them with audience members as they pass through the presentation area. You never know who will pass by and take interest in your poster. Use this as an opportunity to meet psychologists and other students and expand your professional network.

Oral Presentations

The abstract accepted by the conference review committee is an outline and basis for the paper presentation (McCabe & McCabe, 2000). As you prepare your presentation, consider the overall message: What is the one take-home message the audience should leave with? Write the presentation to convey that message.

A large part of an effective presentation lies in the overheads. Convert much of your abstract to overheads, adding and eliminating detail when needed, so that your project is explained clearly and succinctly. Use your overheads to organize your talk. Avoid excessive information. It is tempting to tell the audience all that you know, but that is overwhelming. Overheads should enhance your presentation. If they are so detailed and include so much superfluous material, they will confuse or bore the audience who then may focus so closely on the overheads that they do not listen to you (Cohen & Greco, 2003; McCabe & McCabe, 2000). With regard to format, keep overheads simple with few colors used consistently and a large font. You do not want the overheads to draw attention away from your presentation. The audience will strain to read a tiny font and will miss out on your message.

How many overheads are enough? The general rule is 1½ overheads per minute, or about 15 for a 10-minute talk (McCabe & McCabe, 2000). Simple overheads such as photos or phrases might take 30 seconds each, but more complex slides illustrating procedures or data analyses will require up to 2 minutes. Organize your talk with overheads as follows: two for the introduction, one for the purpose, one to three for the methods, three to five for the results, and one to two for conclusions (McCabe & McCabe, 2000).

A cardinal sin in making oral presentations is to run over your allotted time. One solution is to always run early: If 12 minutes are allotted, plan a 10-minute talk because presentations are nearly always longer than intended. A 10-minute talk is difficult because you have lots to convey in a short time. The organization must be tight without overwhelming the audience with too many details or too quick a delivery pace (McCabe & McCabe, 2000). Prepare your overheads first, and then use the overheads to prepare your comments. If you work from your overheads, you will be more likely to speak directly about them and emphasize important ideas, reducing extraneous comments that eat up your presentation time.

In addition to preparing excellent overheads and preparing your talk alongside those overheads, a critical component in your success as a speaker is practice. Prepare your overheads weeks ahead of time and practice presenting them; revise them as needed, and continue to practice. Try to present your work with minimal notes. If you work from your overheads, you will find that you require few notes to support your presentation. Practice speaking slowly because people tend to talk faster when they are nervous (McCabe & McCabe, 2000). Practice as often as possible because it reduces anxiety and improves your performance. Be sure to practice in front of others, such as graduate students who can provide feedback and ask questions that will prepare you for the question-and-answer period, which is often feared by novice and even more advanced speakers. Sometimes good presentations are sabotaged when the presenter cannot answer simple questions from the audience.

Tip

If you must use notes to give your oral presentation, write them on printouts of your overheads, with two or three slides per page. Then write your notes on each slide. This way you'll view your notes reminding you of what you'd like to say along with your slides.

Question-and-answer sessions are typically conducted at the end of a presentation. It is an opportunity to correct misinterpretations, clarify points, get feedback on work, and interact with audience members. The most important thing to remember during question-and-answer sessions is that you are not under attack and there is no need to defend yourself. Discuss ideas, and separate yourself from your work. Similar to the question-and-answer period during the proposal and dissertation defense, it is essential that you maintain a professional demeanor and are not defensive. Attempt to treat all questions—even ones that might seem insulting, aggressive, or objectionable—as legitimate and well intentioned and respond with poise (McCabe & McCabe, 2000). Never make patronizing remarks or answer in way that makes the questioner feel or appear incompetent or foolish (Cohen & Greco, 2003).

If you are presenting in a large room, restate questions so that all audience members can hear. If the question is complicated or unclear, you can ask the person to repeat or rephrase to buy time. Just as in the dissertation defense, it is okay to pause and organize your thoughts before answering. Prepare for the range of questions beforehand, and you will be prepared for much of what you hear. Several kinds of difficult situations can be expected. How do you handle the challenging situations that may arise (Cohen & Greco, 2003)?

- *Unanswerable questions.* Remark that it is a good question and admit your unfamiliarity with the question. Ask the questioner for his or her thoughts. Make a guess based on the literature and acknowledge that it is a guess.
- *Irrelevant questions.* Avoid digressing from the topic; move on to the next question. Offer to talk about it after the session.
- *Nonsensical questions or novice questions.* Offer a brief explanation and move on. Never insult the questioner. Offer to discuss it in more detail later after the session.
- *Offensive questions.* Avoid becoming defensive. Never repeat offensive language. Explain your perspective and acknowledge differences as well as larger debates in the field as a whole.
- *Vague questions.* Ask for clarification. Restate the question in more simple terms.

Oral presentations are a challenge to students and professionals alike. Effective presentations are the result of planning, practice, and basic presentation skills. The section on job talks in chapter 13 offers additional information on making oral presentations.

JOURNAL ARTICLES

At this point in your academic career you are well aware that publications will help your career. Publishing in scholarly journals is especially valued because journals use peer review. Every article that is published in a given journal has undergone extensive review by several experts in the field (Kazdin, 2003). Publishing your research in scholarly journals attests to its merits.

Selecting a Journal

One of the most important parts of the process of preparing manuscripts is selecting the journal. This should be the first step in writing the manuscript because the choice of journal may influence how to present data because there are often subtle stylistic differences among journals. Selecting a journal is a challenging task but for a good reason: There is no shortage of journals to which to submit manuscripts. The APA publishes journals in nearly all areas of psychology. Many more journals are published by other professional societies, such as the APS, SRCD, and so on. In psychology, journals published by large professional associations, such as APA, APS, and SRCD, are more prestigious than stand-alone journals that are not affiliated with a professional organization. Prestige is accompanied by high rejection rates, as high as 80% to 90% for some journals (Cone & Foster, 2006).

As you consider journals, turn to those that published the articles that you used in your own research. If many of the studies reviewed in the introduction come from a particular journal, consider it as a potential outlet for your work. A useful resource for locating publishing outlets is PSYCLINE (http://www.psycline.org), an online index of journals, which provides links to the Web pages of nearly 2,000 journals in psychology and the social sciences.

To decide among journals, read the guidelines for submission, published in each issue of the journal as well as on the journal's Web site. Does your paper fit the publication guidelines with regard to content? Consider the journal's rejection rate, its visibility, and its audience. Will your work be exposed to the scientists in your field? Examine the quality of articles published in the journal and compare that with your project; is your work a good fit? Some authors want to publish in only the most prestigious journals, whereas others feel that an important article will be recognized no matter where it is published. For junior authors, it is sometimes more important that the work is published than where it is published. Generally, it is advisable to choose the best journal in which you have a chance of being published.

Tip

Carefully consider publishing in electronic journals. Online journals tend to be less well known. It may be easier to get published in these, but you might want to consult with colleagues first. Early critics argued that publishing online might hurt more than help, but online journals are becoming more commonplace, given the ubiquity of the Internet. In general, it is best to carefully consider online journals because they are new and have not yet gained credibility among some of the more established academics (Kazdin, 2003). Again, the best way to judge is to examine the journal and determine its quality before submitting your work.

Writing the Article

If you have presented your project at a conference, use the abstract as an initial outline for your article. The article will tell a "story" about your data. The introduction should move from general to specific, from broad statements introducing the area to the problem at hand, why it is important, as well as theory and research pertinent to your question (McCabe & McCabe, 2000). Close with a specific statement of purpose and hypotheses. Your introduction sets the tone for your story in about two to five manuscript pages (Kazdin, 2003). The method section explains how you conducted your research (who was studied, how, with what measures, apparatuses, and procedures) in enough detail to permit replication. The quality of the method section affects the credibility of the results and ensuing conclusions; clearly explain the *how* of your research.

The results section provides detailed information about the analyses and findings. What statistical tests were selected, and how were they carried out? The results section should clearly address each of the hypotheses articulated in the last part of the introduction (Kazdin, 2003). The introduction section began telling a story. The discussion continues it and explains how the current data contribute to the story. Discuss your results and then broaden the discussion to include an explanation of how your study fits with and contributes to the theory and research that you described in your introduction section (McCabe & McCabe, 2000). What are the implications and limitations of your research study? What should future work tackle (i.e., what now?)? Clarity and brevity are essential because the discussion section should comprise only about three to five manuscript pages (Kazdin, 2003).

The title and abstract are often considered afterthoughts, but it is in your best interest to carefully plan these critical elements of your manuscript. The title is sometimes the only thing that a potential reader will see. Use this valuable real estate to attract readers by conveying the purpose and special features of your study (Kazdin, 2003; McCabe & McCabe, 2000). In about 10 to 12 words, capture the problem at hand, variables, and population studied. The abstract is the first impression—and sometimes the only impression—a reader gets of your work (Kazdin, 2003). Take special care in drafting the abstract because it will be read more often than your article. It will be accessible through the Internet, in online library searchers, and on the publisher's Web site. The abstract is usually the last part of the article written, but it is perhaps the most important. Do not let its small size fool you; review multiple drafts of your abstract to ensure that it says exactly what you wish. Review APA's *Publication Manual* (5th ed.) for additional information about the various parts of an article (APA, 2001).

Prepare the Manuscript for Submission

Once the manuscript is complete, review it several times, incorporating revisions as needed. Check that you have cited articles from the journal to which you are submitting your manuscript. By citing articles form the journal, you send the message that your own work falls within the mission and scope of the journal. As with all papers, presentation is important: Attend to details and proofread your work. Check for missing citations and extra citations in the reference list. Typographical errors and grammatical mistakes create a poor impression. If the manuscript is sloppy, it implies that your work, and thus the research described in your article, is sloppy too.

Pay close attention to the submission guidelines. APA's *Publication Manual* provides detailed guidelines for submitting manuscripts (APA,

2001). Follow these. In addition, attend to the specific guidelines set by the journal to which you are submitting your work. Journals differ with regard to things such as page length (many require manuscripts of no more than 25 pages; Cone & Foster, 2006), number of copies, and material that must be included in letters accompanying submissions. Believe what you read. For example, it may say that the cover letter should include a statement that the research was conducted in accord with APA guidelines and that it is not under review elsewhere. It may seem obvious, but it is essential that you write your cover letter in accord with these statements because failing to do so will slow you down when you are asked to submit a new cover letter or your manuscript is rejected outright.

Manuscript Review

Once the manuscript is out the door, it is time to wait. On receipt, the editor determines whether the paper is appropriate for the journal. If it does not fit submission guidelines or if the presentation is especially poor, the editor will return the manuscript unreviewed. If the manuscript passes the editor's initial reading, then it will be sent out for review by two or three reviewers who are familiar with the topical area. You will be notified that the manuscript is being reviewed and when to expect a decision. The reviewers will evaluate the manuscript with regard to the extent to which (a) the question is important in the field, (b) the design and methodology are appropriate, (c) the statistical analyzes are appropriate to the data and question, (d) the interpretations follow clearly from the design and findings, and (e) the findings contribute to the knowledge base (Kazdin, 2003).

The review process can take several weeks or even months. Typically the editor receives the reviews 3 to 4 months after receiving the manuscript. He or she then will reread the article, consider the reviewers' comments, and make a decision. Several things can happen: The manuscript can be accepted outright, pending minor changes (highly unlikely); it can be rejected with encouragement to resubmit (more likely); or it can be rejected. Anticipate rejection. Nearly all manuscripts are initially rejected; however, take a very close look at that rejection letter because many that look like rejection letters are actually revise and resubmit letters that encourage the author to resubmit the article after completing substantial revisions.

> One student recalls, "The first time I sent a manuscript out and waited seemingly endlessly for the reviews, I was crushed. The editor's letter was long and detailed. The enclosed reviews were brutal. In retrospect, I see that two included some positive comments, but all I could see was the criticism. The third letter was the worst; it recommended rejection, was about a paragraph long,

stated that my work was sloppy and flawed, and offered no suggestions for improvement. Reviews are painful to read. I brought them to my mentor, who replied that the editor's letter and two constructive reviews were very helpful—and that the manuscript wasn't rejected. The recommendation was to revise and resubmit. I figured that was basically a rejection, but my mentor, fortunately, knew otherwise. We revised and resubmitted it, and it is being published!"

Most published manuscripts initially received the recommendation of revise and resubmit (Cone & Foster, 2006). It is nearly impossible to produce the perfect manuscript. New authors often become discouraged by reviews and ignore the encouragement to revise and resubmit. Develop a thick skin to withstand criticism. Do not take the comments personally. Painful as it is, read through the reviews once and then put them and the manuscript aside for at least a week to distance yourself from the manuscript and permit more objective consideration of the reviews.

Tip

Expect the review decision to be late. About a month or two after the expected decision date, if you haven't heard from the editor, e-mail him or her. Though unlikely, the reviews may have been lost in the mail.

Revising the Manuscript

Remember that if revision and resubmission are encouraged, it means that you have a shot; the manuscript has potential. Editors and reviewers are busy people. If your paper was not in the ballpark, an editor would not waste time requesting (and evaluating) a revised version. Unfortunately, too many novices read the initial rejection, ignore the encouragement for resubmission, and give up. Do not give up. Just as in graduate school, endurance contributes to much of success in academic and professional psychology.

Carefully read reviews because they provide guidance for revision. Reviewers are experts in your field; their job is to make constructive suggestions for improving the paper. Take them! Take the reviews seriously. Remember that the editors ask reviewers to offer suggestions for improving the manuscript. It takes more space to explain weaknesses, so even quite positive reviews may seem negative (Cone & Foster, 2006). Do not be discouraged because the suggested changes will strengthen the paper. Sometimes comments by reviewers may indicate that they have misunderstood the paper. Do not overlook these because they suggest that the writing was not clear. If a reviewer did not understand part of the manuscript, you can bet that a reader will not either.

Pay close attention to the editor's letter. The editor frames the reviews and points to important issues. Sometimes reviewers are so thorough that they ask for too many changes. The editor will highlight what is important. If you address all the comments and make the changes outlined in the editor's letter that are feasible, your manuscript will have a good chance at being accepted (McCabe & McCabe, 2000). Make a series of lists that note every point the reviewers make, such as analyses to run and literature to check. Attend to all of the comments and suggestions because reviewers will want to see the changes (and the changes really will improve your manuscript). The resubmission letter to the editor should address each change requested by the reviewers. It is permissible to disagree with the advice of a reviewer and to not make a suggested change, but you must justify your position. Do not fear constructive criticism, but stand up for your point of view. Your letter should thank the editor and reviewers and praise their insights.

There is much to learn from reviews, even if your manuscript is rejected outright. It is considered unprofessional to submit your manuscript to a second journal without revising it. Consider the reviews and make changes where you feel doing so is appropriate before submitting the manuscript to a second journal. The modifications will strengthen the manuscript, and it is a very small world indeed; it is not uncommon for a reviewer to be contacted from a second journal to review your paper, simply by coincidence (Cone & Foster, 2006), and the reviewer will not appreciate that his or her comments went unaddressed. Finally, remember that there is a place for nearly every manuscript; the trick is locating the right outlet.

Finding your professional voice marks your entry into the profession and the beginning of your identity as a psychologist. Develop your professional voice by participating in the field of psychology, through professional associations, conferences, networking, and scholarship.

Recommended Reading

Cohen, L. L., & Greco, L. A. (2003). Presenting your research. In M. J. Prinstein & M. D. Patterson (Eds.), *The portable mentor: Expert guide to a successful career in psychology* (pp. 73–84). New York: Kluwer Academic/Plenum Publishers.

Dodgen, D., Fowler, R. D., & Williams-Nickelson, C. (2003). Getting involved in professional organizations: A gateway to career advancement. In M. J. Prinstein & M. D. Patterson (Eds.), *The portable mentor: Expert guide to a successful career in psychology* (pp. 221–234). New York: Kluwer Academic/Plenum Publishers.

Kazdin, A. E. (2003). Publishing your research. In M. J. Prinstein & M. D. Patterson (Eds.), *The portable mentor: Expert guide to a successful career in psychology* (pp. 85–100). New York: Kluwer Academic/Plenum Publishers.

McInerney, D. M. (2001). *Publishing your psychology research: A guide to writing for journals in psychology and related fields.* Thousand Oaks, CA: Sage.

Nichol, A. A. M., & Pexman, P. M. (2003). *Displaying your findings: A practical guide for creating figures, posters, and presentations.* Washington, DC: American Psychological Association.

Silva, P. J. (2007). *How to write a lot: A practical guide to productive academic writing.* Washington, DC: American Psychological Association.

12 Developing an Identity as a Psychologist

Most students of psychology adopt the perspective that human development is a life span phenomenon, taking place well beyond childhood and over the entire span of adulthood. The process of becoming a psychologist entails its own set of developmental transitions. In this chapter I discuss the personal side of graduate study, in particular, the implications of training for students' sense of self.

Developmental Transitions Over the Course of Graduate Study

Professional development, an ongoing phenomenon that takes place over a career, begins in graduate school. Graduate study entails a number of transitions in which students' concerns, attitudes, functioning, and sense of self shift.

TRANSITIONS OF FIRST-YEAR STUDENTS

Most first-year students begin graduate study feeling somewhat insecure and nervous. What will graduate school be like? What level of performance is expected? Can they cut it and meet those expectations? What will their lives be like over the next few years? This initiation period is marked by doubts about whether they have made the right choice to attend graduate school, a lack of self-confidence, and fears that they will not be able to perform and meet the demands of graduate study (Adler & Adler, 2005). The students experience feelings of inadequacy and self-consciousness about their undergraduate pedigree, uncertain about whether their alma matter measures up to those of their peers and whether they are really prepared for the great undertaking that is graduate study. New graduate students go from being the stars of their undergraduate departments to rookies in a cohort of new students; their previous identities as superior students hold no weight because their new student colleagues are similarly accomplished.

The overall experience of first-year students often varies with the makeup of the cohort of incoming students. Often the cohort gels and becomes a cohesive group, providing members with academic support (study groups, course-related discussion, and note sharing) and socio-emotional support (opportunities to form friendships, share experiences, and seek affiliation). Sometimes the first-year cohort is not cohesive and instead is competitive and argumentative. Beginning graduate study in an unwelcoming and competitive environment compounds students' feelings of insecurity, low self-esteem, and anxiety. Throughout the first year—this tumultuous transition period—graduate students look for guidance from faculty (Hess, 2001).

Many students are assigned a mentor when they arrive at graduate school. The first year of graduate study entails getting to know the mentor, working on his or her research projects, and beginning to consider one's own research program. Although assigning mentors ensures that students have contacts with faculty upon beginning graduate study and do not fall through the cracks, it takes time for a true mentoring relationship to form, and many student–faculty pairings are less than optimal. Other programs do not assign mentors; it is the responsibility of students to make contact with, get to know, and form mentoring relationships with faculty. The pressure of determining who will guide their academic career and broaching a relationship with him or her can be overwhelming to students. Chapter 5 discussed the mentoring relationship; later in this chapter I discuss the developmental progression of mentor–student relationships.

TRANSITIONS OF SECOND-YEAR STUDENTS

By the second year of graduate study most students overcome their initial insecurities and feelings of incompetence. During the second year students often begin to take more specialized courses, and the first-year cohort breaks up into more specialized groupings of students. Students now begin to define themselves by their specialization (e.g., clinical, developmental) and are grouped with peers who share their academic interests (Adler & Adler, 2005). Many students are awarded teaching assistantships during their first and second years of graduate school. Although students' feelings of academic competence generally rise over the course of the first and into the second year of graduate study, initial forays into teaching may increase feelings of self-doubt. Teaching entails its own developmental trajectory, as discussed later in this chapter.

Second-year students face many hurdles in addition to coursework. Doctoral programs that award master's degrees to second-year students will often require the completion of master's comprehensive exams, similar in content to doctoral comprehensive exams but much less broad and comprehensive in scope. Students will find that a great deal of planning, studying, and stress goes into preparing for master's comprehensive exams.

Graduate students learn how to become independent researchers by completing increasingly challenging research tasks and projects over the course of graduate school. Many students conduct their first independent research project during their second year of graduate study. This project is often referred to as the *predoctoral research project,* sometimes called a *second-year project* or *master's thesis* (for students seeking master's degrees or those enrolled in doctoral programs that award students a master's degree along the way). This often is the first opportunity for graduate students to work closely with their mentor on their own research. Students quickly learn that planning and carrying out a research project from beginning to end is challenging.

Students may first become aware of the academic politics during the second year of graduate study. As they consider their own research program, they realize that their choice of subject matter is influenced by their mentor. The choice of mentor may limit opportunities to pursue particular research avenues because of turf wars among faculty or infighting that restricts opportunities for collaboration. Students may become aware of academic and personal splits within the department. Learning that academia is a largely political enterprise may cloud students' idealized image of academia as an intellectually welcoming and value-neutral place.

TRANSITIONS OF ADVANCED STUDENTS

As students near the end of coursework, it is not uncommon for them to feel somewhat apathetic; they have completed several years of intense training but they are far from finished. Students feel that they have proven themselves; they can write papers and pass classes.

> "All I can think about is getting through comps and figuring out what to do for my dissertation," one student tells a friend. "Thinking about the comps makes me sick. There's so much to do. How will I read it all? How will I remember it? Will I be able to use what I know to answer the questions? All of this is swirling in my head—and Dr. Smith wants me to write a term paper? I've written what feels like a million papers. I can write a paper practically in my sleep. Honestly, I feel so beyond this. This semester is just

> something I need to slog through to get to my real work. I resent having to do a paper because I've already shown that I can."

Some students may even resent writing class papers, feeling that they have already demonstrated their competence and assigned class papers are beneath them, trivialities to complete.

As students complete coursework, they begin preparing for the doctoral comprehensive exam. Ending coursework often sets students adrift. A radical change occurs with little to no regular contact with other students, mentors, or members of the department. Students immerse themselves in reading, studying, and preparing for the doctoral comprehensive exam. This period is much less structured than the graduate school experience to date. Students typically are on campus only to teach, meet with mentors, and conduct research but spend the rest of their time preparing for the comprehensive exam.

After completing the comprehensive exam and becoming doctoral candidates, students are faced with a great deal of unstructured time as they begin to write the dissertation. Most students devote the body of their attention to the dissertation, visiting campus only to teach or meet with their mentor. Many students find the unstructured time challenging. Developing the dissertation proposal is a long and trying experience. Even the best of students are likely to feel dissociated from the department because they are focused on important problems that take all of their concentration and they do not come to campus. As students advance toward completion of the dissertation, the job hunt begins, marking the transition to the professional role.

Developments in several competencies—practice, teaching, and research—take place over the graduate school years. Each competency entails a developmental trajectory. The graduate student is faced with navigating several professional development tasks and making strides in several professional competencies at once. Relationships with mentors and supervisors also change over the course of graduate study, and these changes influence students' professional development. Later sections of this chapter examine developmental transitions in relationships and competencies during the graduate school years.

Developmental Transitions in the Mentor–Student Relationship

The mentor–student relationship, as discussed in chapter 5, is a critical part of the graduate school experience and is integral in learning how to think and behave like a psychologist. The mentoring relationship changes over the graduate school years along with students' professional development. Not surprisingly, the most active phase of the mentoring relationship occurs during the graduate school years (Johnson & Huwe, 2003). Some students maintain contact with their mentors for many years after graduation, of course in a much more limited capacity than as students. Other mentoring relationships end once the dissertation is defended and the final copy is submitted. The mentor–graduate student relationship has a limited life span and evolves over the course of the student's progression through graduate school (Johnson & Huwe, 2003; Kram, 1985). The mentoring relationship progresses through four phases corresponding to changes in students' circumstances and needs (Johnson & Huwe, 2003; Kram, 1985).

INITIATION

The first phase, initiation, marks the beginning of the mentoring relationship (Johnson & Huwe, 2003; Kram, 1985). As the mentor and student get to know each other, they interact more frequently and the mentoring alliance forms. The mentoring relationship forms over the first year of graduate school. Students managing the physical and emotional transition to graduate school—with the accompanying stress, anxiety, isolation, and role ambiguity—feel a heightened sense of vulnerability and dependency. Faculty mentors offer guidance and a sense of stability. Many students bond with faculty easily. The initiation phase is marked by excitement as student and mentor learn more about each other, discover shared interests, and become aware of the potential for a productive and satisfying relationship (Johnson & Huwe, 2003).

The developmental task for students during the initiation phase is to establish roles and boundaries. Graduate students must adopt the role of student and create professional boundaries between themselves, their peers, and faculty. Students often hold idealized views of mentors or hold unrealistic expectations for the mentoring relationship. For example, they may not be able to view their mentor's work objectively. Students may try to be exactly like their mentor, cloning the mentor rather than developing an autonomous professional identity (Johnson & Huwe, 2003). Students may have high needs for approval from the mentor; mentors should provide acceptance, confirmation, coaching, and role modeling.

CULTIVATION

Cultivation, the second and longest phase of the mentoring relationship, is the most active period of the mentoring relationship (Johnson & Huwe, 2003; Kram, 1985). It is during this phase that mentors provide a full range of support for career, academic, and psychosocial growth and students demonstrate the greatest leaps in professional development. The cultivation phase extends throughout the body of the graduate school years. This period tends to be stable, productive, and enjoyable for both student and mentor. As students become more accomplished, they gain a sense of competence and feel confirmed and respected by their mentors.

It is during the cultivation phase that the student first consolidates professional knowledge, skills, and attitudes into a stable sense of self, a professional identity (Johnson & Huwe, 2003). With the establishment of professional identity comes a growing awareness of one's capacities, strengths, and weaknesses, and a healthy awareness of professional limitations coupled with self-confidence about abilities and willingness to take risks. During this phase students become better able to accept feedback, are less competitive with peers, and feel more secure in the professional role of psychologist.

In addition to increasing skills and knowledge about how to be a psychologist, during the cultivation phase students learn about the interpersonal side of being a professional psychologist. Students learn how to navigate professional relationships: how to build collegial relationships and manage interpersonal conflict. As they begin to adopt the professional identity of psychologist, they also internalize the values of the profession, adopting a sense of ethical standards that makes them more aware of ethical issues in their work, better able to identify specific issues as they arise, and more likely to take appropriate action.

The mentor's task is to help the student become competent and foster self-awareness while offering guidance, protection, and boundaries. Effective mentors challenge students to take risks, balancing autonomy-granting with protection and limit-setting. Students' attempts at practice, teaching, and scholarship—conducting their first assessment, teaching their first class, or presenting their first paper at a professional conference—all entail risk. The mentor is also taking risks as students' performance holds consequences for the mentor's reputation and credibility.

The mentor acts as a catalyst to professional development by providing support and professional visibility as well as protection. The mentor helps students identify with the profession of psychology and increases visibility by introducing students to professionals in the field and sponsoring or endorsing them. The mentor presents students with challenges that are appropriate to their developing abilities, increasing the difficulty as students become more competent while not overwhelming them and supporting and reassuring students. The mentor offers emotional support, affirmation, and encouragement. Over time self-disclosure on the part of student and mentor increases and their relationship strengthens.

SEPARATION

Changes in circumstance and students' professional advancement trigger the third phase of the mentoring relationship, separation (Johnson & Huwe, 2003; Kram, 1985). This phase occurs as the end of graduate study is in sight, with the dissertation in its final stages and students spending less time on campus. The transition to internship, graduation, and the job search marks a shift toward ending the formal mentoring relationship. Some student–mentor dyads gradually separate, interacting less and less often; others experience more sharp declines in contact. As students' professional competencies near the level of mastery, the mentor grants greater autonomy and the relationship changes, becoming more collegial and reciprocal in nature. Students begin the job search and consider life after graduate school. During this phase the student begins to see the mentor in more realistic light, recognizing that the mentor holds both strengths and weaknesses and is not perfect.

During the separation phase the task for students is to become aware and accept the changing relationship: the loss of the most active phase of mentorship and the increasing responsibility for their own professional decisions and development. Students face the job hunt with its myriad stresses, including fierce competition, potential relocation, and uncertainty about the future. Students may become more cynical about the value of their education and whether it was worth the time and effort. They may become temporarily ambivalent about moving on. Students who have had a warm and productive relationship with their mentor often feel a sense of loss during the separation phase. They may feel abandoned as the mentor focuses on incoming students. The student's task is to say goodbye. The mentor's task is to continue to foster a sense of autonomy and independence in the student, engaging in more collegial interactions, and welcoming the student into the profession. As with students, some mentors have difficulty accepting the changing relationship.

REDEFINITION

The final phase, redefinition, occurs after the student is an independent professional and has separated from the mentor (Johnson & Huwe, 2003; Kram, 1985). The mentoring relationship, if it continues, transitions into a more informal relationship characterized by peerlike interactions. Some mentoring relationships end completely when the student graduates. Others continue through informal contact, occasional calls and e-mail, and catching up when they meet at professional conferences. Sometimes the student and mentor continue close interaction as independent collaborators in scholarly work. The frequency and nature of interaction changes substantially.

> Drew and his mentor continued to collaborate on papers after he graduated. Even though they worked at institutions on opposite sides of the country, they communicated often by e-mail, discussing their work and sharing personal details. At conferences they reconnected, had dinner, and met with other colleagues.

Very close relationships such as that of Drew and his mentor are unusual. However, many students and mentors remain in contact in the years after the student graduates.

During this redefinition phase the mentoring relationship either ends completely or takes on a new form that is based in friendship. Any resentment on the part of students or mentors dissipates and a reciprocal relationship forms. The developmental task for students is to accept their role as psychologist and colleague to the mentor.

Developmental Transitions in Supervisory Relationships

Training in psychological practice is hands-on, with students engaging in applied activities early in their graduate school careers. Supervision is critical to students' learning. Ideally supervisors become mentors to students. The supervisory relationship is much shorter than that of the mentoring relationship, which spans the length of graduate study. Most students will practice in several settings and be supervised by several different professionals. Like the mentoring relationship, the supervisory relationship progresses through several stages.

Stages in supervisory relationships entail shifts in awareness of self and other, motivation, dependence, and autonomy (McNeill, Stoltenberg, & Romans, 1992). Early in the relationship, students depend on supervisors for guidance and are anxious about their competence and lack of experience (McNeill et al., 1992). During the second phase, students feel more autonomous but are still dependent on their supervisors (McNeill et al., 1992). This period is likely to have more conflicts as students attempt to become more autonomous and supervisors continue to set limits and rein in overzealous students. Finally, at the last stage the students function at more autonomous levels (McNeill et al., 1992).

Supervisory relationships shape professional identity. Attachment theory has often been applied to the supervisory relationship (Riggs & Bretz, 2006). The bond between student and supervisor entails elements similar to that of parent and child: trust, protection, autonomy granting, encouragement, and support in developing competence. Attachment theory posits that early relationships influence the course of human development. Attachment processes influence the effectiveness of supervision. The supervisory relationship is intended to promote student growth and be accompanied by attachment responses involving issues of authority and individuation. Supervisors act as a secure base from which students can learn to practice, exploring professional identity while knowing that a supervisor is there for support (Riggs & Bretz, 2006). Students who see themselves as securely attached to supervisors tend to evaluate supervision more positively than students who view the relationship as insecure (Riggs & Bretz, 2006).

The progression of supervisory relationships and the correspondence to students' professional development are especially evident during internship year, a time of transition from student to professional (Kaslow & Rice, 1985). The beginning of internship is stressful for nearly all students who are still developing a sense of professional identity; supervisory feedback is important in helping students see themselves in a professional light. Supervisors provide specific information and guidance. By midyear, students shift their focus outward, acting as semiautonomous professionals, growing apart from supervisors, and desiring more collegial relationships with supervisors (Kaslow & Rice, 1985). Toward the end of the internship year, students function more independently, taking leading roles in intervention, treating more challenging patients, and planning for the following year. This transition from intern to professional is stressful, and there is often some turmoil as students push for more autonomy and supervisors continue to provide guidance (Kaslow & Rice, 1985). The close of the internship year marks a change in the relationship between supervisor and student. Like the redefinition phase of the mentoring relationship, ongoing relations between students and supervisors vary.

Developing a Sense of Identity as a Psychologist

The process of becoming a professional in any field involves a transformation of identity. Graduate study itself is a catalyst for identity development. Navigating an unfamiliar environment that poses enormous academic, interpersonal, and emotional demands forces students to revise their sense of self (Bruss & Kopala, 1993; Ducheny, Alletzhauser, Crandell, & Schneider, 1997). All psychology students, practitioners and academics alike, undergo basic shifts in identity as they move from inexperienced students, through training and socialization, to emerge as new professionals.

PROFESSIONAL IDENTITY AS A PRACTICING PSYCHOLOGIST

Students undergo much personal development over the course of learning to practice psychology (Borders, 1989). Beginning student-practitioners are characterized by black-and-white thinking, little self-awareness, and poor problem-solving skills. They often doubt their competence, rightly so, and heavily depend on supervisors' guidance. Then they shift toward becoming more confident of their abilities but mindful of limitations as well as more empathetic, aware of, and tolerant of clients (Borders, 1989). Students begin to appreciate the contributions of a wider range of theoretical approaches and create more comprehensive treatment plans. In the late stages of development, the student is capable of considering a range of issues at once and design treatment programs and interventions that are more comprehensive (Borders, 1989).

Beginning practitioners are often focused on their own experiences as practitioners. The emerging practitioner is characterized by self-consciousness, feelings of anxiety, and emphasis on her or his own internal experiences of providing therapy, sometimes to the exclusion of attending to the client (Stoltenberg, 2005; Worthington, 2006). As practitioners turn their attention to their clients, their begin to emphasize direct service work. Practitioners become more comfortable with the process of providing therapy, and the focus of their awareness and attention shifts to the client (Stoltenberg, 2005). Now students can simultaneously reflect on the experiences of clients as well as their own thoughts, emotions, and behavior in relation to clients (Stoltenberg, 2005). Some students adopt a standard approach to therapy that is applied uniformly to all clients (Worthington, 2006). When therapy is not effective the student may attribute it to his or her inability to follow the theory and provide the therapy prescribed by the theory. As students become more reflective, they can vary the therapeutic process and adapt their technique in response to the situation and evaluations (Stoltenberg, 2005). With advances in professional development, practitioners become able to reject the universal application of a theory in favor of eclecticism, thereby becoming more flexible practitioners (Worthington, 2006).

Students often enter the world of practice with a sense of being overwhelmed, feeling that it is a great booming, buzzing confusion (Hess, 2001). It is. Early attempts at providing therapy may range from inflexible and universal application of a given theory or approach to applying a mishmash of therapeutic techniques gleaned from readings, observations, instructions from supervisors, or expectations based on media depictions (Hess, 2001). The attempts often feel hollow to the student. Graduate study is a period that entails demystifying therapy, moving from feelings of incompetence and inadequacy to competence and adequacy (Hess, 2001). It requires time to learn how to enter the therapeutic relationship and establish the boundaries that are part of that relationship, that is, to establish a professional identity as a practitioner.

PROFESSIONAL IDENTITY DURING THE INTERNSHIP YEAR

The internship year is an important period of professional development for practitioners, sometimes seen as separate from academic and post-internship experiences and possessing a developmental span of its own (Guinee, 1998). New interns are concerned with gathering information, sizing up the agency, and creating a place for themselves (Lamb, Baker, Jennings, & Yarris, 1982). During the initial weeks of internship, they may struggle for independence and experience fluctuations in confidence as they are confronted with the overwhelming number of new responsibilities, new clinical activities, and more clients than they have seen before (Guinee, 1998). As students transition to the internship, they begin to feel the need to revaluate themselves in light of their new status and responsibilities. This, coupled with feeling more comfortable in the agency setting, leads students toward the second phase of intern development: intern identity (Lamb et al., 1982).

During the second phase of intern development, interns become used to the evaluative component of internship, accustomed to the organization, and immersed in the intern role. They experience greater role differentiation and self-doubt. Interns become more introspective about their work, acknowledge their strengths and limits, and are often preoccupied with their shortcomings (Lamb et al., 1982). The task in this phase is to take risks in confronting their weaknesses, and interns struggle with defining their own goals for professional development and client treatment while working under necessary but sometimes unwanted supervision (Guinee, 1998). Interns experience the turmoil of being more than students but not quite independent professionals; this in-between time is challenging on professional and personal levels.

The latter part of the internship year is marked by the student's shift in status to emerging professional, characterized by greater independence, increased sense of competence, and resolution of the intern role (Lamb et al., 1982). Interns separate from the agency and move on to the next phase in professional development. The transition out of the internship often is marked by mixed feelings: satisfaction and relief over completing another phase in the route toward becoming a professional psychologist, and uncertainty over what the next phase of professional development holds in store as well as feelings of loss when terminating relations with clients and supervisors (Guinee, 1998).

Tip

An obstacle to students as they take on professional roles as therapists, instructors, and researchers is the feeling that they are not as competent as they appear and have somehow deceived others. This fear that one is simply acting out a role, faking it, is known as the *impostor syndrome* (Clance & Imes, 1978; Henning, Ey, & Shaw, 1998). The impostor syndrome is common among high-achieving and successful individuals and, not surprisingly, is associated with feelings of distress (Henning et al., 1998).

PROFESSIONAL IDENTITY AS AN ACADEMIC PSYCHOLOGIST

Becoming an academic psychologist—a teacher and scholar—entails its own developmental trajectory. The task for students who wish to be academic psychologists is to gain competence in both teaching and research.

Most graduate students express concern about beginning to teach. Often they are close in age to their students and find it challenging to exert authority in a class of age mates, fearing that undergraduate students will not respect their expertise and knowledge. Many begin as teaching assistants and have some experience in the classroom before teaching their own course; this transition to teaching may be more gradual and comfortable. Others are immersed in teaching without any prior classroom experience other than that of student.

Early on, teaching demands a great deal of attention as the instructor must create lectures and assignments, plans, and grading rubrics. The constant tinkering required to keep pace and modify a class in response to student needs can become all consuming. The course deadlines are real, and balancing personal and professional obligations becomes more difficult. As graduate students obtain more experience, they become more comfortable in their role, spend less time preparing class, and feel more confident in class (Adler & Adler, 2005). Once they begin to teach their own classes, graduate students are free from restrictions placed by professors and are given a wide berth of autonomy. They create their own syllabi, exams, and procedures, as well as evaluate students. Many students relish these responsibilities.

Becoming a scholar is a gradual process that begins on entry to graduate school. Students learn to think like researchers and to do research as they interact with their mentor, work on their mentors' projects, and begin to develop and carry out their own research projects. Graduate school entails an apprenticeship model in which students work alongside master scholars and gradually gain competence in the skills underlying scholarship.

As a scholar, the critical transition is moving from consumer of knowledge, absorbing it, to being a creator of knowledge (Adler & Adler, 2005). Accomplishing this transition requires that students grasp the theoretical and methodological basis of current work, determine gaps in their current knowledge, devise and carry out conceptually and methodologically sound scholarship that addresses those gaps, and draw appropriate conclusions. Conducting sound research does not ensure success as a scholar; one must also disseminate it.

The student's first conference presentation is a career milestone (Adler & Adler, 2005). Having posters or papers accepted for presentation at a conference affirms and legitimatizes students' identities as scholars. Presenting at a conference offers professional challenges, such as how to present a complicated research project concisely and how to respond to questions from the audience. As presenters, students attend the conference as participants rather than observers and often are more likely to engage other scholars at conferences. Many students find the external validation of their work encouraging.

Submitting a paper to a journal is another professional milestone. Preparing a paper for submission is an achievement of its own that many mentors and students celebrate. The journal review process offers another opportunity into the transition from student to professional. Most scholars never forget the first decision letter and set of manuscript reviews that they receive. Most students will receive rejection letters or invitations to revise and resubmit their work. Even students who are accustomed to receiving criticism of their work often recoil upon reading journal reviews. Most reviews offer constructive criticism, although some can be harsh. It is difficult to learn that the paper that resulted from months of effort is unacceptable for publication. Experiencing and learning this inevitability of academic life is an important step in students' professional development as scholars.

Promoting Professional Development

The professional identity is a synthesis of professional knowledge, skills, attitudes, interests, and values that is not static but changes over the course of a career (Ducheny et al., 1997). Throughout the career individuals move through a series of experiences that require redefining the professional identity and increasing levels of competence (Cross & Papadopoulos, 2001; Ducheny et al., 1997).

Personal reflection is an essential part of professional development over the duration of a career. Progression in developing a sense of identity as a psychologist requires openness to experience, flexibility, and critical reflection (Cross & Papadopoulos, 2001). Self-knowledge provides the insight to shape professional development. At regular intervals, spend time exploring how you define yourself, identifying your needs for professional development, determining if they are being satisfied, and, if they are not, devising ways of fulfilling them. Periodically evaluate how you are progressing toward your professional development goals. Have your goals shifted? Set in place a regular schedule of evaluating and revising your professional development goals to ensure that you grow throughout your career (Ducheny et al., 1997).

In addition, understanding yourself as a professional entails considering how your experiences and background influence your work as a practitioner, teacher, and scholar. Consider the following (Cross & Papadopoulos, 2001):

- How does my experience with my family influence my work?
- How might interaction styles among family members influence my work?
- How does my own experience—life events and history—influence my personality and behavior? How might these experiences influence my work?
- How does culture influence my work? Are there ways in which my culture influences how I interact with others?
- How do my experiences with members of particular ethnic or cultural groups influence my cognitions and behaviors?
- How might cultural issues lead to problems or misunderstandings in my work?
- How does gender influence my work? What does it mean to be male or female? How might gender influence how others perceive me or how I perceive them?
- How do my personal morals and values relate to codes of professional ethics?

Finally, reflective psychologists, especially practicing psychologists, are open to seeking personal therapy (Norcross, 2005). About three quarters of mental health professionals have received at least one episode of personal therapy (Norcross, 2005). Personal therapy is associated with empathetic ability, self-awareness, improved self-esteem, and self-reported increases in emotional relief and functioning as a therapist (Norcross, 2005). However, therapy is only one instrument in the psychologist's toolbox. The most critical component of professional development is self-awareness.

Professional identity develops and undergoes dramatic change as students progress through graduate school. As they advance in competency and assume greater responsibility in clinical work, planning and conducting research, and teaching courses, their sense of professional identity shifts and changes. Graduate study marks the beginning, but professional development and identity change is a career-long endeavor.

Recommended Reading

Baker, E. K. (2003). *Caring for ourselves: A therapist's guide to personal and professional well-being.* Washington, DC: American Psychological Association.

Cross, M. C., & Papadopoulos, L. (2001). *Becoming a therapist.* New York: Taylor & Francis.

Darley, J. M., Zanna, M. P., & Roediger, H. L. (2003). *The complete academic: A career guide* (2nd ed.). Washington, DC: American Psychological Association.

Hess, A. K. (2001). Learning psychotherapy. In S. Walfish & A. K. Hess (Eds.), *Succeeding in graduate school: The career guide for psychology students* (pp. 249–262). Mahwah, NJ: Erlbaum.

Johnson, W. B., & Huwe, J. M. (2003). *Getting mentored in graduate school.* Washington, DC: American Psychological Association.

Keller, P. A. (1994). *Academic paths.* Hillsdale, NJ: Erlbaum.

Kottler, J. A., & Hazler, R. J. (1997). *What you never learned in graduate school: A survival guide for therapists.* New York: Norton.

Norcross, J. C. (2005). The psychotherapist's own psychotherapy: Educating and developing psychologists. *American Psychologist, 60,* 840–850.

Career Moves for Emerging Psychologists

13

The dissertation is all-consuming. Doctoral candidates use tunnel vision to keep their dissertations moving forward. Frequently, doctoral candidates approach their dissertation defense and the culmination of graduate study as if they are coming out of a deep sleep, and they are taken aback at the next task that confronts them: seeking employment. In this chapter I explore the tasks that face the emerging psychologist, including creating a curriculum vitae, seeking postdoctoral training, getting a job in practice or academic settings, and considering alternative careers for psychologists.

Constructing a Curriculum Vitae

The first impression that many potential mentors, supervisors, and employers form of an applicant is based on his or her curriculum vitae (CV). Every academic job application, whether it is a position as a clinician, professor, researcher, or postdoc, requires the submission of a CV, or scholarly resume. The CV is a comprehensive yet concise presentation of an applicant's experiences and competencies; it grows over the course of a career. Early career academics tend to have short CVs of two to three pages, depending on their experiences; the CVs of experienced and accomplished academics are many pages long.

An effective CV is comprehensive and accurately portrays the applicant's experience and competencies. CVs are a component of many professional documents, such as applications for grants, jobs, promotion and tenure, and appointments to committees of professional organizations, as well as invitations to present seminars or invited talks, and more (McCabe & McCabe, 2000). Because CVs are requested frequently and the experiences included on CVs are the currency of professional psychology—the ticket to funding, publication, and career opportunities—keep your CV current so that the entire body of your work is represented. Update and add to your CV at regular intervals throughout your career (e.g., each semester or more often). As their careers progress, most psychologists become much busier. With time, it becomes difficult to remember details of presentations and professional activities. Recording new information as it arises is easier and more accurate than backtracking later. Also, those who request a CV, such as potential employers, grant reviewers, and committee chairs, may be offended by receiving out-of-date documents.

COMPONENTS OF THE CV

The CV presents a clear and extensive portrait of an individual's experiences, competencies, and body of work. The following subsections discuss the content areas covered by the CV. CVs tend to be similar regardless of psychological specialty, and they even are similar across fields such as mathematics, English, or history, with very few differences. Note that not all of the content areas indicated are appropriate to all psychologists. Practitioners should emphasize the material concerning psychological practice by, for example, making the sections relating to practice (e.g., Licensure, Clinical Experience) more prominent and excluding sections that are irrelevant or for which they have no experience. Academic psychologists who are applying for postdocs, for research positions, or to institutions that favor research over teaching should emphasize their research experience by placing Research Experience and Statistical Experience sections more prominently (and sections for practitioners, like Clinical Experience and Licensure, may be deleted entirely from some CVs if they are not relevant). Similarly, academic psychologists who are applying for teaching-intensive positions or to institutions whose missions emphasize teaching should make sections relevant to teaching more visible.

Contact Information

Ensure that those who read your CV will be able to contact you if needed. Provide your name, address, phone, fax, and e-mail address for home and office (if applicable). Use permanent phone numbers and e-mail addresses; if you are graduating, use your own personal e-mail account rather than the university e-mail account that will expire on your graduation. Use a professional e-mail address that includes your name (your first initial and last name, full name, etc.) rather than an informal and potentially unprofessional e-mail address (e.g., butterfly16@ domain.com).

Education

Provide a complete overview of your educational background, including institutions, degrees, major/specialty, and dates of attendance. If you have not yet completed the doctoral degree, indicate your status (e.g., doctoral candidate) and an expected graduation date. Some students include the title of their thesis or dissertation and the name of their mentor or thesis/dissertation chair; others include this information in the Research Experience section, which occurs later in the CV. Your choice of where to place information about your thesis or dissertation will depend on your particular case. If you have no other research experience, then it may be more appropriate to include the dissertation under Education.

Licensure and Certification

Practicing psychologists indicate the state in which they are licensed and their license number. Indicate any other certifications and provide documentation.

Honors and Awards

List each honor or award, including the granting institution and date awarded. This includes election to honor societies, fellowships, and scholarships. If you have only one award, you might consider including it under Education (under the granting institution).

Grants Awarded

Document any grant funding for your research or other projects. Include the project title, awarding agency, dollar amount, and date. Consider describing the project in one to two lines.

Clinical Experience

Post relevant clinical experience including practica, externships, and paid work. Include the institution, your title, supervisor, and dates. Discuss the responsibilities and activities for each position (e.g., conducted assessments, provided group therapy to adolescents diagnosed with major depressive disorder).

Research Experience

Document relevant research experiences. Include research assistantships, research practica, and unpaid research experiences. For each position, list the title or nature of the position (e.g., research assistant), institution, supervisor, and dates. Explain your responsibilities and duties (i.e., What did you do? What was the project? What experience and skills did you gain?).

Statistical Experience

This section is particularly important for applicants to postdoctoral research positions. Faculty who hire postdoctoral researchers are interested in applicants' skill sets, in particular, how applicants can support faculty research. Applicants who are not applying to postdoctoral research positions often omit this section. Discuss experiences that enhance your capacities for conducting research and make you a desirable candidate for research positions. List statistics courses you have taken, data analysis techniques that you have experience with, statistical and computer programs in which you are proficient, and any unusual methodological skills that you have acquired.

Teaching Experience

Document all of your experiences with teaching, from guest lectures to teaching assistantships to full responsibility for teaching courses. For each experience note the course; institution; role held in each; and, for teaching assistantships, the supervisor. It is especially important to discuss your responsibilities in teaching assistantships because teaching assistantship experiences vary. Some students grade essays and never see a student, whereas others lead discussion sections and provide guest lectures. Provide the reader with comprehensive information about your experience.

Publications

Present your publications in American Psychological Association (APA) style. Many students list their most recent publication first and work backward so that their current work is most visible.

Conference Presentations

Record your conference presentations, using APA style. Create separate subsections for posters and papers so that readers can easily differentiate the two (and avoid the perception that posters are inaccurately portrayed as paper presentations).

Unpublished Manuscripts

This section documents manuscripts that are in preparation or under review. Be careful to note only those manuscripts that are in progress (i.e., in draft form). The reader may request more information about the manuscript or to review it. If you cannot provide additional information or produce a manuscript, it may appear as if the CV is padded and inaccurate.

Professional Service

Under this section, catalog service activities at the department, university, and community level. This includes department committees, university committees, student associations, committee memberships, administrative work, editorial activities (e.g., reviewing manuscripts; working on a departmental journal), service with professional associations (e.g., American Psychological Association of Graduate Students committees), and community activities that are professionally relevant (e.g., volunteering to help an organization with conducting research on its programs). For each, identify both the committee and your role and activities.

Professional Affiliations

List the professional associations to which you belong, such as APA, Association for Psychological Science, Society for Research in Child Development, and so on.

Research Interests

List four to six descriptors to identify your research interests. What key words or phrases might be used to describe your work? For example, "adolescent risk behaviors," "ethical issues in teaching," or "HIV prevention with African American youths."

Teaching Interests

List courses you have taught, those you are prepared to teach, and those that you would like the opportunity to teach. Be honest in recording teaching interests because employers and job search committees may use this information in making decisions about which applicants to interview and hire.

In general, place the most important information first in your CV. Education is the first item. What comes next varies by the applicant's emphasis. Practitioners should include Clinical Experience, followed by Licensure and Certification, and so on, ordering the section by professional importance. Researchers should include Grants, Honors and Awards, Research Experience, Publications, and so on. Teachers should include Honors and Awards, Grants and Awards, Teaching Experience, Teaching Interests, and so on. Use judgment in determining the order in which to present information on your CV. One size does not fit all. Exhibits 13.1, 13.2, and 13.3 illustrate CVs of academic and practitioner psychologists.

DOS AND DON'TS OF CV WRITING

The challenge of CV writing is to present professional experiences in a comprehensive, honest, concise, and positive light. It is a challenging task and one that most students do not master overnight. Although CVs are highly individualized, there are some general rules for constructing them. The following are some dos and don'ts (Dittmann, 2003):

Dos in Preparing CVs

- *Do use a consistent format.* The three sample CVs presented use three different formats that include differences such as whether dates are listed in the left or right margin. Such a decision is a personal choice (although I prefer to see dates listed in the right-hand margin so that the left margin, which the eye tends to gravitate toward, easily contains important content). Once you make a decision about where to place dates, for example, apply your decision consistently.
- *Do be concise.* Make every word count. Although all entries must be described, do not use more than a few lines for any one entry. An exception may be for describing clinical experiences in which details such as patient populations and specific activities are particularly relevant.
- *Do talk with others about CV writing.* Discuss CV writing with your mentor and other faculty. It is especially important to speak with your peers and students who are more senior to gain insight into how early career psychologists prepare CVs. CVs of junior professionals are quite different from those of senior professionals. Do not be frightened by a mentor's CV. Faculty members' CVs reflect years of experience. Peers offer better comparison points. Solicit peers' CVs and discuss CV writing together.
- *Do seek feedback.* Once you have drafted your CV, ask peers, faculty, and family to review it. They will spot weaknesses and have suggestions for improvement that you will not have considered.

EXHIBIT 13.1

Sample Curriculum Vitae for a Teaching-Oriented Student

David Smith
212 West 52nd Street
New York, NY 11012
(212) 555-9899
David.Smith@gmail.com

Education

Sam University, New York, NY, 2004–present
Doctoral Candidate, Experimental Psychology (PhD Anticipated May 2008)
Dissertation: Cognitive, Affective, and Developmental Predictors of Depression
Mentor: James Simpson, PhD

MA, Experimental Psychology, 2006
Thesis: Antidepressant Medication: Friend or Foe?
Mentor: William Jones, PhD
Honors: Oscar Mayer Scholarship, 2004–2006

Jones University, New York, NY, 2000–2004
BA, Psychology, 2004
Honors: Psi Chi, 2003; Phi Beta Kappa, 2004

Teaching Experience

Senior Teaching Fellow, Sam University, 2008–2008
Assumed full responsibility for teaching two undergraduate courses in Introduction to Psychology as well as supervising two graduate teaching assistants

Teaching Fellow, Sam University, 2006–2007
Assumed full responsibility for teaching two undergraduate courses in Introduction to Psychology

Teaching Assistant, Sam University, 2005–2006
Led discussion sections of undergraduate psychology courses, including Introduction to Psychology, Social Psychology, and Applied Developmental Psychology

Publications

Smith, D. (2008). Religiosity, risk-taking, and stress during the transition to college. *Journal of Depression, 105,* 99–100.

Smith, D., & Cite, W. E. (2006). The impact of stress on depression. *Journal of Depression, 103,* 100–110.

Conference Presentations

Paper Presentations

Smith, D. (2008, August). Overcoming procrastination. In W. E. Cite (Chair), *Procrastination management.* Symposium conducted at the annual meeting of the American Procrastination Association, San Francisco.

(Continued)

EXHIBIT 13.1 *(Continued)*

Smith, D., & Cite, W. E. (2007, August). The impact of Cracker Jacks in lowering procrastination. In J. Simpson & W. E. Cite (Co-chairs), *Cracker Jacks: Wonder drug of the 90s?* Symposium conducted at the annual meeting of the American Cracker Jack Association, New York.

Poster Presentations

Cite, W. E., & Smith, D. (2006, May). *The developmental correlates of finishing your Cracker Jacks.* Poster session presented at the biennial meeting of the Society for Research in Child Development, Washington, DC.

Smith, D. (2004, July–August). *On Cracker Jacks and you.* Poster session presented at the annual meeting of the American Psychological Association, Honolulu, HI.

Unpublished Manuscripts

Submitted for Review

Smith, D., & Simpson, J. (under review). *Predicting depression among college students.*
Smith, H. J., & Smith, D. (under review). *The effects of Cracker Jacks in reducing depression.*

Works in Progress

Smith, D. (in preparation). *Ethical ambiguities in research on Cracker Jacks.*
Smith, D., & Simpson, J. (in preparation). *Effects of Cracker Jacks consumption on moral development.*

Research Experience

Research Associate, The Village Center for Care, 2007–present
Research design and analysis for the nursing home and skilled nursing facilities. Various projects have included the analysis of acute care needs within the New York City geriatric population and protease use among residents.
Supervisor: Elwin Smith, PhD

Research Intern, The Darkhouse, 2006–2007
Collected interview data for a National Institute of Mental Health–sponsored, 5-year study on friendship and adaptation to change. Aided in the collection and coding of data for an AARP-funded stress rehabilitation and family services intervention. Examined age differences in coping strategy use among older persons with stress via archival data from a repeated measures 2-year longitudinal study.
Supervisor: Don Jones, PhD

Religion as a Moderator of Risky Behavior, 2005–2006
Investigated the moderating role of religious attitudes, beliefs, and behavior in college students' risky behavior in a cohort-sequential sample.
Supervisor: Kathleen Shapiro, PhD

Professional Affiliations

American Cracker Jacks Association
American Procrastination Association
American Psychological Association
Society for Research in Child Development

EXHIBIT 13.1 *(Continued)*

References

W. E. Cites, PhD
Department of Psychology
Smith University
1188 Sam Ave.
New York, NY 06810
(212) 666-8899
Cites@smith.edu

[Two other references follow]

- *Do use page numbers.* Create a header for your CV that includes your last name (at minimum) and page number, permitting the CV to be reconstructed should the pages be separated.
- *Do proofread, proofread, proofread.* Typos, misspellings, and grammatical mistakes are indefensible. The CV must be free of errors.
- *Do attend to presentation.* Create an inviting presentation format that is professional, uncluttered, and easy to read. Use a laser printer and print your CV on white paper that is of good quality but is not the heavy bond paper that is common among resumes in business settings. Although color and quality of paper are sometimes used to make business resumes stand out, they are not preferred by most psychologists (especially those in academia) and may convey that the writer is unaware of the norms of academia, which can turn a reader off (Kronenfeld & Whicker, 1997).

Don'ts in Preparing CVs

- *Don't pad your CV.* Extrawide margins, large font, and irrelevant material (e.g., high school activities and accomplishments) give the impression that applicants are inflating CVs to make them appear more impressive.
- *Don't provide excessive detail.* Although an explanation of the activities entailed in each position you have held is essential, take care not to provide excessive detail. For example, a description of research activities that includes "I composed the ad to solicit participants, scheduled their visits, greeted them" is too detailed. Anyone who has conducted research (and even those who have not) can deduce these details.
- *Don't provide irrelevant personal information.* Do not include information about your age, marital status, number of children, ethnicity,

EXHIBIT 13.2

Sample Curriculum Vitae for a Research-Oriented Student

David Smith
212 West 52nd Street
New York, NY 11012
(212) 555-9899
David.Smith@gmail.com

Education

2003–present	Doctoral Candidate, Sam University Area of Study: Developmental Psychology PhD Expected Spring 2009
2003–2004	Master of Arts, Sam University
1988–2003	Bachelor of Arts, College of Rhode Island Major: Psychology

Honors/Fellowships

2008–2009	Doctoral Dissertation Award, Hypnosis Foundation
2007	Summer Fellowship, Hypnosis Foundation, Utah Chapter
2006–2007	Graduate Assistantship, Sam University
2005–2006	Teaching Fellowship, Sam University
2004–2005	Presidential Scholarship, Sam University
2003–present	Member of Psi Chi, National Honors Society for Psychology
2002	Who's Who Among Students in American Universities and Colleges

Research Experience

2007–2008	Examined the effects of age and type of disorder on coping with stress and depression.
2007–2008	Designed and conducted program evaluation of Depression Voices Care program at Bellevue Hospital, New York City.
2005–2007	Developmental Research Internship, The Darkroom, Inc. Coded open-ended responses for initial stages of content analysis of qualitative data on older adults coping with depression. Conducted telephone interviews of older adults and their family members for a study on older adults' adaptation to depression. Screened and interviewed older adults in the community as part of a study on the role of friends and family in the adaptation to depression.
2005–2006	Research Assistant, New York City Department for the Unstable Conducted content analysis of qualitative data in a study on senior center satisfaction of older adults. Other responsibilities include interviewing older adults, data auditing, and literature review.
2005–2006	Examined the effects of coping strategies on individuals with depression. Secondary analysis of data collected for an evaluation course.
2004–2005	Lab Assistant, Sam University

EXHIBIT 13.2 *(Continued)*

	Instructed students in Introduction to Psychology Lab and Perception Lab. Responsibilities included creating and/or supervising educational lab projects, grading homework assignments, exams, and papers.
2004–2005	Rated interviews about identity formation in a college sample for the purpose of establishing interrater reliability.
2003–2004	Collected data on HIV and risk perception in a college sample.
2002–2003	Developed a questionnaire and collected and analyzed data on health risk behaviors and AIDS.
2002–2003	Collected and analyzed data on peripheral vision, aging, and attention.

Publication

Smith, D. (2008). Religiosity, risk-taking, and stress during the transition to college. *Journal of Stress, 105,* 99–100.

Manuscripts Under Review and In Preparation

Smith, D., & Simpson, H. J. (under review). *Predicting depression among college students.*
Smith, D. (in preparation). *Ethical ambiguities in research on Cracker Jacks.*

Conference Presentations

Smith, D. (2008, August). Overcoming procrastination. In W. E. Cite (Chair), *Procrastination management.* Symposium conducted at the annual meeting of the American Procrastination Association, San Francisco.

Smith, D., & Cite, W. E. (2007, August). The impact of Cracker Jacks in lowering procrastination. In J. Simpson & W. E. Cite (Co-Chairs), *Cracker Jacks: Wonder drug of the 90s?* Symposium conducted at the annual meeting of the American Cracker Jack Association, New York.

Statistics and Computer Experience

Statistics Packages:	SAS SPSS AMOS
Statistics Courses:	Introduction to Psychological Statistics Research Methodology Statistics Seminar Applications of Statistical Software Analysis of Variance Regression Analysis Structural Equations Modeling
Analysis Experience:	Multivariate Analysis of Variance Multiple Regression Multisample Path Analysis Structural Equations Modeling

(Continued)

EXHIBIT 13.2 *(Continued)*

Research Interests

Adolescence and Early Adulthood
Emphasis on risk behaviors common to these age groups such as substance use, delinquency, adolescent pregnancy, and sexually transmitted disease.

Reasoning and Decision Making
Emphasis on adolescent and young adult reasoning about life choices and engagement in risk behaviors.

Teaching Experience

2006–2007	Adjunct Instructor, Sam University Assumed full responsibility for teaching two undergraduate courses in Introduction to Psychology
2005–2006	Teaching Assistant, Sam University Assumed full responsibility for teaching undergraduate psychology courses, including Introduction to Psychology, Social Psychology, and Applied Developmental Psychology
2003–2004	Tutor in Psychology, Sam University Higher Education Opportunity Program Tutored undergraduate psychology students in Introduction to Psychology, Research Methods, and Statistics

Professional Affiliations

American Cracker Jacks Association
American Procrastination Association
American Psychological Association
Society for Research in Child Development

References

[Three are listed]

political affiliation, religious affiliation, sexual orientation, place of birth, height, weight, and hobbies. These items are irrelevant and invite bias on the part of reviewers.

- *Don't use category headings that are inaccurate.* For example, a section titled Grants and Publications is inaccurate if only one item is listed (i.e., it is either a grant or a publication).
- *Don't worry about the length.* Your CV should depict your experiences and competencies accurately. The number of pages entailed to accomplish that goal does not matter. CVs grow with careers.

The CV is an important document that is a needless source of stress for many young professionals. Accurate records and a clean and organized presentation style are all that is required for an effective CV. The

EXHIBIT 13.3

Sample Curriculum Vitae for a Clinically Oriented Student

CHRIS HEATH
14 East West Street
Any Town, ST 14000
305.555.9898
cheath@gmail.com

Education

Doctoral (PsyD) Candidate in Clinical Psychology — Anticipated, September 2008
Psychology University, Any Town, ST

Bachelor of Arts in Psychology, Cum Laude — May 2004
Psychology University, Any Town, ST

Honors and Awards

Roberts Service Award, Psychology University, July 2008
2007 Student of the Year, Psychology University
Cum Laude graduate, Psychology University
Psi Chi, National Honor Society in Psychology, inducted 2002

Clinical Experience

Clinical Psychology Intern — September 2007–September 2008
North Edwards Psychiatric Center, Any Town, ST

Served as a full-time psychology intern in an American Psychological Association–accredited psychiatric facility. Completed rotations in neuropsychology, medical consultation, posttraumatic stress disorder, and behavioral medicine. Gained experience with biofeedback, chronic pain management, group therapy, day treatment, HIV/AIDS support, and Eye Movement Desensitization and Reprocessing.

Clinical Psychology Extern — September 2006–August 2007
South Edwards Psychiatric Center, Any Town, ST

Performed duties of sole staff psychologist-in-training on a multidisciplinary medical team within a primary care community-based health-care facility. Provided long- and short-term psychotherapy to patients. Consulted with staff on the psychological and physical health of patients. Demonstrated positive results by monitoring outcomes and patient feedback through assessments.

Clinical Psychology Trainee — September 2005–August 2006
West Edwards Psychiatric Center, Any Town, ST

Administered, scored, and interpreted psychological assessment batteries within a private practice setting. Evaluations were done for psychological disability determination, cognitive and personality assessment, differential diagnosis to inform treatment, suitability for chemical dependency treatment programs, and learning disability determination.

Supervision

Psychology Department, Psychology University, Any Town, ST
Supervised a graduate student treating a client with panic disorder

(Continued)

EXHIBIT 13.3 *(Continued)*

Psychology Department, Psychology University, Any Town, ST
Supervised undergraduates in conducting interviews for a treatment study of panic disorder.

Publications

Heath, C. (2008). Religiosity, risk-taking, and stress during the transition to college. *Journal of Stress, 105,* 99–100.

Heath, C., & Coyote, W. E. (2006). The impact of Cracker Jacks on stress. *Journal of Stress, 103,* 100–110.

Conference Posters and Presentations

Heath, C., & Coyote, W. E. (2007, August). The impact of Cracker Jacks in lowering procrastination. In H. J. Simpson & W. E. Coyote (Co-chairs), *Cracker Jacks: Wonder drug of the 90s?* Symposium conducted at the annual meeting of the American Cracker Jack Association, New York.

Heath, C. (2006, May). *The developmental correlates of finishing your Cracker Jacks.* Poster session presented at the biennial meeting of the Society for Research in Child Development, Washington, DC.

Heath, C. (2004, July–August). *On Cracker Jacks and you.* Poster session presented at the annual meeting of the American Psychological Association, Honolulu, HI.

Heath, C., & Higfish, C. B. (2003, October). *Effects of social support from family and friends on adaptation to depression.* Paper presented at the annual meeting of the State Society on Depression of New York, Albany.

Teaching Experience

Adjunct Instructor 2009–2012
Something College, Anywhere, ST
Taught: Introduction to Psychology, Clinical Psychology, Abnormal Psychology

Research Experience

Research Assistant January 2004–August 2004
Psychology University, Any Town, ST
Collaborated in research examining measures of emotion. Assisted in designing research methods, ran subjects, collected/compiled data, and wrote manuscripts.
Supervisor: G. Goose, PhD

Research Assistant May 2002–August 2002
Psychology University, Any Town, ST
Assisted in research examining infant attachment
Supervisor: G. Goose, PhD

Professional Memberships

American Psychological Association, student affiliate (2004–2008).

References

[Three are listed]

recommended readings at the end of this chapter list additional resources to aid in crafting a CV.

Considering the Postdoctoral Fellowship

Postdoctoral fellowships, or postdocs, are becoming more common in psychology (Simon & Spirito, 2003) because employers seek to hire early career psychologists who have experience, competence, and can hit the ground running. Postdoctoral fellowships are the way to get that experience, allowing you to develop new skills and gain research and clinical experiences that will advance your professional career. Research postdocs are especially valued in academia, especially at research-oriented institution, because they give new psychologists the opportunity to learn methodologies, build their research programs, and gain publications. Clinical postdocs provide practitioners with additional training and the opportunity to specialize in a topical area or with a particular population while they gain experience that is necessary for licensure. Although students often seek postdoctoral training to advance their careers, some consider postdoctoral training because there are no job offers. Typical settings that hire postdoctoral fellows include hospitals, medical centers, universities, government agencies, and private industries. In sum, postdocs are employed wherever psychologists are found.

Some postdoctoral fellowships are advertised through the publications and Web sites of national professional associations such as the American Psychological Association, Association for Psychological Science, and American Psychological Association of Graduate Students. However, the majority of postdoctoral training opportunities are advertised through word of mouth and electronic announcements on professional listservs. Speak with your mentor and other faculty committee members, and they might make a few calls and tap into the hidden network of opportunities. Applications for postdoctoral positions generally require a CV, a cover letter, and letters of recommendation from your mentor and perhaps other faculty. Some may simply request names of referees. Other applications may request a research statement. Interviews can range from informal phone discussion to extensive in-person interviews.

Recognize that there is great variability in postdoctoral positions in terms of training standards and opportunities (Simon & Spirito, 2003). In considering postdoctoral positions, ask the following questions:

- What are the clinical demands (e.g., billable hours or direct patient care)?
- What is the supervisory structure?

- What is the level of satisfaction among current postdocs?
- Are there are enough clinical hours offered to meet licensure requirements?
- What are research requirements and opportunities?
- How is the position funded?
- How is research funded? Are your own projects funded?
- Will you have enough time to complete your work (i.e., will your postdoctoral fellowship last throughout a project)?

Carefully consider the supervisor because he or she is a critical part of the postdoctoral experience, similar to the graduate school mentor who shapes much of the graduate school experience. What are the supervisor's expectations? How many postdocs has he or she trained, and where have they gone afterward? What are the supervisor's policies on authorship with postdocs? Will he or she have sufficient time to mentor you? All of the considerations about selecting mentors for graduate study are also relevant here. A postdoctoral fellowship is an important training opportunity; select a site that will offer you the training you desire, provide the support needed for professional development, and respect and foster your emerging professional autonomy.

Getting a Job in Clinical Practice

Psychologists practice in a variety of settings: university counseling centers, community mental health centers, private practice, group practice, and more. In each setting, psychologists engage in the range of clinical activities, including assessment, therapy, program development and evaluation, administration, consultation, and outreach (Hinkelman, 2005).

When considering any practitioner position, examine the size and type of placement setting. University counseling centers, for example, are found in a wide variety of institutions from small private colleges to large public universities, and they serve a diverse range of students across settings. Similarly, community mental health centers vary by geographic setting (from rural to urban) and client population (from homogeneous to highly diverse in ethnicity, income, religion, and culture).

Solo private practice—practicing on one's own after licensure (or under supervision before obtaining a license)—entails considerations such as startup costs, which include office space, furniture, utilities, and malpractice insurance, and developing a client base (Vineberg, 2005). To survive, a private practice requires a steady flow of referrals and new clients. Practitioners in private practice must also understand and apply business practices; classes and instruction in accounting practices, investment strategies, and tax planning are essential because a private practice is a small business (Barnett & Henshaw, 2003; Vineberg, 2005).

In contrast to solo private practice, *group practice* refers to a group of practitioners who share resources and work under one roof. Group practices vary in how they are organized, how resources are shared, the number and specialties of providers, and the kind of services that are provided (Habben, 2005). Like psychologists in solo practice, psychologists in group practice hold much autonomy to determine hours, clients, and treatment methods, as long as they complete the number of contact hours with clients required by the practice (Habben, 2005). A big difference between private and group practice is that the risks, expenses, and work of running a practice is shared among group members, potentially reducing the stress of private practice (Barnett & Henshaw, 2003; Habben, 2005).

In general, when searching for a job as a practitioner, regardless of setting, the fewer geographic restrictions you place on your search the more likely you will find a position quickly. Search for openings in professional publications, such as the *APA Monitor* (and APA Web site) and state psychological association newsletters, local newspapers, and psychologist listservs. Also search electronic databases of jobs, such as those at Monster.com and CareerBuilder.com, where you may also post an abbreviated CV for employers to view (note that you may post a CV on the APA Web site as well).

A large proportion of job openings are not advertised other than through word of mouth. How do you learn about these openings? Network. Tell everyone you know that you are looking for a practice position. Professors and colleagues are important sources of information about job openings. Meet as many professionals as you can. Informal conversations can lead to e-mails and phone calls, interviews, and job offers. As you network, be sure to have your CV and other information prepared so that you can act quickly when you hear about a job opening. Psychologists looking to enter group practice might consider making contact with all practices in the area. Send a letter of introduction and CV to all group practices in the area in which you would like to work. You may not hear from many group practices, but if you hear from one or two, it will be time and effort well spent.

Getting a Job in Academia

The first step in seeking a position in a college or university is to locate job openings. Job advertisements are published in publications of national organizations, such as the American Psychological Association and Association for Psychological Science, and national publications such as *The Chronicle of Higher Education* and *The New York Times.* Many positions are advertised by word of mouth and on electronic listservs. Academic job openings are few and far between, and competition is fierce. Applicants without geographic restrictions, who can move anywhere, are more likely to be successful in obtaining an academic position. The typical application for a faculty position at a college or university consists of a CV, cover letter, and references. Depending on the institution, it may include the research statement, the teaching statement, or both.

Tip

Many doctoral candidates consider going on the job market before their dissertation is complete. Think twice before entering the job market as an ABD ("all but dissertation"). Most institutions prefer candidates who have completed the doctoral degree. Some will consider ABD candidates. Completing a dissertation is challenging enough without juggling the responsibilities and stresses of a new job as a professor. After teaching, grading, committee work, and other faculty duties, when will there be time to work on the dissertation? Beginning a faculty position before completing the dissertation is a recipe for disaster—for never completing the dissertation and never advancing beyond ABD.

COVER LETTER AND REFERENCES

Some search committees receive hundreds of applications. Usually the first round of reviews is split up among several faculty, and one or two may view each application to determine who makes the first cut. Cover letters set the stage for the application; a poor cover letter is detrimental.

> "A lot of the cover letters that come in are awful," one faculty member complained. "They show no understanding or awareness of what happens in our department or school. They look like they are simply word-processed form letters that go out to everyone. We reject about half of our applicant pool simply by throwing out applications with form letters. It indicates a lack of real interest in the program. An excellent cover letter, on the other hand, may make us consider someone more closely than we might have otherwise."

The above comments from a faculty member are on target. The cover letter matters. Take the time to tailor the letter to the university and department. It takes research, time, and effort to write a good cover letter. Successful cover letters demonstrate the fit of the candidate and position. Aim for the following organization in crafting your cover letter (Kronenfeld & Whicker, 1997; Reis, 1997):

In the first paragraph, explain the following:

- How you learned of the position ("I'm applying for the position of assistant professor, advertised in the *APA Monitor*").

- Who you are ("I am a doctoral candidate in social psychology, scheduled to defend my dissertation this April").
- Why you are interested in the position and department ("I am especially interested in this position because . . .").

In the middle paragraph(s),

- provide an overview of your research,
- demonstrate how your achievements and qualifications make you the right person for the position and indicate how your competencies meet the specific needs identified by the department, and
- express interest in the department and institution.

In the final paragraph,

- indicate the materials that you have enclosed in your application (e.g., CV, research statement, teaching statement, sample syllabi, and reprints),
- offer to provide additional materials, and
- thank the committee for its consideration and mention that you look forward to meeting with them.

Other suggestions include the following:

- Find out enough about the school to show the connection between what you offer and what the school needs.
- Always address the letter to a specific person, be sure to use the correct title, and spell the person's name correctly.
- Try to limit the cover letter to one page.
- Use simple and direct language.
- The cover letter (and your entire application) should be error free. Committees are particularly unforgiving of typos and spelling errors because they indicate carelessness.

Although cover letters are critical in guiding readers through your application, references often determine whether your application makes it to the next step of evaluations. Some search committees will request that candidates ask referees to submit letters before the application will be reviewed. In these cases applicants are to contact referees and request that they send reference letters to the search committee. Other search committees request that applicants include a list of referees; they then contact referees to request letters for applicants who show promise.

Your referees must speak very highly of you because all reference letters are extremely positive; a neutral letter is damaging to your application. Seek letters from faculty who know you well and can speak to your promise as a research, teacher, and colleague. Not all referees can cover all of the bases, so choose at least one referee who can speak to your teaching and at least one (preferably more) who can speak to your research. The same basic rules of seeking letters of recommendation for graduate school and internship apply here.

STATEMENTS OF TEACHING AND RESEARCH

A statement of teaching philosophy increasingly is required at both teaching- and research-oriented institutions. The teaching statement is a description of your teaching philosophy, experience, and interests. Describe what you do in the classroom and why you do it. What is the basis for the decisions you make about how to organize and run your classes?

Discuss your teaching experience, including experiences as a teaching assistant. What courses have you taught and what are you prepared to teach? Discuss how you have taught your courses and move beyond simply listing courses that appear on your CV. Which student populations interest you? What methods do you use: discussion, lecture, group work, cases, in-class activities? Provide examples and how you use them to achieve goals. What is the role of technology in your classroom? Discuss your beliefs about why your methods work. What are your goals as teacher and how do you meet these goals? Demonstrate that you are thoughtful in your teaching process, and provide justification for the teaching choices that you make.

The teaching statement should be one to two pages in length. Most teaching statements are written in the first person. Proofread the document; errors are unacceptable. Seek feedback from others, especially others whom you deem excellent teachers. Include sample teaching materials as appendixes to your teaching statement (e.g., cases, assignments, teaching strategies). Choose only a few samples very carefully, and ensure that the samples reflect how you wish to be perceived.

While the teaching statement describes the philosophy that underlies your teaching, the research statement discusses your program of research and why it is important. Search committees are interested in learning about your *program* of research rather than individual research projects. In other words, discuss how the research studies you have conducted fit together to examine a given problem or set of problems in your field; what story does your work tell? Some students are puzzled as to how to present their research as a cohesive whole. Consider the topic of each of your research studies. In what ways are they similar? Even if they do not focus on the same topic, it is likely that there are commonalities in approach and content emphasis. For example, one student who conducted research studies on group think, social influences on coping, and adolescents' perception of risks entailed in alcohol use determined that the common element across the studies was social cognition, that is, how people process and understand social information and make decisions in the world. Most students will find a common theme that links their research, but it usually requires that students consider their work from a global perspective, looking at the broad research question examined in each study rather than focusing on the specific variables of any one study.

Tip

In constructing your research statement, describe how your work is related to others' work but demonstrate that your research is your own. Avoid too many references to your mentor's work because it is important that you demonstrate your autonomy and that you are a competent, independent researcher.

In addition to summarizing and tying together your past research, discuss your current work. How does your dissertation fit into this line of research? Discuss future directions for your work. How will you continue this line of research over the next 3 to 5 years? As you discuss the future, emphasize that your research is programmatic. Identify a specific aspect of your prior work that you will study in depth and discuss how you will do so. Briefly discuss the research questions that you intend to study and how the next set of research studies will do so. Why is this work important? What gaps in the literature will your research program fill? What are the applied implications of your work? Finally, discuss funding: What funds have you received from outside sources, and what is your plan for securing grants to fund your research? This is particularly important for research-oriented institutions; however, teaching-oriented institutions increasingly are becoming interested in applicants' potential to secure outside funding.

All of these details of your research statement should comprise about one or two pages in length, but no more than three. Writing in the first person is permissible. Write with a general audience in mind; avoid technical terms and jargon. Define terms. Use headings to organize the content and make it easier for readers to grasp the components of your research statement. Seek feedback from your mentor, other faculty, and colleagues to ensure that the document is clear, concise, and sends the message that you intend. Finally, proofread the document, and ask someone else to proofread it as well. Spelling and grammatical errors on any part of your application are the kiss of death for your candidacy.

THE INTERVIEW AND JOB TALK

Once the search committee receives your application and the deadline for submissions has passed, they review the applications. Many searches yield 100 applications or more; therefore, the review process can take some time. The top candidates are selected and, if they have not yet been received, references are requested. After much discussion, the search committee narrows down the candidates. Sometimes they cannot decide which candidates to invite to a campus interview or they have limited funds for inviting candidates to interview. In these cases the search committee may conduct an interview by phone to screen candidates. Once the list of candidates is narrowed down to five or six, the committee invites the top three applicants to a campus interview. The academic interview is very different from interviews for nonacademic positions.

Academic interviews typically take place over 1 to 2 days. Candidates are often met at the airport or given directions on how to get to the hotel. You will meet many people during your interview. Most departments make applications available for interested readers to permit department members the opportunity to learn about you before you arrive. Not all department members do the preparatory reading. It is likely that you will meet with some faculty who do not know the foggiest thing about you.

Before your visit, try to get an agenda that will outline your visit: when you will speak, meals and social events, and the people you will meet. Obtaining this material before your visit will help you to prepare and plan. Expect to meet with the faculty chair, dean, provost, faculty who conduct similar research, and perhaps graduate students. In addition to longer meetings with the department chair and administrators, you will also have many one-on-one sessions with faculty that might last 15 to 30 minutes.

In your meetings, ask about the department and university, but ask informed questions that indicate that you have done your homework. Ask questions in each of your meetings with faculty to compare responses. Faculty may offer different responses to questions such as whether the institution's mission regarding research and teaching is changing. Look through the course catalog, department homepage, and faculty Web pages. Show that you are interested in the department and university, that you think highly of them, and that you are very interested in joining them. Your enthusiasm confirms the search committee's decision to invite you to campus. Know a little bit about the faculty, especially those with whom you will meet: their research, background, and where they earned their degrees. Show that you know something about their work; it is flattering and demonstrates sincere interest (Sternberg, 2003). Try to determine common ground with the faculty. How can you connect? It is by forming connections, on an intellectual and personal level, that you win support that is crucial to advancing your candidacy.

Tip

Remember that social events, though informal, are part of the interview. Your interactions and behavior will be carefully observed. Be wary of alcohol consumption and remember that you are always on display and are always the potential candidate, not a friend.

What does the search committee look for in interviews? They want a colleague who is well matched to the department, which means that he or she will fit in, share values concerning teaching and scholarship, and be a good colleague (Sternberg, 2003). Search committees also look for candidates who are a good fit to the position, who can teach the desired courses and are trained and conduct research in the desired subarea. All institutions, regardless of research orientation, value teaching. Desirable candidates are good teachers (Sternberg, 2003). Search committees also look for candidates who are good scholars and fit into the departmental and university profile regarding scholarship. For example, research-oriented institutions seek candidates with research experience, publications, well-defined research plans, and the potential to secure grant funding. Institutions that are more oriented toward teaching may seek candidates who are interested in conducting quality research that integrates students, informs teaching, and is conducted at a pace that is conducive to a heavy teaching load.

The most nerve-wracking part of the academic job interview is the job talk. Typically, the job talk entails presenting your research program to the department's faculty and graduate students. Sometimes the job talk entails teaching an undergraduate class; this is more common in teaching-oriented institutions as compared with research-oriented institutions. Occasionally, a department may request candidates to teach a class and give a research presentation.

If you are invited to teach a class, remember that the faculty are interested in how you connect with students, but they also understand that it is difficult to establish rapport when teaching a one-shot deal, in a single class. Questions that they will consider in evaluating your teaching include the following:

- *Interaction style.* Are you clear, and are your points easy to understand? Do you encourage student questions? How do you respond to student questions? What kind of questions do you ask, and how do you react to student responses (or lack thereof)?
- *Organization.* Does the lesson have an identifiable beginning, middle, and end? Is the organization apparent to students? Are the organizing themes clear?

- *Methods.* How much lecture and discussion do you use? Do you use cases or other activities to achieve class goals? How do you integrate the various components—cases and discussion—into the lesson, and do you draw conclusions from these components that students can grasp? Do your teaching techniques encourage active learning and critical thinking?
- *Technology.* What technology do you use? If you use PowerPoint, how effective are your overheads? How easy are they for students to grasp? Are they overly complex? How do you use the whiteboard? Are major points emphasized through overheads, handouts, or use of the whiteboard?

The research presentation usually is the central element of the job interview. The same procedure and strategies that work for conference presentations also apply here; however, the research presentation is a much longer talk and should be tailored for your specific audience. In most cases, 1 hour is allotted to the presentation. Prepare to speak for about 40 to 45 minutes, which permits 15 minutes for questions. However, also take into account that most job talks do not start on time, so a 40-minute presentation will permit 10 to 15 minutes of questions, assuming that you begin a few minutes late.

Begin preparing your presentation as soon as you are able. Remember that this is not simply a presentation of your dissertation. Instead you are expected to go well beyond your dissertation to include a discussion of your earlier work (if it relates to the dissertation) and where you will go next in this line of research (from your research statement; Reis, 1997).

Prepare for a general audience. Some of the jargon and technical terms that you use will be new to audience members who do not conduct research in your area (McCabe & McCabe, 2000). Your challenge is to not insult the audience by defining elementary terms (remember that your audience is composed of psychologists) yet to not lose the audience by using technical terms that are not defined (Sternberg, 2003). Seek input from colleagues, especially graduate students and faculty in different subfields of psychology, to determine whether your presentation is appropriate for a general audience of psychologists.

Rehearse your presentation often. Ensure that you do not finish too quickly or run over your allotted time. Presentations often are longer than you realize. Running over is common because you speak more slowly to an audience than you do in everyday conversation. It is embarrassing to finish very quickly, allowing too much time for questions (20–30 minutes) and increasing your likelihood of hearing crickets chirp. On the other hand, running out of time frustrates your audience because you must either speed up to get through your presentation or stop early, having left out critical information; either way, audience members usually are left confused. Prepare well to present a polished performance. Presentations run smoothly and appear off-the-cuff only after a great deal of preparation and practice (Sternberg, 2003). Preparation is what permits you to be spontaneous and to handle the unexpected.

Organize your presentation with a clear beginning, middle, and end. Explain why your work is interesting and important. Use a concrete example at the beginning of your talk to make the value of your work clear (Sternberg, 2003). Use examples and relevant anecdotes to maintain audience interest (Reis, 1997). Lead the audience through your talk by telling them what you are going to demonstrate, demonstrating it, and then telling them what you have demonstrated. As you progress through the talk, reiterate the purpose and what each step in the presentation means with regard to that purpose.

Cite relevant work, especially that of audience members. Discuss the antecedents to your own work and acknowledge the work of others. Place your work in the broader context of research (Reis, 1997). Leave the audience with a take-home message about your purpose, what you tried to show, what it meant, and why they should care. As you prepare, consider what you want your audience to consider and remember when they leave (Reis, 1997; Sternberg, 2003).

Prepare for questions (Sternberg, 2003). Sometimes candidates give an excellent talk yet are not prepared to answer questions and blow it. Think about the questions you are likely to receive. Practice responding to questions. Overall, the same techniques for preparing for proposal and dissertation defense as well as conference presentations work here.

Considering Skills, Considering Careers

Doctoral training in psychology imparts skills that are generalizable to a wide variety of settings. Although the majority of psychologists work in human service and academic settings, a substantial number of psychologists work in nontraditional settings, such as business and government settings. For example, 18% of 2003 doctorate recipients held full-time positions in business schools, government, and other settings (compared with 42% in human services, 28% in academia, and 11% in schools; Wicherski & Kohout, 2005).

The most critical skills that graduate students develop include information gathering, analysis and synthesis, methodological design, and statistical reasoning (Kuther & Morgan, 2007). Graduate study entails specialized training in how to work with information: how to identify needs, collect information, critically evaluate and synthesize information, and draw conclusions and recommendations. Employers value these skills. More specifically, they look for the following:

Information management skills:

- Ability to define, plan, and oversee projects.
- Ability to identify a problem and generate questions, especially from ambiguous data.
- Ability to recognize that there are multiple ways of addressing a problem or studying a question and to consider and critically evaluate each.
- Ability to create a plan to address a research question, including identifying steps needed to complete the project.
- Ability to identify needed resources, secure them, and manage them to complete the project.
- Ability to oversee a team that carries out a project.

Methodological and statistics skills:

- Ability to design experimental, quasi-experimental, and qualitative studies.
- Ability to detect potential confounds in variables or problematic designs and procedures.
- Statistical reasoning and analysis skills.
- Ability to summarize and draw conclusions from data.
- Ability to present results and conclusions of research to nontechnical audiences.

Thinking skills and understanding of human behavior:

- Understanding that people approach problems from different perspectives.
- Ability to take perspective of others.
- Recognition that there are advantages to all perspectives.
- Understanding of qualitative characteristics of human development and behavior, such as cognitive, perceptual, physical, emotional, and social capacities.

General skills:

- Ability to learn quickly.
- Ability to work well with people.
- Ability to take initiative.
- Dependability.
- Computer literacy.

Psychologists who seek nontraditional careers should assess their skill set as they consider potential careers. Although all psychologists are trained in the above skills, they vary in their strengths and weaknesses. Examine yours. There are many career options. Consider how you would like to spend your time. Which activities are most interesting to you? Examples of positions held by psychologists include but are not limited to the following (Kuther & Morgan, 2007; Morgan, Kuther, & Habben, 2005): management consultant, quantitative analyst, usability specialist, trial consultant, social policy researcher, acquisitions editor, science writer, technology consultant, research analyst, market research consultant, executive search consultant, and executive coach. The recommended readings at the end of this chapter offer resources that provide information and guidance on alternative careers in psychology.

Developing a career as a professional psychologist, whether clinical or academic, entails a variety of skills that are not taught in graduate school. Learn how to construct a CV and a solid job application, interview well, and you will have an advantage over the mass of job applicants who are unprepared. Applying for a position is a risk; there is always the opportunity to fail. However, there is risk in every aspect of professional development. Do not be afraid to take risks because it is through taking risks and managing their consequences that people grow. All psychologists, especially beginning psychologists, make mistakes. Do not dwell on your mistakes but learn from them. Successful psychologists recognize that professional development is a career-long enterprise. Embark on this journey early and reap the professional rewards.

Recommended Reading

Barnett, J. E., & Henshaw, E. (2003). Training to begin a private practice. In M. J. Prinstein & M. D. Patterson (Eds.), *The portable mentor: Expert guide to a successful career in psychology* (pp. 145–156). New York: Kluwer Academic/Plenum Publishers.

Kottler, J. A., & Hazler, R. J. (1997). *What you never learned in graduate school: A survival guide for therapists.* New York: Norton.

Kronenfeld, J. J., & Whicker, M. L. (1997). *Getting an academic job: Strategies for success.* Thousand Oaks, CA: Sage.

Morgan, R. D., Kuther, T. L., & Habben, C. J. (2005). *Life after graduate school: Opportunities and advice from new psychologists.* New York: Psychology Press.

Pope, K. S., & Vasquez, M. J. T. (2005). *How to survive and thrive as a therapist: Information, ideas, and resources for psychologists in practice.* Washington, DC: American Psychological Association.

Simon, V. A., & Spirito, A. (2003). Recommendations for a postdoctoral fellowship. In M. J. Prinstein & M. D. Patterson (Eds.), *The portable mentor: Expert guide to a successful career in psychology* (pp. 269–285). New York: Kluwer Academic/Plenum Publishers.

Sternberg, R. (2003). The job search. In M. J. Prinstein & M. D. Patterson (Eds.), *The portable mentor: Expert guide to a successful career in psychology* (pp. 297–309). New York: Kluwer Academic/Plenum Publishers.

Sternberg, R. (2006). *Career paths in psychology: Where your degree can take you* (2nd ed.). Washington, DC: American Psychological Association.

Afterword

Throughout this book we have seen that the great deal of autonomy granted graduate students acts as a double-edged sword. Autonomy permits students to use their time as they see fit, grapple with questions of their own choosing, and carve out a professional identity of their own. At the same time, many students are unprepared to take advantage of the autonomy afforded them. Perhaps the most important theme of this book is that success in graduate school requires that students be proactive and take control of their own learning and professional development. All of the following take-home messages flow from the assumption that students must take initiative and responsibility for their own professional development.

Be your own best advocate.

No one cares as much about your success or will advocate for your interests as well as you. You cannot expect anyone to keep track of your progress, hold your hand, or tell you what to do. Successful students recognize that it is their responsibility to take initiative, monitor their own progress, ask questions, and seek assistance.

Keep the big picture in mind.

Managing the day-to-day tasks of graduate study—reading, writing papers, completing research tasks—can eat up all of your time and energy. While these tasks are essential, don't forget to look ahead at the big picture: What's the next step in your program and how are you getting there? Keep the dissertation and your ultimate career goals in mind. Plan ahead to prepare for each stage of graduate school, keep progressing towards your ultimate goal, and avoid unpleasant surprises.

Don't neglect your personal life.
The demands of graduate school can take over your life and make you neglect your own personal needs. Don't let this happen. Treat graduate school like a job. Put in full-time hours, scheduling time to work during the week and perhaps some evenings or weekends, but also schedule time off. Don't let graduate school stop you from interacting with family and friends and making time for you. View your training within the broader context of your life and life plans. Set your professional goals and priorities, but also set personal priorities and schedule your time with both in mind.

Be reflective.
During the graduate school years you will develop a sense of professional identity. This entails learning about yourself, becoming aware of your issues, defining your values, and understanding how your perspective influences your work. Personal reflection is an essential part of professional development over the duration of a career. At regular intervals, reflect on your professional goals, training experiences, and personal and professional needs.

Take risks and make mistakes.
Some students play it safe. They study problems to which they already know the answers, avoid difficult cases, and rarely take classes they know will entail a struggle. Don't be that student. Take intellectual risks. Try something challenging. Open up the possibility for mistakes. It is through taking risks and managing their consequences that we grow as professionals. Recognize that you will make mistakes. Everyone does. Learn from them and avoid repeating them.

The graduate school years are a wondrous time of opportunity. Take advantage of this time to shape your personal and professional identity. The key to success in graduate school is to embrace the autonomy afforded, be open to new experiences, and be reflective enough to learn from your mistakes and grow as a psychologist.

References

Adler, P. A., & Adler, P. (2005). The identity career of the graduate student: Professional socialization to academic sociology. *American Sociologist, 36,* 11–27.

Aldwin, C. M. (2005). *Stress, coping, and development: An integrative perspective.* New York: Guilford Press.

American Psychiatric Association. (2000). *Diagnostic and statistical manual of mental disorders* (4th ed., text revision). Washington, DC: Author.

American Psychological Association. (1986). *Accreditation handbook.* Washington, DC: Author.

American Psychological Association. (2001). *Publication manual of the American Psychological Association* (5th ed.). Washington, DC: Author.

American Psychological Association. (2002). Ethical principles of psychologists and code of conduct. *American Psychologist, 57,* 1060–1073.

Arney, K. (2003). *The scientific conference guide,* from Science's Next Wave. Retrieved November 30, 2007, from http://sciencecareers.sciencemag.org/career_development/previous_issues/articles/2380/thescientificconference_guide_or_how_to_make_the_most_of_your_free_holiday

Association of Psychology Postdoctoral and Internship Center (APPIC) Board of Directors. (2006). *2006 APPIC Match: Survey of internship applicants.* Retrieved November 30, 2007, from http://www.appic.org/match/5_2_2_4_8_match_about_statistics_surveys_2006.htm

Association of Psychology Postdoctoral and Internship Center (APPIC) Board of Directors. (2007). *2007 Match statistics.* Retrieved November 30, 2007, from http://www.appic.org/match/5_2_2_1_9_match_about_statistics_general_2007.html

Barnett, J. E., & Henshaw, E. (2003). Training to begin a private practice. In M. J. Prinstein & M. D. Patterson (Eds.), *The portable mentor: Expert guide to a successful career in psychology* (pp. 145–156). New York: Kluwer Academic/Plenum Publishers.

Billings, A. C., & Moos, R. H. (1982). Stressful life events and symptoms: A longitudinal model. *Health Psychology, 1,* 99–117.

Bloom, D. F., Karp, J. D., & Cohen, N. (1998). *The Ph.D. process: A student's guide to graduate school in the sciences.* New York: Oxford University Press.

Boggs, K. R., & Douce, L. A. (2000). Current status and anticipated changes in psychology internships: Effects on counseling psychology training. *Counseling Psychologist, 28,* 672–686.

Boice, R. (2000). *Advice for new faculty members.* Boston: Allyn & Bacon.

Borders, L. D. (1989). Developmental cognitions of first practicum supervisors. *Journal of Counseling Psychology, 36,* 163–169.

Bruss, K. V., & Kopala, M. (1993). Graduate school training in psychology: Its impact upon the development of professional identity. *Psychotherapy, 30,* 685–691.

Charlesworth, E. A., & Nathan, R. G. (2004). *Stress management: A comprehensive guide to wellness.* New York: Ballantine Books.

Clance, P. R., & Imes, S. (1978). The imposter phenomenon in high achieving women: Dynamics and therapeutic intervention. *Psychotherapy Theory: Research and Practice, 15,* 241–247.

Clark, R. A., Harden, S. L., & Johnson, W. B. (2000). Mentor relationships in clinical psychology doctoral training: Results of a national survey. *Teaching of Psychology, 27,* 262–268.

Clemence, A. J., & Handler, L. (2001). Psychological assessment on internship: A survey of training directors and their expectations for students. *Journal of Personality Assessment, 76,* 18–47.

Cohen, L. L., & Greco, L. A. (2003). Presenting your research. In M. J. Prinstein & M. D. Patterson (Eds.), *The portable mentor: Expert guide to a successful career in psychology* (pp. 73–84). New York: Kluwer Academic/Plenum Publishers.

Colón Semenza, G. M. (2005). *Graduate study for the twenty-first century: How to build an academic career in the humanities.* New York: Macmillan.

Cone, J. D., & Foster, S. L. (2006). *Dissertations and theses from start to finish: Psychology and related fields* (2nd ed.). Washington, DC: American Psychological Association.

Cross, M. C., & Papadopoulos, L. (2001). *Becoming a therapist.* New York: Taylor & Francis.

Curzan, A., & Damour, L. (2000). *First day to final grade: A graduate student's guide to teaching.* Ann Arbor: University of Michigan Press.

Dearing, R. L., Maddux, J. E., & Tangney, J. P. (2005). Predictors of psychological help seeking in clinical and counseling psychology graduate students. *Professional Psychology: Research and Practice, 36,* 323–329.

Dee, P. (2001, May 18). *Yours transferably: Ruthless reading.* Retrieved January 16, 2007, from http://sciencecareers.sciencemag.org/career_development/previous_issues/articles/0980/yours_transferably_ruthless_reading/

Denicola, J. A., & Furze, C. T. (2001). The internship year: The transition from student to professional. In S. Walfish & A. K. Hess (Eds.), *Succeeding in graduate school: The career guide for psychology students* (pp. 335–349). Mahwah, NJ: Erlbaum.

Dingfelder, S. F. (2005). Breaking into peer reviews. *GradPsych, 3*(2). Retrieved November 30, 2007, from http://gradpsych.apags.org/mar05/peerreview.html

Dittmann, M. (2003). CV dos and don'ts. *GradPsych, 1*(2). Retrieved November 30, 2007, from http://gradpsych.apags.org/sep03/cv.cfm

Dodgen, D., Fowler, R. D., & Williams-Nickelson, C. (2003). Getting involved in professional organizations: A gateway to career advancement. In M. J. Prinstein & M. D. Patterson (Eds.), *The portable mentor: Expert guide to a successful career in psychology* (pp. 221–234). New York: Kluwer Academic/Plenum Publishers.

Ducheny, K., Alletzhauser, H. L., Crandell, D., & Schneider, T. R. (1997). Graduate student professional development. *Professional Psychology: Research and Practice, 28,* 87–91.

Dunkley, D. M., Blankstein, K. R., Halsall, J., Williams, M., & Winkworth, G. (2000). The relation between perfectionism and distress: Hassles, coping, and perceived social support as mediators and moderators. *Journal of Counseling Psychology, 47,* 437–453.

Fowler, R. D. (1999). Managing a professional association. In W. O'Donohue & J. E. Fisher (Eds.), *Management and administration skills for the mental health professional* (pp. 275–291). New York: Academic Press.

Frank, F., & Stein, K. (2004). *Playing the game: The street-smart guide to graduate school.* New York: iUniverse.

Gloria, A. M., Castillo, L. G., Choi-Pearson, C. P., & Rangel, D. K. (1997). Competitive internship candidates: A national survey of internship training directors. *Counseling Psychologist, 25,* 453–472.

Goplerud, E. N. (2001). Stress and stress mastery in graduate school. In S. Walfish & A. K. Hess (Eds.), *Succeeding in graduate school: The career guide for psychology students* (pp. 129–140). Mahwah, NJ: Erlbaum.

Gross, S. M. (2005). Student perspective on clinical and counseling psychology practica. *Professional Psychology: Research and Practice, 36,* 299–306.

Guinee, J. P. (1998). Erikson's life span theory: A metaphor for conceptualizing the internship year. *Professional Psychology: Research and Practice, 29,* 615–620.

Habben, C. J. (2005). Group practice: Adapting private practice to the new marketplace. In R. D. Morgan, T. L. Kuther, & C. J. Habben (Eds.), *Life after graduate school in psychology* (pp. 97–112). New York: Psychology Press.

Hall, R. G., & Hsu, J. (Eds.). (1999). *Internships and postdoctoral programs in professional psychology: APPIC directory 28th edition, 1999–2000.* Washington, DC: Association of Psychology Postdoctoral and Internship Centers.

Hall, R. G., & Hsu, J. (Eds.). (2000). *Internships and postdoctoral programs in professional psychology: APPIC directory 29th edition, 2000–2001.* Washington, DC: Association of Psychology Postdoctoral and Internship Centers.

Hartley, J., & Davies, I. K. (1978). Note-taking: A critical review. *Programmed Learning and Educational Technology, 15,* 207–224.

Hasan, N. T., Fouad, N. A., & Williams-Nickelson, C. (2008). *Studying psychology in the United States: Expert guidance for international students.* Washington, DC: American Psychological Association.

Henning, K., Ey, S., & Shaw, D. (1998). Perfectionism, the imposter phenomenon and the psychological adjustment in medical, dental, nursing, and pharmacy students. *Medical Education, 32,* 456–464.

Hess, A. K. (2001). Learning psychotherapy. In S. Walfish & A. K. Hess (Eds.), *Succeeding in graduate school: The career guide for psychology students* (pp. 249–262). Mahwah, NJ: Erlbaum.

Hinkelman, J. M. (2005). University counseling center: Bridging the gap between university counseling centers and academia. In R. D. Morgan, T. L. Kuther, & C. J. Habben (Eds.), *Life after graduate school in psychology* (pp. 73–86). New York: Psychology Press.

Institute of Medicine of the National Academies. (2006). *Sleep disorders and sleep deprivation: An unmet public health problem.* Washington, DC: National Academies Press.

Johnson, W. B., & Huwe, J. M. (2003). *Getting mentored in graduate school.* Washington, DC: American Psychological Association.

Kaslow, N. J., Pate, W. E., II, & Thorn, B. (2005). Academic and internship directors' perspectives on practicum experiences: Implications for training. *Professional Psychology: Research and Practice, 36,* 307–317.

Kaslow, N. J., & Rice, D. G. (1985). The psychological stresses of internship training: What training staff can do to help. *Professional Psychology: Research and Practice, 16,* 253–261.

Katell, A. D., Levant, R. F., & Loonstra, A. S. (2003). Gaining clinical experience in and after graduate school. In M. J. Prinstein & M. D. Patterson (Eds.), *The portable mentor: Expert guide to a successful career in psychology* (pp. 135–143). New York: Kluwer Academic/Plenum Publishers.

Kazdin, A. E. (2003). Publishing your research. In M. J. Prinstein & M. D. Patterson (Eds.), *The portable mentor: Expert guide to a successful career in psychology* (pp. 85–100). New York: Kluwer Academic/Plenum Publishers.

Keilin, W. G. (2007). The match. In C. Williams-Nickelson & M. J. Prinstein (Eds.), *Internships in psychology: The APAGS workbook for writing successful applications and finding the right match* (pp. 93–98). Washington, DC: American Psychological Association.

Keilin, W. G., & Constantine, M. G. (2001). Applying to professional psychology internship programs. In S. Walfish & A. K. Hess (Eds.), *Succeeding in graduate school: The career guide for psychology students* (pp. 319–333). Mahwah, NJ: Erlbaum.

Keilin, W. G., Thorn, E. E., Rodolfa, E. R., Constantine, M. G., & Kaslow, N. J. (2000). Examining the balance of internship supply and demand: 1999 Association of Psychology Postdoctoral and Internship Centers' match implications. *Professional Psychology: Research and Practice, 31,* 288–294.

Korn, J. H. (2001). Developing teaching skills. In S. Walfish & A. K. Hess (Eds.), *Succeeding in graduate school: The career guide for psychology students* (pp. 221–232). Mahwah, NJ: Erlbaum.

Kram, K. E. (1985). *Mentoring at work: Developmental relationships in organizational life.* Glenview, IL: Scott Foresman.

Krieshok, T. S., Lopez, S. J., Somberg, D. R., & Cantrell, P. J. (2000). Dissertation while on internship: Obstacles and predictors of progress. *Professional Psychology: Research and Practice, 31,* 327–331.

Kronenfeld, J. J., & Whicker, M. L. (1997). *Getting an academic job: Strategies for success.* Thousand Oaks, CA: Sage.

Kuther, T. L., & Morgan, R. (2007). *Careers in psychology: Opportunities in a changing world* (2nd ed.). Belmont, CA: Thomson/Wadsworth.

Lamb, D. H., Baker, J. M., Jennings, M. L., & Yarris, E. (1982). Passages of an internship in professional psychology. *Professional Psychology 13,* 661–669.

Lazarus, J. (2000). *Stress relief and relaxation techniques.* New York: McGraw-Hill.

Levine, I. (2005). *Are science trainees driven to drink?* Retrieved November 30, 2007, from http://sciencecareers.sciencemag.org/career_development/previous_issues/articles/3430/mind_matters_are_science_trainees_driven_to_drink

Levine, I. (2006, July 28). *Forty winks: Science and sleep.* Retrieved November 30, 2007, from http://sciencecareers.sciencemag.org/career_development/previous_issues/articles/2006_07_28/forty_winks_science_and_sleep/(parent)/158

Lewis, B. L., Hatcher, R. L., & Pate, W. E., II. (2005). The practicum experience: A survey of practicum site coordinators. *Professional Psychology: Research and Practice, 36,* 291–298.

Lopez, S. J., & Draper, K. (1997). Recent developments and more internship tips: A comment on Mellott, Arden, and Cho (1997). *Professional Psychology: Research and Practice, 28,* 496–498.

Lopez, S. J., & Prinstein, M. J. (2007). Goals and essays. In C. Williams-Nickelson & M. J. Prinstein (Eds.), *Internships in psychology: The APAGS workbook for writing successful applications and finding the right match* (pp. 23–29). Washington, DC: American Psychological Association.

Lovallo, W. R. (2004). *Stress and health: Biological and psychological interactions.* Thousand Oaks, CA: Sage.

Madson, M. B., Aten, J. D., & Leach, M. M. (2007). Applying for the predoctoral internship: Training program strategies to help students prepare. *Training and Education in Professional Psychology, 1,* 116–124.

Maki, D. R., & Delworth, U. (1995). Clinical supervision: A definition and model for the rehabilitation profession. *Rehabilitation Counseling Bulletin, 38,* 282–293.

Malley-Morrison, K., Patterson, M. D., & Yap, L. (2003). Proposing and completing your dissertation. In M. J. Prinstein & M. D. Patterson (Eds.), *The portable mentor: Expert guide to a successful career in psychology* (pp. 117–130). New York: Kluwer Academic/Plenum Publishers.

Martin, R. P. (2001). Preparing and defending theses and dissertations. In S. Walfish & A. K. Hess (Eds.), *Succeeding in graduate school: The career guide for psychology students* (pp. 303–317). Mahwah, NJ: Erlbaum.

McCabe, L. L., & McCabe, E. R. B. (2000). *How to succeed in academics.* San Diego, CA: Academic Press.

McKarney, L. (2001, April 20). Peer-review techniques for novices. *ScienceCareers.org.* Retrieved November 30, 2007, from http://sciencecareers.sciencemag.org/career_development/previous_issues/articles/0980/peer_review_techniques_for_novices

McKeachie, W. J. (1994). *Teaching tips: Strategies, research, and theory for college and university teachers* (9th ed.). Lexington, MA: D.C. Heath.

McNeill, B. W., Stoltenberg, C. D., & Romans, J. S. C. (1992). The integrated developmental model of supervision: Scale development and validation procedures. *Professional Psychology: Research and Practice, 23,* 504–508.

Megargee, E. I. (2001). *Megargee's guide to obtaining a psychology internship* (4th ed.). New York: Brunner-Routledge.

Meyers, S. A., & Prieto, L. R. (2000). Training in the teaching of psychology: What is done and examining the differences. *Teaching of Psychology, 27,* 258–261.

Miller, W. R., & Thoresen, C. E. (2003). Spirituality, religion, and health: An emerging research field. *American Psychologist, 58,* 24–35.

Mitchell, L. (1996). *The ultimate grad school survival* guide. Princeton, NJ: Peterson's.

Morgan, R. D., Kuther, T. L., & Habben, C. J. (2005). *Life after graduate school: Opportunities and advice from new psychologists.* New York: Psychology Press.

National Institute on Alcohol Abuse and Alcoholism. (2008). *How to cut down on your drinking.* Retrieved January 16, 2008, from http://pubs.niaaa.nih.gov/publications/handout.htm

Norcross, J. C. (2000). Psychotherapist self-care: Practitioner-tested, research-informed strategies. *Professional Psychology: Research and Practice, 31,* 710–713.

Norcross, J. C. (2005). The psychotherapist's own psychotherapy: Educating and developing psychologists. *American Psychologist, 60,* 840–850.

O'Neill, J. M., & Wrightsman, L. S. (2001). The mentoring relationship in psychology training programs. In S. Walfish & A. K. Hess (Eds.), *Succeeding in graduate school: The career guide for psychology students* (pp. 111–128). Mahwah, NJ: Erlbaum.

Peters, R. L. (1997). *Getting what you came for: The smart student's guide to earning a master's or Ph.D.* New York: Farrar, Straus, and Giroux.

Pica, M. (1998). The ambiguous nature of clinical training and its impact on the development of student clinicians. *Psychotherapy, 35,* 361–365.

Prinstein, M. J. (2007). The interview. In C. Williams-Nickelson & M. J. Prinstein (Eds.), *Internships in psychology: The APAGS workbook for writing successful applications and finding the right match* (pp. 79–89). Washington, DC: American Psychological Association.

Prinstein, M. J., Lopez, S. J., & Rasmussen, H. N. (2003). Navigating the internship application process. In M. J. Prinstein & M. D. Patterson (Eds.), *The portable mentor: Expert guide to a successful career in psychology* (pp. 157–169). New York: Kluwer Academic/Plenum Publishers.

Rando, W., & Rozenblit, L. (2003). Recommendations for teaching psychology. In M. J. Prinstein & M. D. Patterson (Eds.), *The portable mentor: Expert guide to a successful career in psychology* (pp. 101–116). New York: Kluwer Academic/Plenum Publishers.

Reis, R. M. (1997). *Tomorrow's professor: Preparing for academic careers in science and engineering.* Piscataway, NJ: IEEE Press.

Riggs, S. A., & Bretz, K. M. (2006). Attachment processes in the supervisory relationship: An exploratory investigation. *Professional Psychology: Research and Practice, 37,* 558–566.

Rodolfa, E. R., Vieille, R., Russell, P., Nijjer, S., Nguyen, D. Q., Mendoza, M., et al. (1999). Internship selection: Inclusion and exclusion criteria. *Professional Psychology: Research and Practice, 30,* 415–419.

Rosen, D. (n.d.). *How to be a good practicum student.* Retrieved November 30, 2007, from http://www.apa.org/apags/profdev/goodpracstudent.html

Rossman, M. H. (2002). *Negotiating graduate school: A guide for graduate students* (2nd ed.). Thousand Oaks, CA: Sage.

Rudestam, K. E., & Newton, R. R. (2007). *Surviving your dissertation: A comprehensive guide to content and process* (3rd ed.). Thousand Oaks, CA: Sage.

Rugg, G., & Petre, M. (2004). *The unwritten rules of PhD research.* New York: Open University Press.

Schindler, B. A., Novack, D. H., Cohen, D. G., Yager, J., Wang, D., Shaheen, N. J., et al. (2006). The impact of the changing health care environment on the health and well-being of faculty at four medical schools. *Academic Medicine, 81,* 27–34.

Simon, V. A., & Spirito, A. (2003). Recommendations for a postdoctoral fellowship. In M. J. Prinstein & M. D. Patterson (Eds.), *The portable mentor: Expert guide to a successful career in psychology* (pp. 269–285). New York: Kluwer Academic/Plenum Publishers.

Stedman, J. M. (2006). What we know about predoctoral internship training: A review [Special volume]. *Training and Education in Professional Psychology, 2,* 80–95.

Sternberg, R. (2003). The job search. In M. J. Prinstein & M. D. Patterson (Eds.), *The portable mentor: Expert guide to a successful career in psychology* (pp. 297–309). New York: Kluwer Academic/Plenum Publishers.

Stoltenberg, C. D. (2005). Enhancing professional competence through developmental approaches to supervision. *American Psychologist, 60,* 857–864.

Sumprer, G. F., & Walfish, S. (2001). The politics of graduate programs. In S. Walfish & A. K. Hess (Eds.), *Succeeding in graduate school: The career guide for psychology students* (pp. 77–94). Mahwah, NJ: Erlbaum

Tubesing, D. A. (1981). *Kicking your stress habits: A do-it-yourself guide for coping with stress.* Duluth, MN: Whole Person Associates.

Turner, J. A., Edwards, L. M., Eicken, I. M., Yokoyama, K., Castro, J. R., Tran, A. N.-T., et al. (2005). Intern self-care: An exploratory study into strategy use and effectiveness. *Professional Psychology: Research and Practice, 36,* 674–680.

Vesilind, P. A. (2000). *So you want to be a professor? A handbook for graduate students.* Thousand Oaks, CA: Sage.

Vineberg, D. (2005). Independent practice: Alive or dead? In R. D. Morgan, T. L. Kuther, & C. J. Habben (Eds.), *Life after graduate school in psychology* (pp. 87–96). New York: Psychology Press.

Wicherski, M., & Kohout, J. (2005). *2003 doctorate employment survey.* Washington, DC: American Psychological Association.

Williams-Nickelson, C., & Keilin, W. G. (2007). Getting started: General overview of the internship application process. In C. Williams-Nickelson & M. J. Prinstein (Eds.), *Internships in psychology: The APAGS workbook for writing successful applications and finding the right match* (pp. 3–10). Washington, DC: American Psychological Association.

Worthington, E. L. (2006). Changes in supervision as counselors and supervisors gain experience: A review [Special volume]. *Training and Education in Professional Psychology, 2,* 133–160.

Index

About the Author

Tara L. Kuther, PhD, associate professor at Western Connecticut State University in Danbury, received her PhD in developmental psychology from Fordham University in New York City in 1998. Over the past decade she has taught courses in child, adolescent, and adult development at Western Connecticut State University. Dr. Kuther also has taught courses at the undergraduate and graduate level at Lehman College (City University of New York [CUNY]), Iona College, Fordham University, and Teachers College, Columbia University, all in New York City; and Iona College in New Rochelle, New York. Dr. Kuther is a fellow of the Society for Teaching of Psychology (Division 2 of the American Psychological Association) and has served in leadership roles in the Council for Undergraduate Research and the Society for Teaching of Psychology. Her publications include 10 books, many of which are oriented toward student development, such as *The Psychology Major's Handbook, Careers in Psychology: Opportunities in a Changing World* (with Robert Morgan), and *Life After Graduate School in Psychology: Insiders Advice From New Psychologists* (with Robert Morgan and Corey Habben). Dr. Kuther's scholarly work on risky behavior during adolescence and early adulthood, moral development, ethical issues in research and teaching, and student development has appeared in over 40 articles and chapters and over 70 presentations at regional and national conferences.

About the Author